THE LIFE & ART OF

FRANK MOLNAR, JACK HARDMAN, LEROY JENSEN

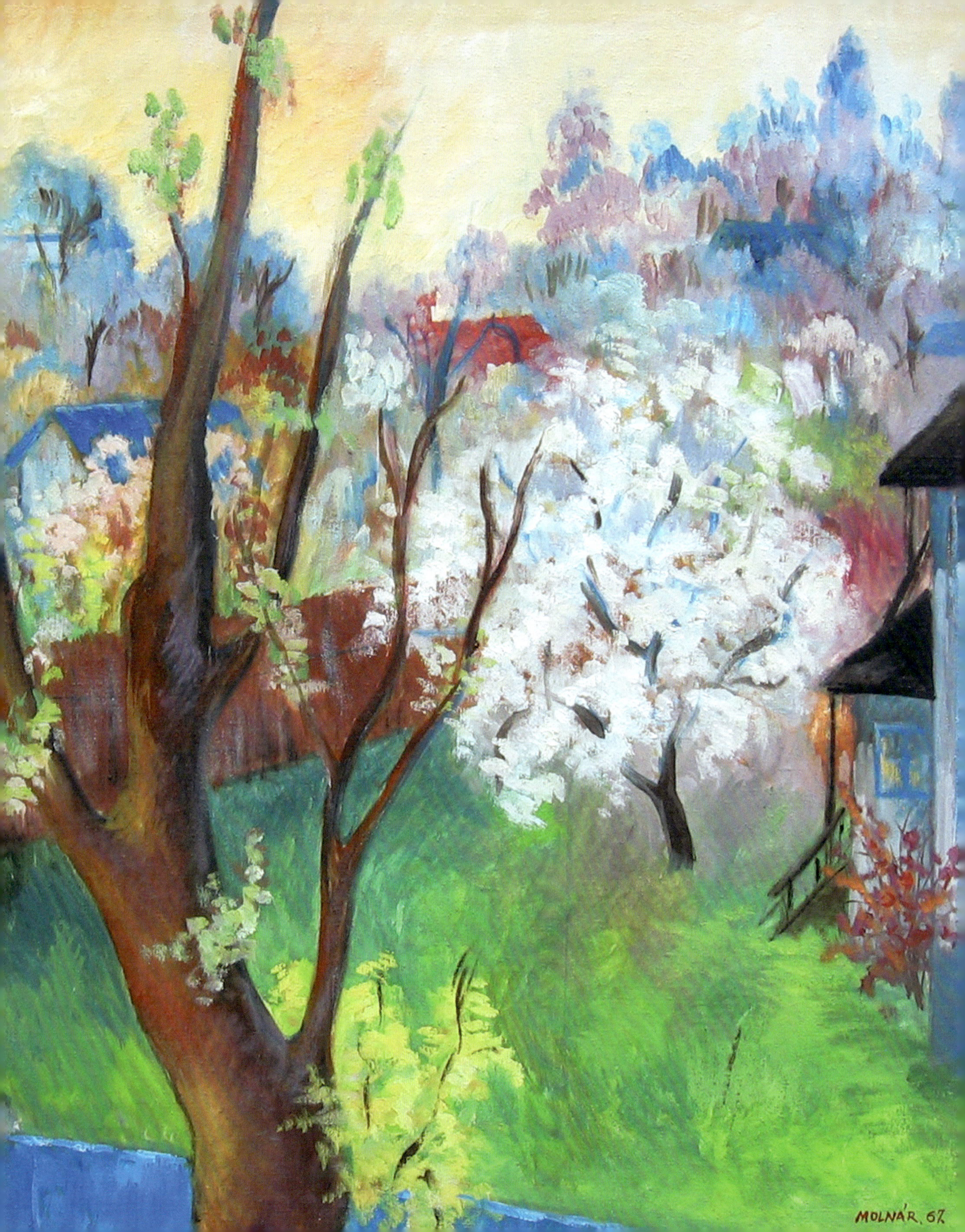
MOLNÁR 67

The Unheralded Artists of BC — 2

THE LIFE & ART OF

FRANK MOLNAR, JACK HARDMAN, LEROY JENSEN

EVE LAZARUS

CLAUDIA CORNWALL

WENDY NEWBOLD PATTERSON

Introduction by MAX WYMAN

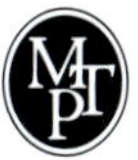

MOTHER TONGUE PUBLISHING LIMITED

Salt Spring Island, B.C.

Canada

PREVIOUS SPREAD:
Untitled [detail], 1967,
oil on canvas, 30" x 33",
Frank Molnar
COURTESY OF
THE WESTBRIDGE
FINE ART GALLERY
PHOTO BY NICHOLAS WESTBRIDGE

Library and Archives Canada Cataloguing in Publication

Lazarus, Eve, 1959-

The life and art of Frank Molnar, Jack Hardman, LeRoy Jensen / Eve Lazarus, Claudia Cornwall, Wendy Newbold Patterson ; introduction by Max Wyman.

(The unheralded artists of BC ; #2)

Includes index.

Contents: Frank Molnar / Eve Lazarus – Jack Hardman / Claudia Cornwall – LeRoy Jensen / Wendy Newbold Patterson.

ISBN 978-1-896949-02-4

1. Molnar, Frank, 1936–. 2. Hardman, Jack, 1923–1996. 3. Jensen, LeRoy, 1927–2005. 4. Molnar, Frank, 1936– —Criticism and interpretation. 5. Hardman, Jack, 1923–1996—Criticism and interpretation. 6. Jensen, LeRoy, 1927–2005—Criticism and interpretation. 7. Artists—British Columbia—Biography. 8. Art, Canadian—British Columbia—History. I. Cornwall, Claudia Maria II. Patterson, Wendy Newbold, 1945- III. Title. IV. Series: Unheralded artists of BC ; #2

N6546.B75L39 2009 700.92'2 C2009-904244-4

Cover design by Mark Hand and Jan Westendorp
Book design, layout and typesetting by Jan Westendorp
Front cover image: *Painting: self portrait*, oil, 1963, by Frank Molnar
Photo of Molnar's painting by Coast Imaging Arts
Back cover photos: Frank Molnar, photographer unknown; Jack Hardman, photo by Basil King; LeRoy Jensen, photographer unknown.

All efforts have been made to locate copyright holders of source material wherever possible.

Printed and bound in Canada by Friesens
Printed on chlorine free paper; inside pages are 10% PCW

Mother Tongue Publishing gratefully acknowledges the assistance of the Province of British Columbia through the B.C. Arts Council

Published by:

Mother Tongue Publishing Limited
290 Fulford-Ganges Road
Salt Spring Island, B.C. V8K 2K6
Canada
phone: 250-537-4155 fax: 250-537-4725

www.mothertonguepublishing.com

Represented in Canada by the Literary Press Group

PUBLISHER'S NOTE

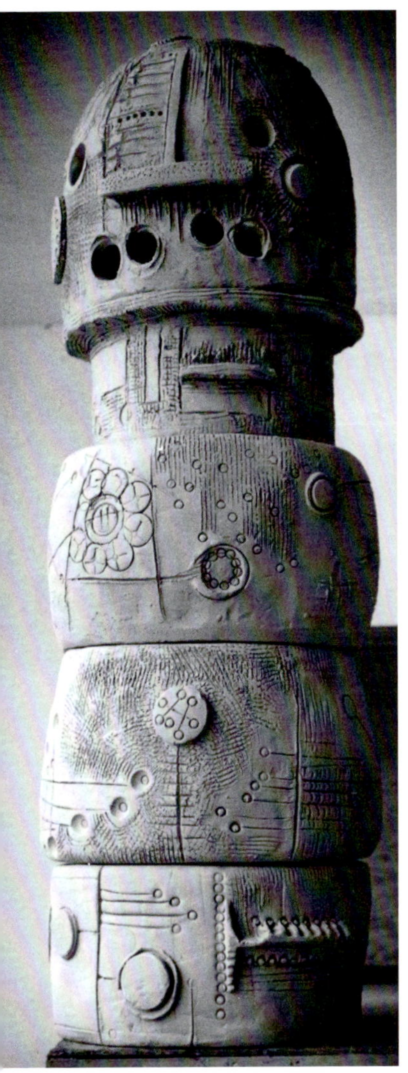

—TO THE UNRECOGNIZED ARTISTS OF CANADA—

WELCOME to the second book in our bold series; *The Unheralded Artists of BC.*

Here, pulled from the shadows of history is a visual feast, an introduction to three wildly creative individuals who emerged as artists in the fertile 1950s and 1960s. Driven to create, they were part of the underground and previously undocumented art scene.

Filled with rare photos, art work, interviews and lively stories, this book will whet your appetite for a deeper, more truthful provincial and national art history.

Opening the door on the forgotten is an enormous job. Much has already been lost, yet so much is waiting to be discovered. This series addresses "absences" and "others", beginning with unheralded artists from early 1900 through to the 1960s in British Columbia, Canada.

Art does not need to be "current" or contemporary to be validated, but waiting for society to acknowledge the achievements of an artist is a road often fraught with disappointment. With this series, we have begun to honour the men and women who travelled before us and who deserve a more lasting visibility.

Visceral Totem, Mid '50s/'60s, ceramic, approx. 4' x 20" x20", missing, Jack Hardman
PHOTO BY JACK V. LONG

CONTENTS

x Introduction—Max Wyman

FRANK MOLNAR
—EVE LAZARUS

2 Preface
—Charles van Sandwyk

5 Flight from Hungary

9 An Artists' Colony

13 Sylvia

17 Exhibitions

23 Capilano College

27 Canadians and the Nude

31 Point Grey

37 Frank's Legacy

42 Frank Molnar Exhibitions

JACK HARDMAN
—CLAUDIA CORNWALL

46 Preface
—Jean François Guimond

49 Artist, Mentor, Enfant Terrible

57 Burnaby: An Artists' Enclave

65 The Professional Sculptor

77 A Mentor's Life

85 Jack Hardman Exhibitions

LEROY JENSEN
—WENDY NEWBOLD PATTERSON

90 Preface
—Roy Patterson

93 Beginnings in Asia

97 Art Student in Denmark and France

101 The Price of Success and the Paradigm of Originality

107 The Teacher and His Students: A Personal Reminiscence

113 The Work

119 Juggling Art, Family and Activism

127 The Last Painting

131 Epilogue: The Dogwood Tree

132 LeRoy Jensen Exhibitions

134 Acknowledgements

137 Endnotes

143 Index

INTRODUCTION

All members of society are worthy of immortality.

—Amadeo Modigliani

Art is a fickle mistress. On some of her acolytes, she bestows great glory in their lifetime, and they live lives of fanfare and luxury. Some she makes the favourites of fashion, and they do what they can with their fifteen minutes of fame. For some she reserves the accolades until they are dead and cannot, so far as we know, appreciate the gift. On many she bestows nothing but oblivion.

No law says an artist deserves to be remembered simply for being an artist, any more than a plumber can expect to be memorialized for his work. But we would serve ourselves better than we do if we were less ready than we are to consign the work of so many of our creative artists, in every field of art, to the scrapheap of history. As a society in the throes of headlong and momentous change, we have acquired an addict-like need for the shock of the new. But attention must be paid—more attention than has been paid to date—if we are not to lose forever our connection with the full scope and benefit of what has gone before.

The spirit of generosity and inclusiveness that is encapsulated in Modigliani's words is what animates the ambitious series of publications that includes this volume. *The Unheralded Artists of B.C.* is designed to shine a lasting light on the legacy of artists whose work, for one reason or another, has been left largely invisible.

This second volume is about three examples of bloody-minded, damn-the-torpedoes creative individualism, three artists rooted in a stubborn belief in the value of what they were saying and the way they were saying it. Others will have to pronounce on the aesthetic merit of the work, and where it fits in the grand continuum, and no doubt there will be plenty to argue with them, whatever they have to say. But whether you like the work, dislike it or remain indifferent to it is, in a sense, beside the point. The point is that we now have a clearer idea of what was going on in our small corner of the world of art than we had before.

These were all artists who had and valued a solid grounding in training and technique. From what we read here, they were difficult men. Many artists are. They were also individuals of character and charisma, persons who left a lasting impression on the people with whom they made contact. For instance, Jean Wolf said she found

Frank Molnar "intimidating and intense... he's not an easy person, although none of them were really." He was, as it is explained here, "like other traditional artists of the '60s and '70s, largely ignored in the public and gallery rush to embrace change."

That last point resonates throughout these stories. Although they found themselves working in a period of effervescent innovation and experiment, in a milieu that was eager to link itself to other crucibles of creative daring, these artists were by no means dedicated followers of fashion. They scorned and spurned the isms of the era and clove instead to the sturdy standards. And the case is made for each that they have suffered for that, most significantly in terms of lack of regard for what they did in their working careers and the resultant loss of public memory of their work.

Perhaps understandably, then, there is a tone of protectiveness, affirmation and fierce attachment in these pages. The alert reader will from time to time pick up hints of pique and resentment, even sardonic bitterness, at the perceived injustices suffered by these individuals at the hands of The System or The Clique. These should be recognized for what they are. In any field of endeavour, disappointment can colour attitudes to the point where regrettable and unsupportable statements can be made about the more successful. In any case, it is unlikely that the slights these men suffered were all imaginary, and their despair over their lack of acceptance or success was no less real. Experience bruised them. Jack Hardman, we are told, was so discouraged he destroyed works; he was by no means the first unfashionable artist to be driven to such extremes.

There are other important themes here: the theme of immigration, and the importation of influences from other, more developed places; and the theme of education and mentoring, the task and duty of passing those influences along. When these men were doing their most mature work, the city was still young and searching for its identity. The process of the creation of that identity goes on. The book in your hands memorializes the contribution of three men, little-known or regarded as it might have been at the time, to that process.

Attention is being paid.

MAX WYMAN
LIONS BAY, BC, AUGUST, 2009

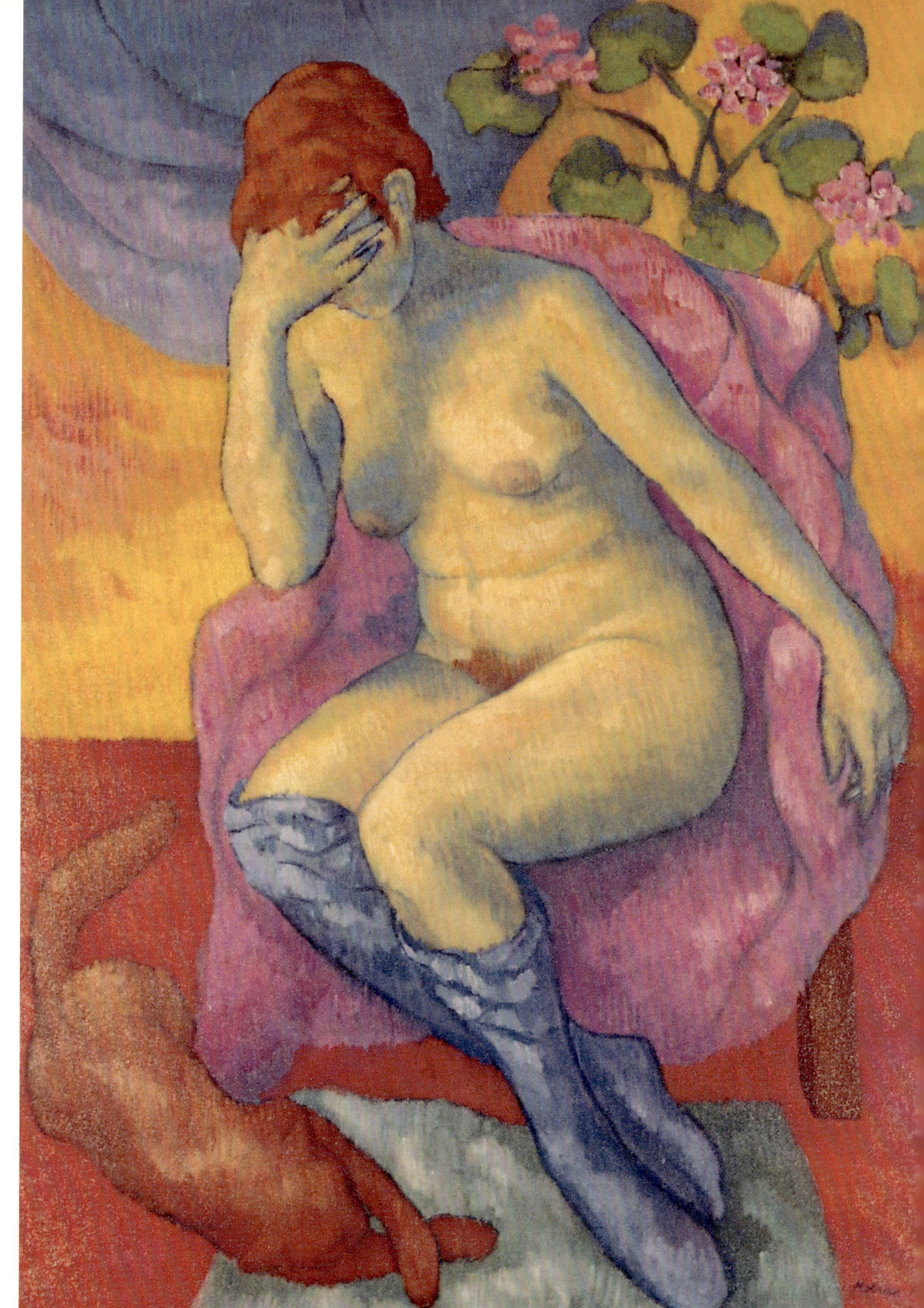

FRANK MOLNAR

—EVE LAZARUS

preface by CHARLES VAN SANDWYK

Preface

‹‹ *Nude With Cat,* 1964,
oil on canvas,
47½" x 34½"
PRIVATE COLLECTION
OF DR. B.M. HYDE

FRANK MOLNAR, the great lover of fine wine, women and song, is sitting in his favourite chair, bent over one of my unfinished drawings—a timid sketch of three mice—stiff and hesitantly drawn. He looks up to see if he has my attention and then begins: "First, Chuck, [he always calls me Chuck] the mice are fabulous... sensitively handled... nice work! I like the composition more or less, though you still have trouble with foreshortening."

Now he gets excited; his arms wave about like a classical conductor, "If you wish to make it more exciting, increase the intensity of the vermilion in the sealing wax, then offset it with a touch of blue in the shadow areas. Don't be shy of colour. Make the edge of the envelope darker; remember: contrasts move forward, subtlety recedes."

And so, with great diplomacy and tenderness, begins one of his brilliant critiques. If the drawing has no hope, he helps consign it to a quick and merciful death. If the drawing shows promise, he is immediately reassuring while he dissects the weak points, analyzing the areas for improvement. I've never met anyone quite so good at it.

Regarding a painting's philosophical content, he says, "That part I never interfere with. You've got to give your art your own meaning."

This is why I'm drawn to Frank. His world, his loves, his painting—they are all interconnected and interchangeable. A man and his art should follow the same path; they share the same integrity, the same meaning.

I've watched his work grow over the years, from his early brooding self-portraits and academic nudes, to the softly painted figures of the 1970s and '80s, right up to the gutsy, complex patterning and impasto which, today, dominate the drawing and composition beneath.

Those great masters of the brush stroke have influenced him: the spareness and hesitancy of Bonnard, the chiselling directness of Van Gogh, the otherworldly colouring of Gauguin. They have all come to play in the field of Frank, and then some. But by now, his style and imagery are all his own.

The evening visit begins with a few strong single malts. The home is formal, though light and airy, filled with European antiques. Frank's vibrant oils hang on the walls. The back porch door is open. The Hungarian peppers are ripening in bowls outside, and their fragrance wafts through the kitchen. The appetizers are brought in casually by Sylvia, Frank's wife. She plumps herself down on the couch next to him and offers breaded mushrooms stuffed with pâté, and joins in.

Not much has changed in Frank's world. He is at the gymnasium regularly; he still lifts barbells like a man 25 years his junior. He still suffers knee pain and arthritis, though perhaps a little more now.

Sylvia brings out a steaming bowl of goulash, together with fried langosh and more wine. We leave the drawing room and head for the dining table. The conversation moves to politics and world events. We have a little bloodletting over coffee, between goulash and dessert, the inevitable reaction to an exclusionary and restrictive art community. His eyes are fiery and passionate, or deep and sensitive, or all of the above—depending on the conversation. Frank has an uncanny perception and a razor-sharp wit. He has an opinion about and a solution for just about every international stupidity known to man.

Then all is pushed aside, and the scotch bottle returns. The talk becomes quieter. We cross to the subject of art—our art... of our intellectual yearnings... experiments we wish to try... inspirations we may be seeking or may have inadvertently found. We analyze the art game and always come back to a place of making plans, of encouragement. He ends with the words, "Appreciate what you've got, Chuck, and make use of it. It's now or never."

I look out the window, and dawn is creeping over the hill. We've been up all night.

Frank and Sylvia are my Paris salon of the 1920s, they are my Bloomsbury set. For hundreds of years, artists have gathered together to do battle over ideas, over intellectual sovereignty and over the desire to forge a common bond.

Their salons have never been so elegant and humane, nor, I suspect, so invigorating as in the company of Frank Molnar.

Charles van Sandwyk is a B.C. artist and writer who was taught by Frank Molnar in art school. They have been friends ever since

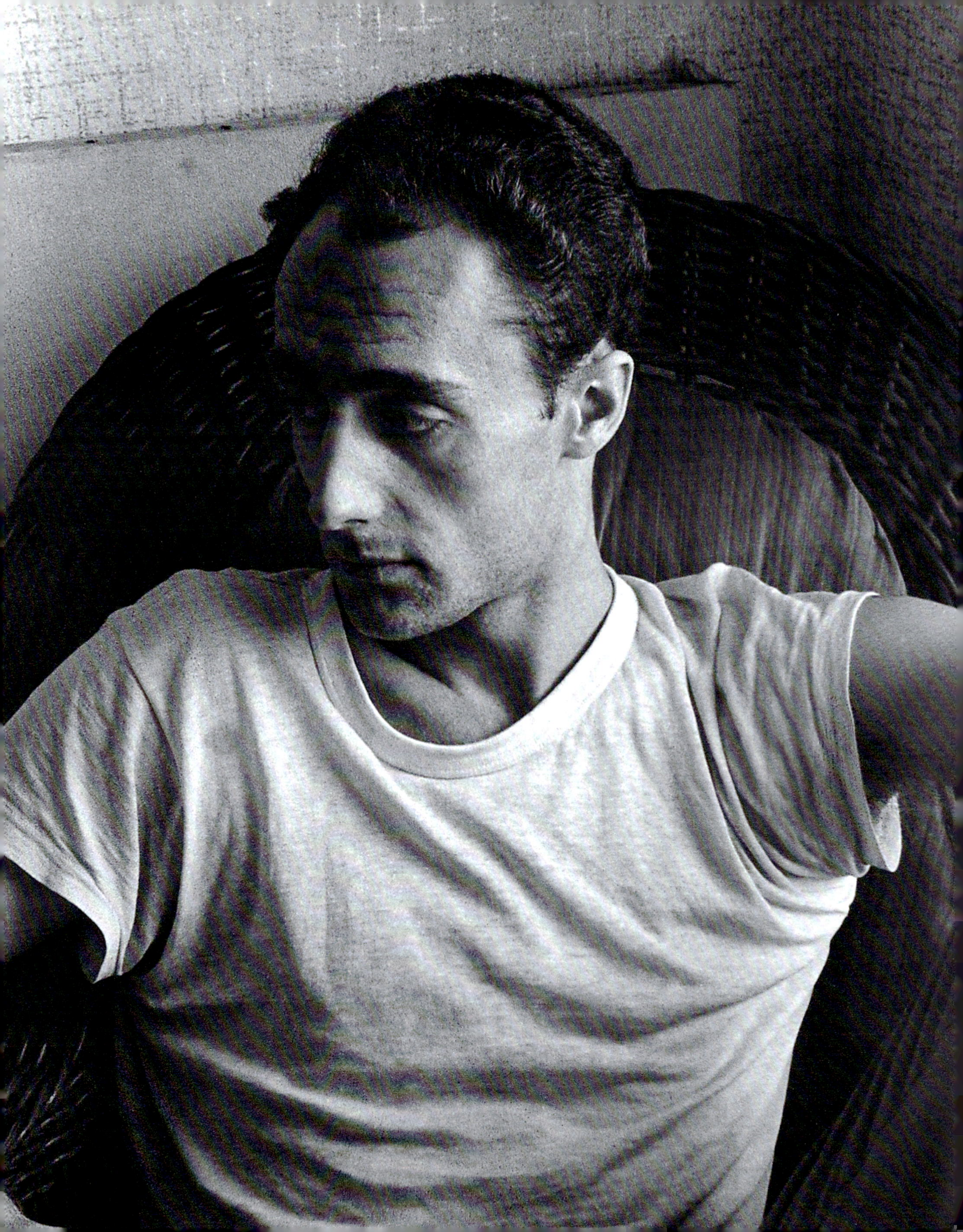

Flight from Hungary

Frank Stephan Molnar was 20 when he fled Budapest during the 1956 Hungarian Revolution. Years of war, Soviet occupation and bombings had turned the city to rubble. He saw starving people and dead bodies in the street; friends would disappear overnight. Young Frank craved the freedom to paint, an impossible dream under communist rule.

‹ Frank Molnar, 1960, Pennsylvania Academy of the Fine Arts, USA

"The communist system is the most repressive, horrible system. People were starving at the time; thousands were banished to Siberia and disappearing into gulags. Art was out of the question," said Frank.[1]

Frank, born in 1936, grew up in a typical working-class home on the outskirts of Budapest, with his parents, Maria and Ferrence, an industrious motor mechanic, and his younger sister, Ilona. After studying agriculture and animal husbandry at a technical high school, he applied to veterinary school, but without family ties to the Party, post-secondary education was impossible. Ferrence flirted with socialism, but did not believe in communism. "At that time in Hun-

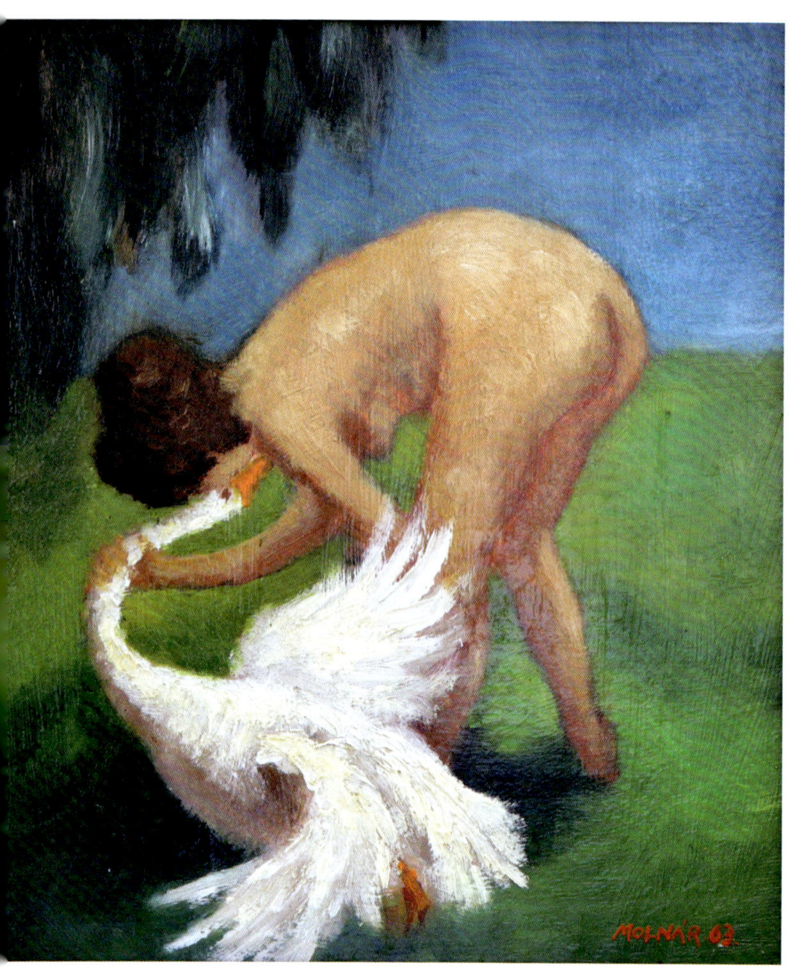

gary if your parents were not part of the communist party your chances of going to university were nil."[2]

By November of 1956, the Hungarian Revolution had failed, Russian troops occupied the country and Hungary became a satellite state of the Soviet Union. For a brief time, Hungarians were free to leave, and an estimated 200,000 did just that. Leaving, said Frank, was something that Hungarians decided almost impulsively: "Either change your life or don't, take a chance or not." He grabbed the chance and with four friends found their way to refugee camps, first in Essen, Austria, then another in Vienna and a third in Munich, before going to America.

Frank scored a fellowship to Saint Vincent College in Pennsylvania where he took general studies and learned English. Benedictine monks encouraged him to send his drawings to the Pennsylvania Academy of the Fine Arts. He spent the next three and a half years there, surviving on a combination of a scholarship, janitorial work and modeling and studying under well-known American artists, including painter Franklin Chenault Watkins. Frank learned different painting techniques, drawing, artistic anatomy, art history and perspective, all the time perfecting his figurative work. "I never had any inclination to do totally abstract painting," he said. "All painting is essentially abstract if you get down to the nitty-gritty, but to be non-figurative and non-representative never interested me."[3]

Leda and the Swan, 1963, oil on canvas, 12" x 10"
PRIVATE COLLECTION
DAN FAIRCHILD PHOTOGRAPHY

Six months later, Frank had a green card, with most of the rights and responsibilities of citizenship. By 1962, his college deferment ended, just as U.S. involvement in the Vietnam War escalated. Draft looked like a certainty. With a year left of his studies, and many friends already fighting, he was tired of a lifetime of war and headed for Canada's "wild west coast." Frank took the train to Montreal and arrived in Vancouver on May 5, 1962. He quickly discovered that Eastern European immigrants were not warmly welcomed in the largely Waspish Vancouver.

Frank's passion for bold dynamic nudes with provocative themes and sensuous colours immediately set him firmly apart from the artistic trends. Inspired by the romantics and the impressionists, he put his own interpretation on goddesses and Greek mythology. In 1963, he painted the first of a series of erotic canvasses depicting Leda and the Swan. He drew from live models and seemed to switch effortlessly from figurative work and still lifes in oil to watercolours, a softer medium better able to capture West Coast land and seascapes.

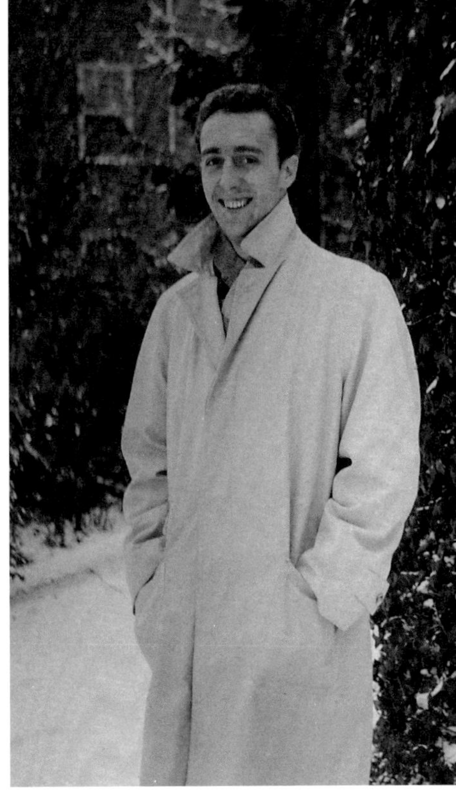
Frank at Pennsylvania Academy of the Fine Arts, 1957

Outside Frank's Kitsilano home and studio, Vancouver was a young city in constant change, and the cultural elite comprised a handful of household names such as Gordon Smith, Jack Shadbolt, B.C. Binning and Toni Onley. These middle-class artists with mostly English backgrounds tapped into the Vancouver Art Gallery (VAG) and taught at the Vancouver School of Art (VSA), while others left to make their name in New York, Paris or London.

"The '60s and '70s were a time of questioning everything," said Paul Wolf. "Art became straight design, but design with emotion, and it was questioning the figurative, questioning cubism, questioning the whole scene. People wanted to see things differently."[4]

Serious, soft-spoken and intellectual, Frank seemed much older than his years. Growing up in the midst of war and deprivation left him no time for abstract expressionism, performance art, photography, popular culture or, by the '70s, conceptualism.

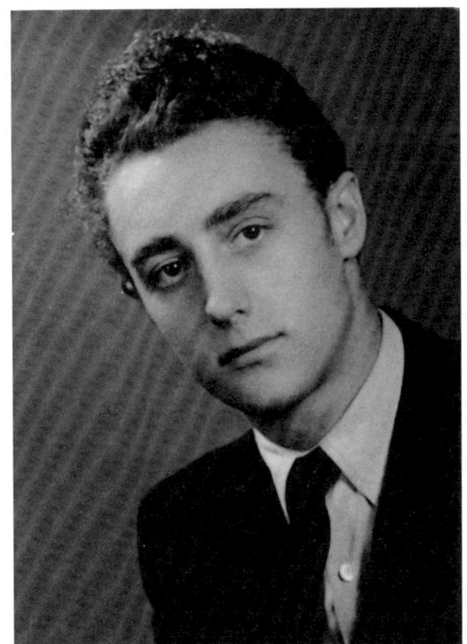
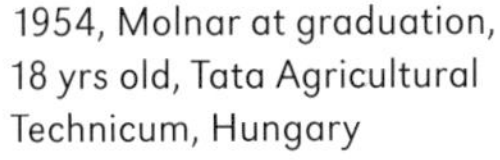
1954, Molnar at graduation, 18 yrs old, Tata Agricultural Technicum, Hungary

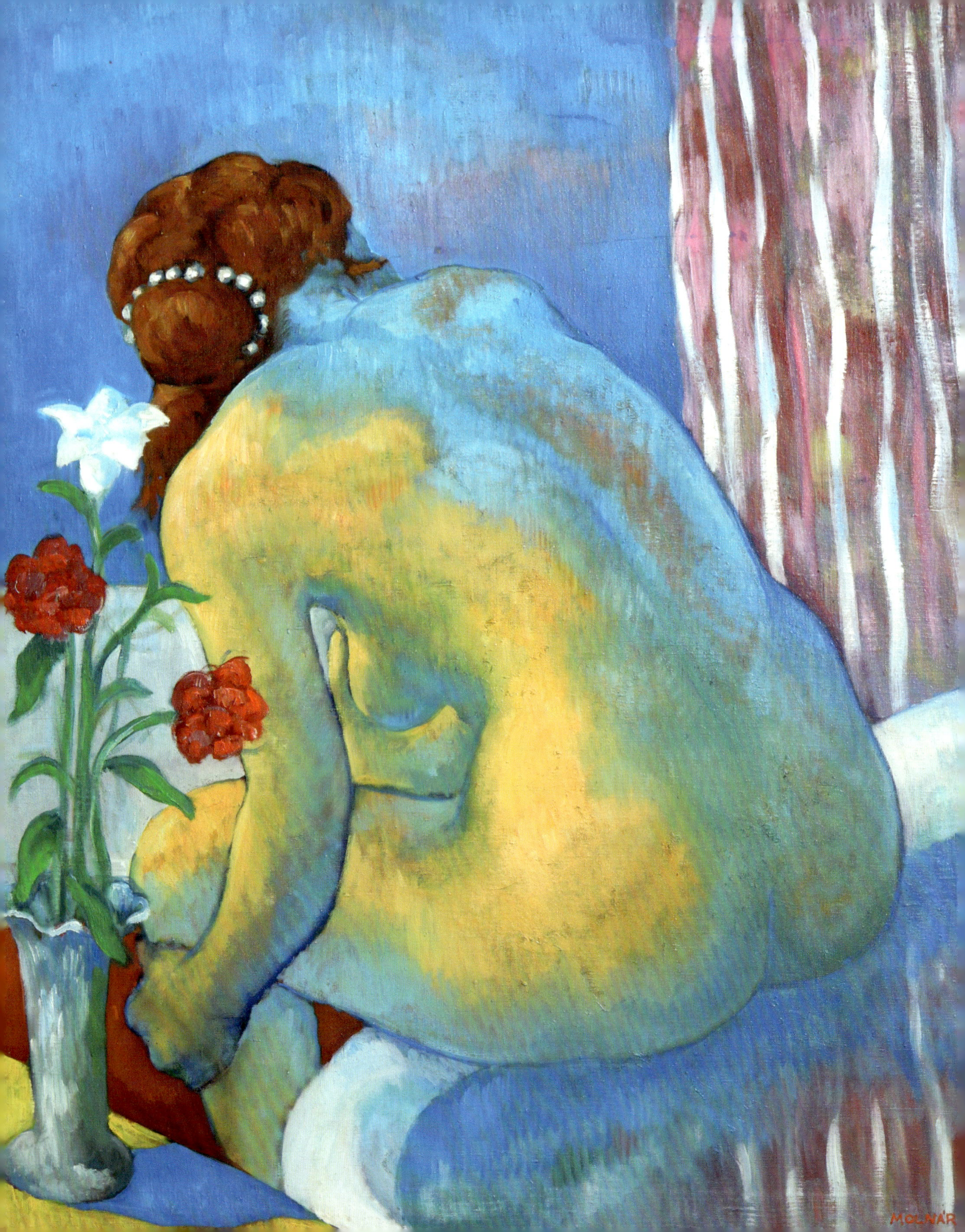
MOLNAR

An Artists' Colony

At the same time that Frank fled Budapest, 300 students, faculty members and their families from the forest engineering faculty at the University of Sopron in Hungary found a safe haven at the newly created Sopron School of Forestry at the University of B.C. By 1962, most had received Canadian citizenship and opted to stay.[5]

‹ *Untitled,* 1965,
oil on canvas, 36", x 30"
DAN FAIRCHILD PHOTOGRAPHY

Reclining Nude, 1964,
oil on canvas, 32" x 48"
PRIVATE COLLECTION

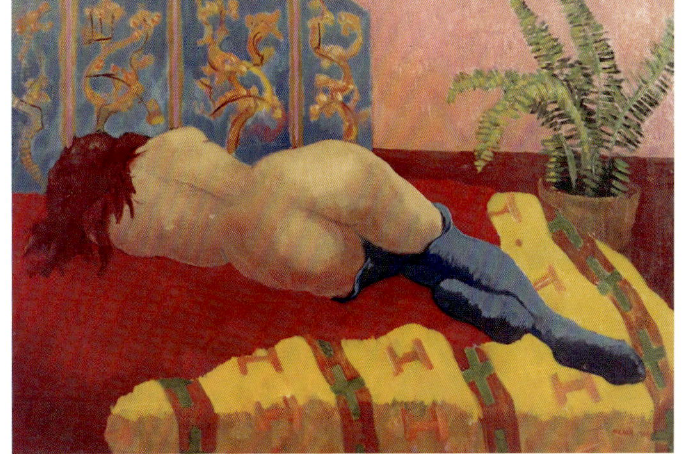

When Frank arrived in Vancouver that year, he quickly met up with a group of Hungarians, including Eddie Apt, a former forestry student now studying art and trying to get established as a sculptor. Frank roomed with Apt's family for a time before moving into an apartment above a grocery store at 2205 West 6th in 1965. There he was surrounded by a lively artists' colony that

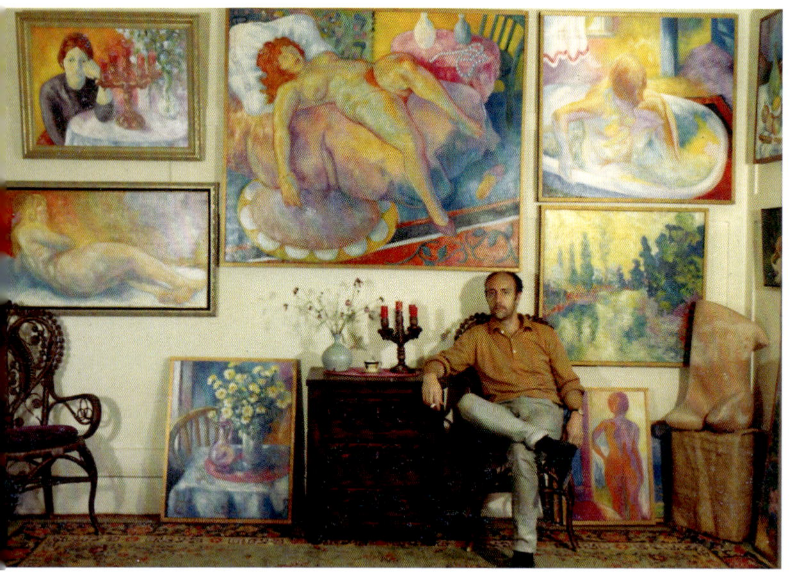

Frank Molnar in Kitsilano apartment, 1960s

included Jack Akroyd, Jock Hearn, Jack Dale, David Denby, Paul Huba and Roy Kiyooka, as well as poets John Newlove, Judith Copithorne and bill bissett.

In the mid-1960s, Kitsilano was filled with two-storey buildings that served as both small businesses and cheap rentals. Many apartments had 12-foot ceilings and room for a mezzanine, perfect for studios. The Molnars paid $65 a month for their two-bedroom apartment with a large kitchen and a fireplace in the living room.

Elek Imredy, a Hungarian refugee and sculptor, lived in an apartment across from Frank and next door to Jack Akroyd. Peggy Imredy said her husband, Frank and Akroyd shared the costs of models for weekly drawing classes in Imredy's studio. The older sculptor frequently paid both painters one dollar an hour to help with the clay and the plaster molds and other labour-intensive parts of sculpture. "Frank and Jack were artists and could always use the money, and he could always use the help," she said.[6] At that point, Imredy had already carved out a solid reputation. His nursery rhyme characters sat in amusement parks, his religious sculptures adorned schools and churches, and by 1972, his most famous commission, *Girl in a Wetsuit*, sat on a big rock on the north side of Stanley Park. Poet Judith Copithorne modeled at the art school and was one of three women who modeled for *Girl in a Wetsuit*. She remembered Frank being, like most artists in the area, "severely underemployed" but always painting and Akroyd as having "a working-man gruff way of talking."

Jack Akroyd, Kitsilano, 1970s, PHOTO BY MARJ TRIM

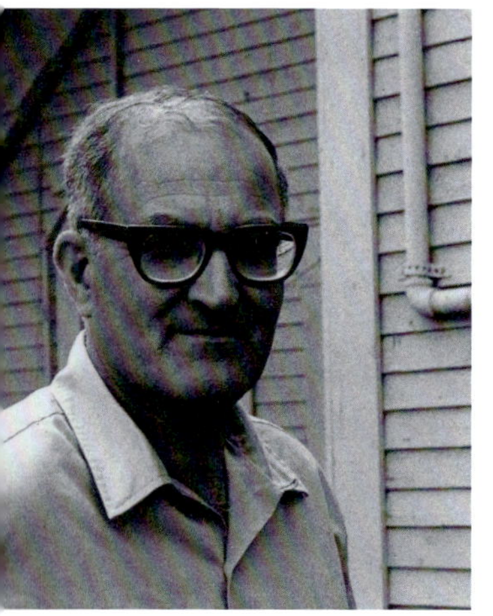

"Jack Akroyd used to paint in his studio right beside the window which was right on the street," Copithorne said. "It was a big window, and he would paint there whenever he had a chance, and he would talk to anybody who would pass by."[7]

Although Frank and Akroyd had vastly different personalities and painting styles, they were close friends. Several times, over about 15 years, they would hit the road in the early spring, drive to Kelowna and paint. They stayed with Akroyd's friends in a cabin by Lake Okanagan and, using that as their base, drove to Osoyoos and Vernon, taking two to three weeks to "follow the blossoms." Frank said they would stop along

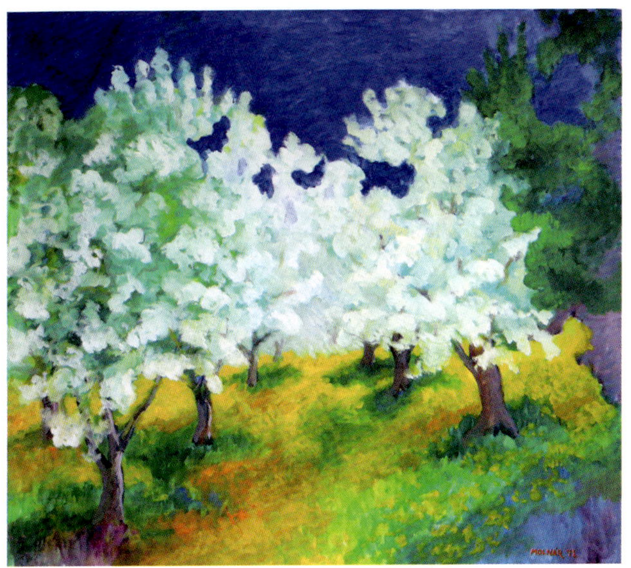

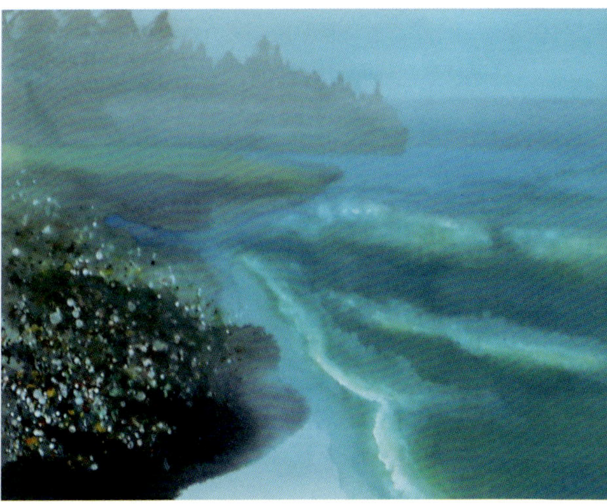

the way to sketch and photograph the orchards to paint when they returned home. "Imagine a beautiful cherry orchard, white as white blossoms in rows and underneath dandelions like a gold carpet," he recalled. "And when you looked through the white of the cherry blossoms to the blue of the sky, it was an unbelievable colour." He added that he has no paintings from that time because the watercolours and oils all sold so quickly.[8]

In the early 1990s Frank switched from painting orchards to seascapes at Long Beach on Vancouver Island. "The light in the Okanagan is completely different from the West Coast. It's a sharp light that tends to flatten out in the distance," explained Frank. "On the West Coast of Vancouver Island you have this constant rain and moisture, and in the summer, there is the fog. Then the fog starts to lift, and the sun comes out and it's unbelievably beautiful, and there is constant change as islands and trees and other things in the distance start to appear."[9]

Most people, he said, believe that fog is grey, "but if you look at it in the changing light it reflects every colour that you can think of because the droplets break the light into the components of the rainbow." Frank said these sensitive colour changes come through best when using watercolours. The medium, he says, gives the painting freshness, and he enjoys the immediacy of it. Because of its delicacy, Frank's method is to sketch and take pictures of the changing scene—sometimes as much as every half-hour then go back to the studio and paint.[10]

Watercolour, 2002,
22" x 28"

Blossoms, 1970,
oil on canvas, 38" x 42"
PRIVATE COLLECTION OF
KAREN AND MAURICE SHU
DAN FAIRCHILD PHOTOGRAPHY

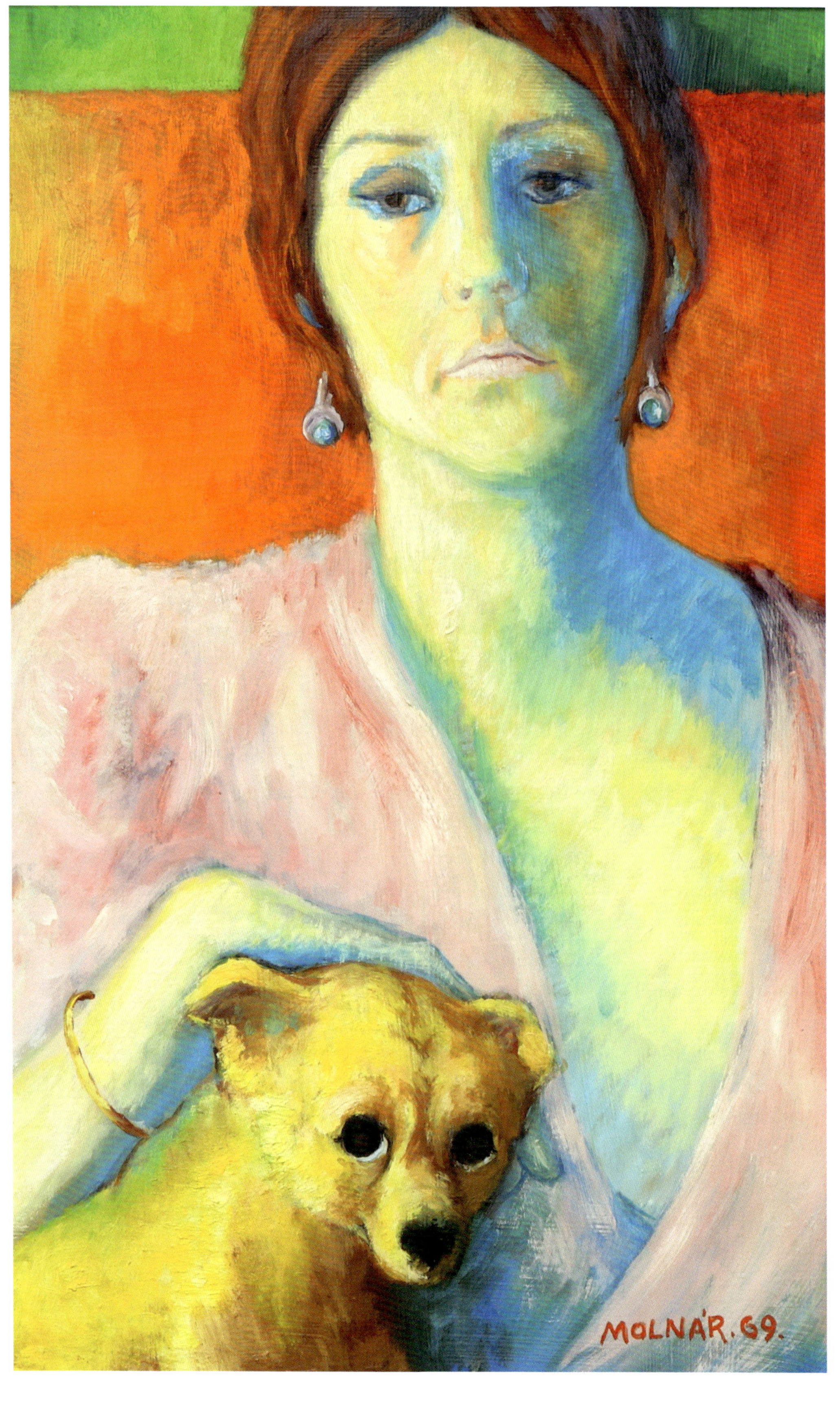
MOLNÁR.69.

Sylvia

‹ *Sylvia,* 1969,
oil on canvas, 18" x 12"
PRIVATE COLLECTION
PHOTO BY DAN FAIRCHILD PHOTOGRAPHY

FRANK HAS EDDIE APT TO THANK for introducing him to Sylvia Pidraziuk, a student at UBC who modeled part-time to help pay for her tuition. Born in Vancouver in 1939, Sylvia is a first-generation Canadian, born to Ukrainian parents. "Eddie said you have to meet this mad Hungarian, all he does is paint," Sylvia said.[11] Shortly after meeting Frank, she switched from home economics to study music and art education, three lifelong loves.

In 1966, Frank and Sylvia married and lived in the large Kitsilano apartment. He painted his big luscious nudes often to the strains of Mozart and modeled many of his figurative work after the beautiful Sylvia. "He is very strong and very passionate about his work, and he loves to paint the nude; he reveres the human body," she said. "He is, I believe, extremely talented, and that's what caught me in a big way. Not only his very strong personality, but his talent—he can really draw."

Sylvia loved to watch him paint. Perched on the edge of an old claw-footed tub in the bathroom, she could see into the small studio at the end of the apart-

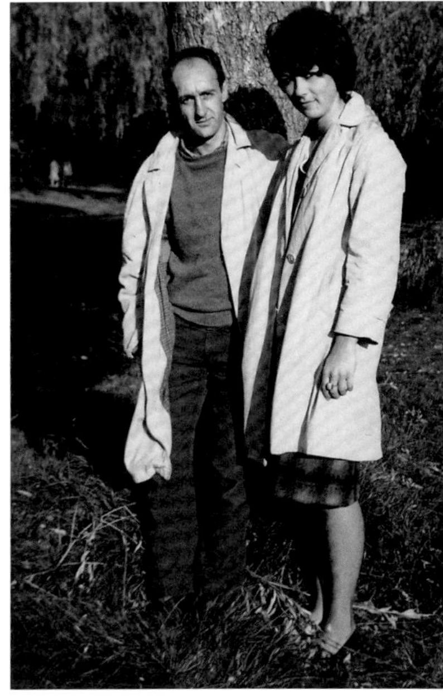

Frank & Sylvia at Stanley Park, Vancouver, 1960s

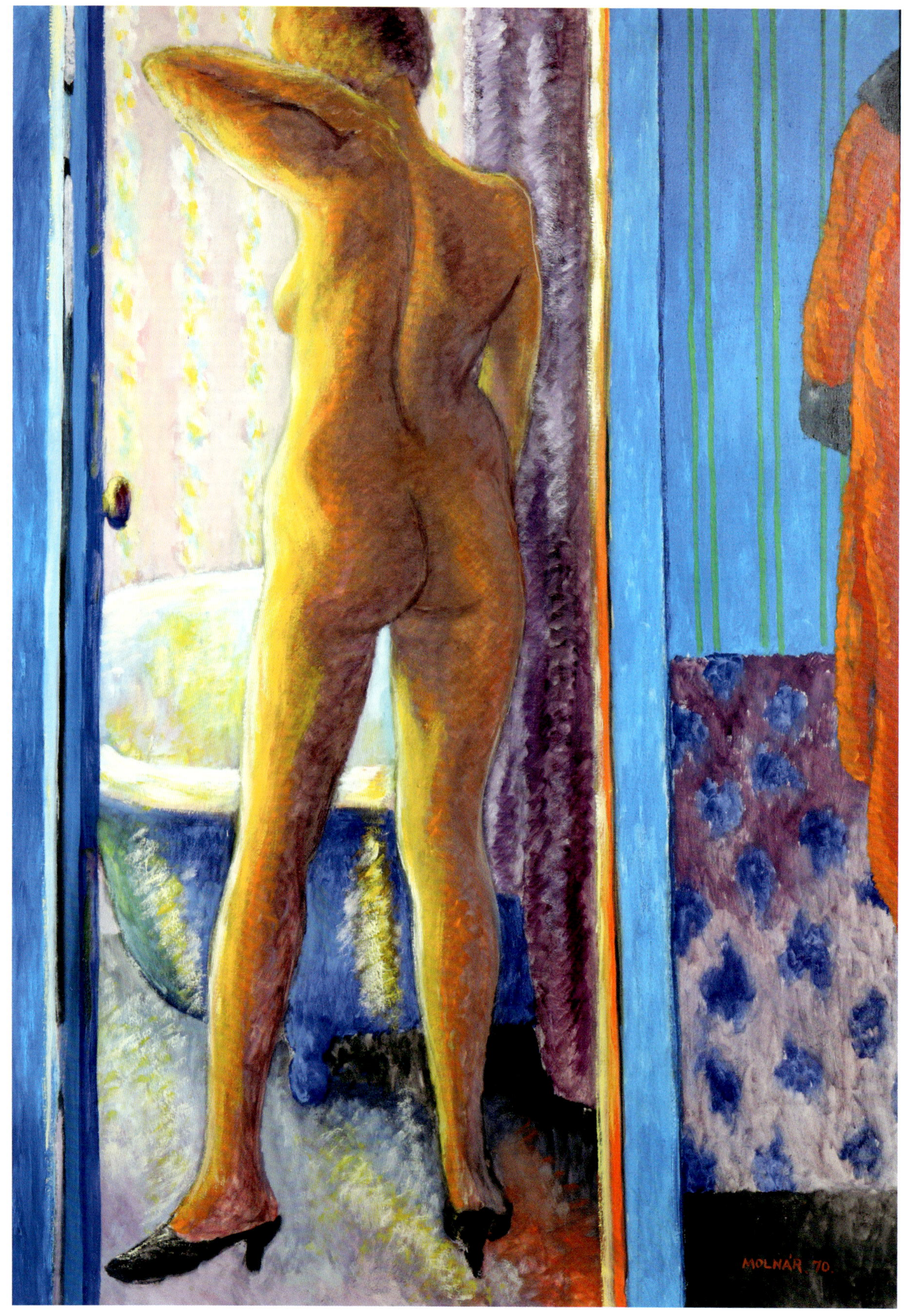
MOLNÁR '70.

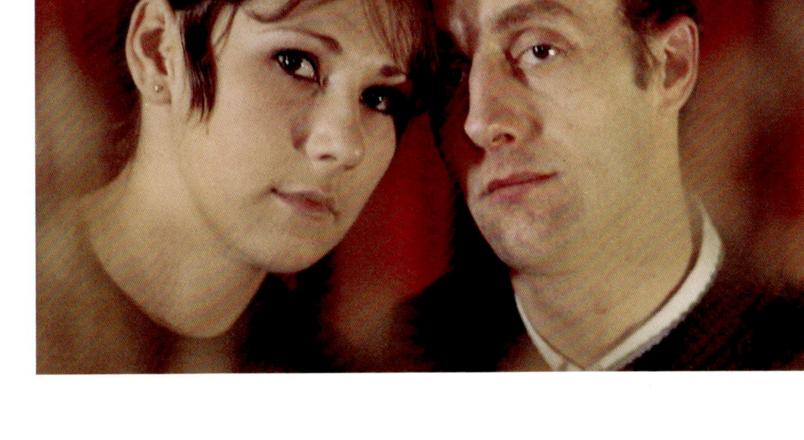

Sylvia & Frank, 1960s, Kitsilano, PHOTO BY JACK DALE

ment. "It's amazing when I think back at the amount of work he produced," she said. "He would just be standing there, and it would flow out, and when it was finished, I always felt that the painting was there on the wall already."[12]

The couple had no children of their own, but Sylvia taught art, social studies, language arts and music for 26 years. While Frank painted, Sylvia introduced food to her elementary social studies and language arts students. "When we studied India, we made roti; when we studied Japan, we made ramen noodles; and when we did Eastern Europe, we cooked cabbage rolls," she said. "When we did Greece, we talked about pastries and all kinds of architecture, and I said to the class, you know you may not remember the names of the columns that we are drawing and building out of clay, but you will never forget the taste of this sweet baklava."

After retiring from teaching in 1995, she started Sylvia's Cooking School, running it from a friend's Point Grey mansion, wrote a food column for *Kontakt* magazine that ran for seven years and hosted *Ukrainian Food Flair* on Nash Holos, a local Ukrainian radio program.[13]

Woman by Bathtub, 1970, oil on canvas, 48" x 34"
DAN FAIRCHILD PHOTOGRAPHY

While Sylvia was heavily involved in her own career, she was always there for Frank. "She was the moving spirit when we had exhibitions. She was the organizer who kept the records, and she would give me 100 percent support every which way," said Frank.

For a time, she became Sylvia Molnar Artists' Agent, representing Georg Schmerholz, Jack Akroyd and others. She would bring potential buyers into the artist's studio, organize exhibitions and negotiate prices on behalf of the artist. "It was very difficult," Sylvia recalled. "I was new on the scene, and it was hard to break through."

During the '60s, Frank and other artists who showed such promise—like Jack Akroyd, David Marshall and George Fertig—remained locked out of the inner circle and were considered irrelevant to the art world. Aiding their obscurity was the problem that there were only a handful of galleries and little chance for exhibition.[14]

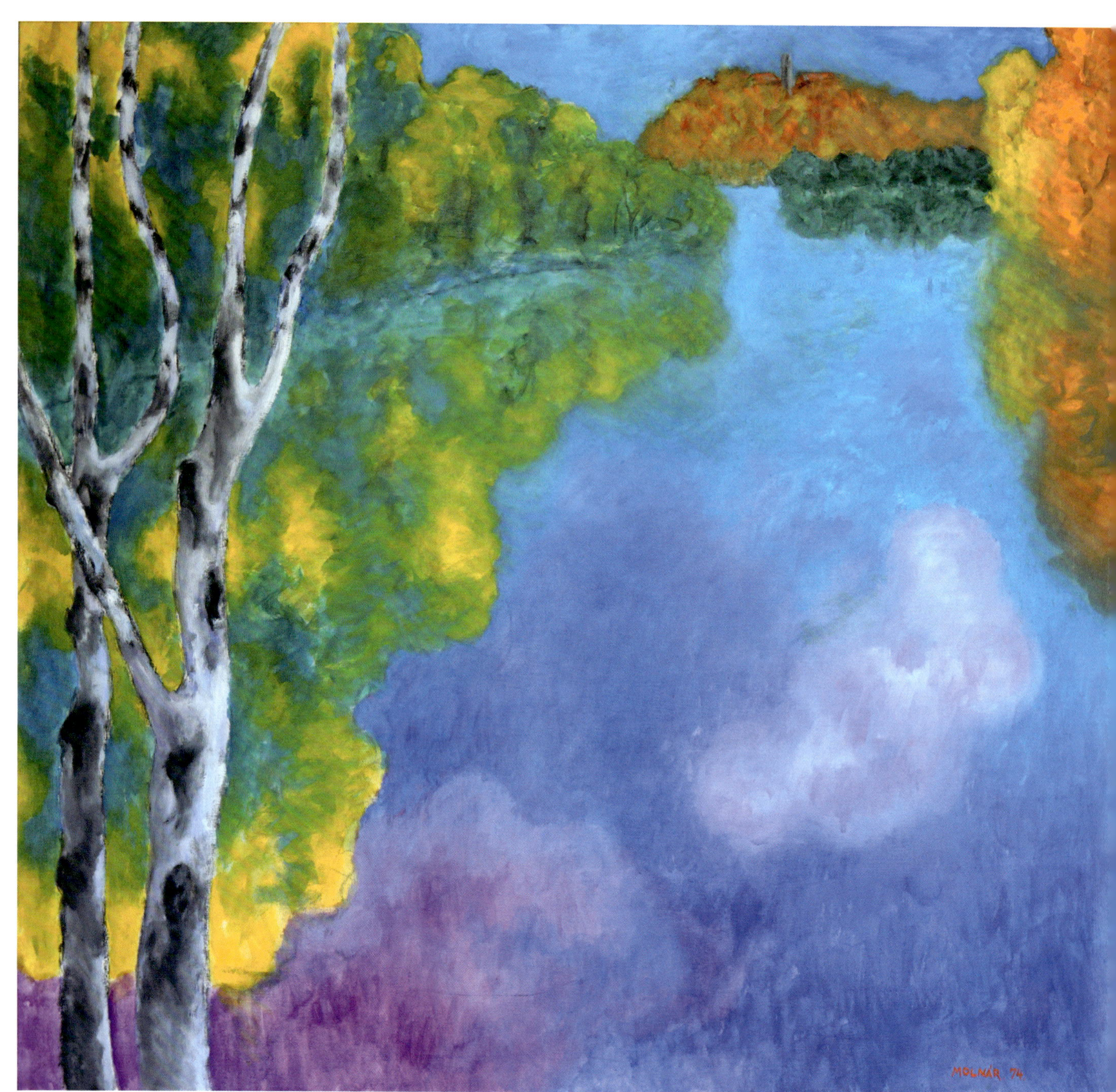
MOLNÁR 74

Exhibitions

‹ *Untitled,* 1974,
oil on canvas, 40" x 40"
PRIVATE COLLECTION OF
KAREN AND MAURICE SHU
DAN FAIRCHILD PHOTOGRAPHY

FRANK HELD FIVE SHOWS at Peder and Anne Pedersen's Danish Art Gallery at 3757 West 10th (at Alma) in Kitsilano, two with Jack Akroyd. His early work showed at the Gallery of B.C. Arts across from Stanley Park, run by Mrs. Clark. With Hungarian-born Georg Schmerholz, he held joint shows in the sculptor's Kitsilano studio at 2277 West 10th (at Vine). "Our work was so different, there was no competition," Frank said.

Twice a year, the Molnars held weekend salon-style art shows in their apartment. On the whole, the shows were successful, but also stressful and expensive for the couple. Sylvia would prepare the invitations, do the mailing and then cater the parties, often for up to 200 guests. "I firmly believe that we were way ahead of our times. We were doing home visits, studio visits, meet the artist, that kind of thing, and people weren't used to it," she said. "We did it with class, but we were very poor."

While today's buyers want to meet the painters and expect to see their work

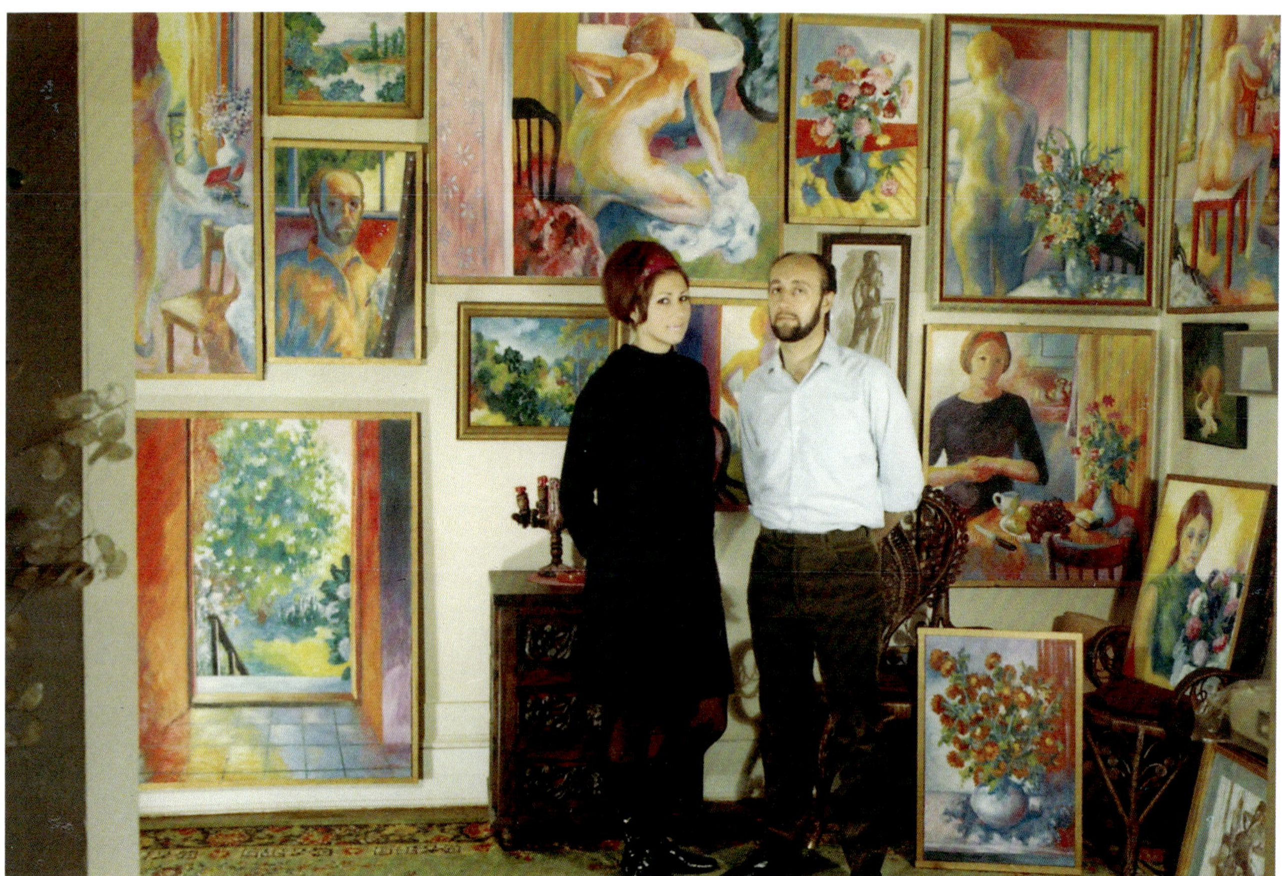

Sylvia & Frank in apartment, 1960s, PHOTOGRAPHER UNKNOWN

displayed in their own studios, bypassing the galleries was considered heresy in the '60s. It's a price Frank continues to pay as he has rarely exhibited his work in public.

As the '60s drew to a close, Frank had no illusion that he would be a career painter, and having no desire to starve, he took a teaching job at the newly formed Capilano College. Now that his students became his priority, he no longer had the time to hold regular shows, but having an income independent of painting freed him to continue painting exactly the way he wanted.

One of the few breaks that came to these emerging artists was meeting Paul and Jean Wolf in the early 1960s. In those days, Paul Wolf worked as a psychiatric nurse alongside artist Jock Hearn. "Paul said there's a really interesting man on my ward; he's a student nurse and he's an artist," recalled Jean Wolf. "I immediately pictured a scruffy looking man wearing a beret. But here's this pink man who looked like he scrubbed his face every day and wore one of those Robin Hood hats with a feather in it. Well, it was Jock Hearn. He was obsessed with cleanliness and totally unlike any artist I've ever imagined."[15]

An Invitation to a Preview Tuesday, Nov. 14th from 7:30 p.m. to 10 p.m. in honour of

FRANK MOLNAR

and

JACK AKROYD

Danish Art Gallery, 3757 West 10th Avenue, Vancouver, B.C.

NOV 7 1967

invitation: Molnar and Akroyd exhibition, 1967 COURTESY VANCOUVER ART GALLERY LIBRARY

Hearn introduced the Wolfs to sculptor David Marshall and painters Roy Kiyooka, David Denby, Jack Akroyd and Frank. "That was the beatnik area," Jean recalled. "It was like living an art lesson." She found Frank "intimidating and intense… Quite frankly he scared me. He's not an easy person, although none of them were really."

After Paul Wolf graduated university and secured a federal government job in Ottawa, the couple quickly realized that little sold in the local galleries except pine trees. "And they still sell them, very successfully," he added.[16] "There were more BAs, MAs and PhDs in Ottawa than anywhere else in Canada, and we thought it might be a good market for art." They set up a gallery in the basement of their Ottawa house, put together a company called Artists West and soon had a rash of eager buyers purchasing work from B.C. artists.

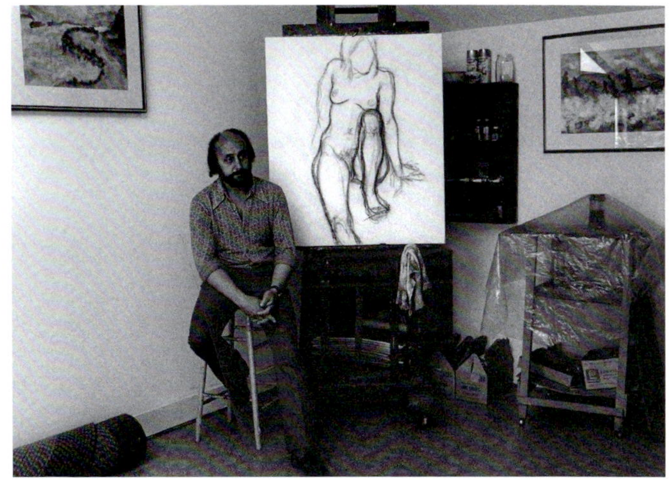

Frank Molnar in studio, 1975, PHOTO BY MARJ TRIM FOR ARTISTS WEST

"I didn't sell as many of Frank's—I don't know why, they were extremely attractive nudes," said Wolf. "The buyers all had a lot of degrees, but they would start looking at art and say 'I'm not sure that goes with the drapes.'"

Akroyd's paintings sold well, as did Denby's designs. "Frank's had more punch, and so it was a limited number of people willing to put punch on their walls and still is," said Wolf. "Basically Canadians really much prefer to buy waters, trees and lakes. His stuff would sell well in Europe."

Frank caught another break in 1970 when he was one of 46 artists selected from over 450 entries to exhibit work at *Survey 70: Realism(e)s*, a co-production of the Montreal Museum of Fine Arts and the Art Gallery of Ontario. Frank exhibited three oil paintings, *View from Mission Abbey, Kalamalka Lake* and *The Slough*, alongside such well-known names as Michael Snow, Toni Onley, Tony Urquhart, Ken Danby and Joyce Wieland. "In trying to limit the number in the present exhibition to a manageable size, we

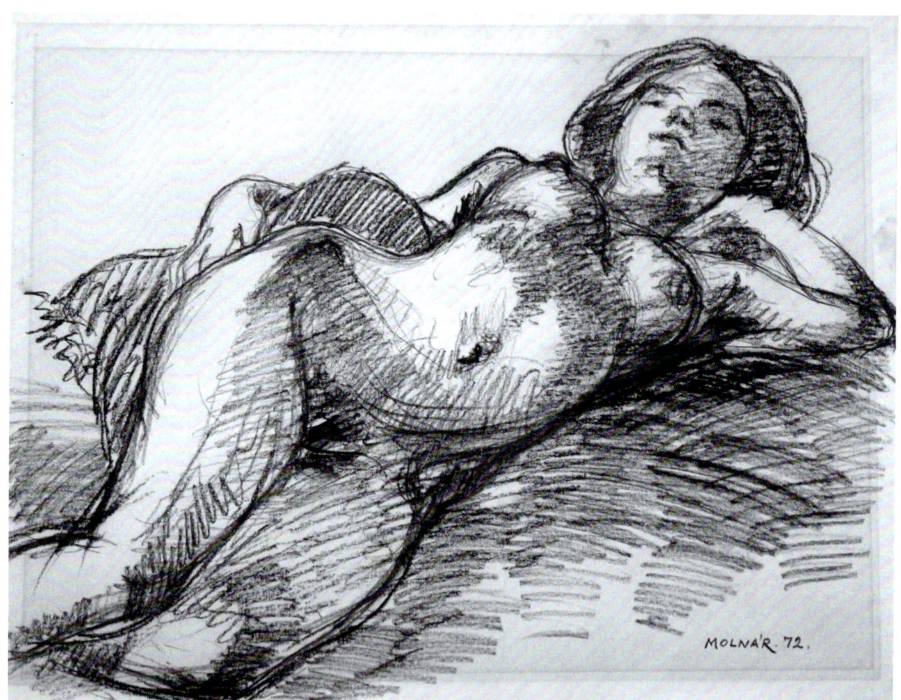

Charcoal on paper, 1972, 18" x 24"
DAN FAIRCHILD PHOTOGRAPHY

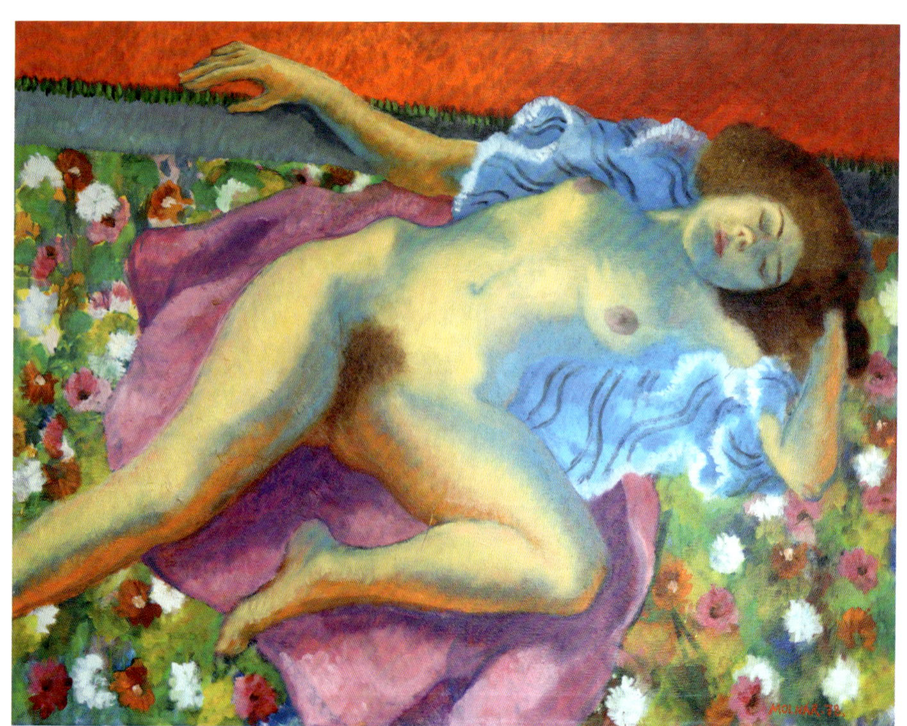

Untitled, 1978, oil on canvas, 40" x 48"
PRIVATE COLLECTION OF KAREN & MAURICE SHU
DAN FAIRCHILD PHOTOGRAPHY.

›~ *Self Portrait – Frank Molnar,* 1968, oil on canvas, 18" x 12"
MOLNAR COLLECTION
DAN FAIRCHILD PHOTOGRAPHY

› Peter Aspell, Molnar's house, Dec 26th 1998

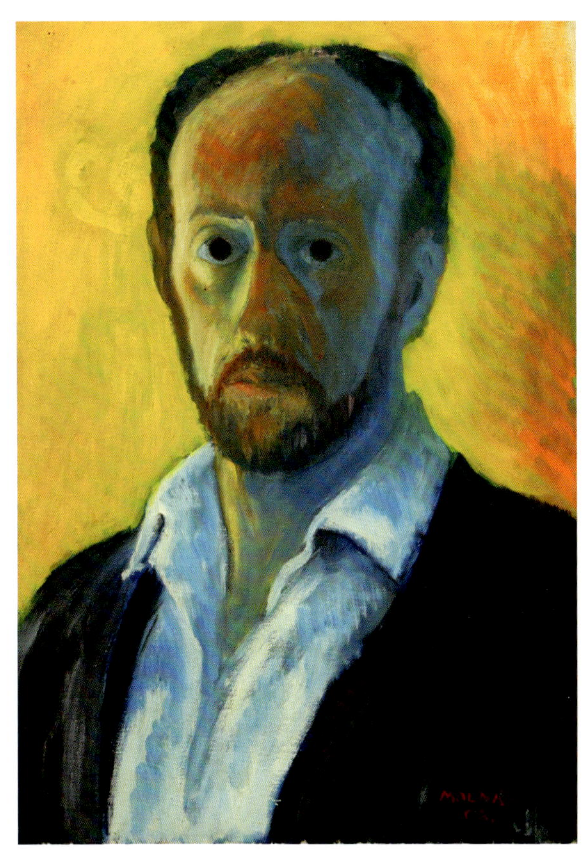

sought out variety and originality, complexity of ideas as well as new techniques," wrote Mario Amaya, the chief curator of the Art Gallery of Ontario, in the catalogue. "It is one's sincere hope that the exhibition will contribute a fuller picture of what is going on at a moment when the art of Canada is assuming an international identity of its own, as well as providing some concrete examples of the talent that abounds."[17]

In Frank's case, neither the public nor the art elite were listening. But he steadfastly refused to compromise either his style of painting or his integrity. And, fortunately for him, he never had to.

Jack Akroyd introduced Frank to Peter Aspell, another figurative painter living in Vancouver. "He said, Frank, you and I are the only sensualists in this damn town," recalled Frank. At the time, Stephen Leskard was establishing a commercial art and design school at Capilano College and looking for instructors. Aspell, who taught at the Vancouver School of Art, suggested he hire Frank.

Before he became one of the College's first art teachers, Frank and Sylvia took an extended trip to Europe in 1968, his first time back in 12 years. They visited art galleries and museums in England, Austria, Germany and Hungary, as well as the Rijksmuseum in Amsterdam. In Paris, Frank paid homage at the studio where Eugene Delacroix (1798–1863) lived, worked and died. Later he marvelled at the artist's murals at the Church of Saint-Sulpice. One of the most impressive paintings he saw was the 1654 oil by Rembrandt van Rijn, *Bathsheba at Her Bath*, at the Louvre, one he revisited many times.

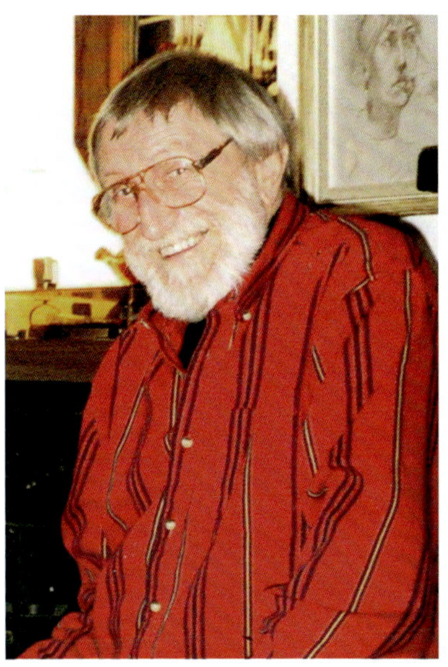

"It's the most beautiful painting. A beautiful life-size nude sitting reading a letter while an old lady washes her feet," explained Frank. "The woman looks at the letter with such unbelievable humility as she accepts her fate, I have seen people sit down and have tears in their eyes. Not too many people could paint it that way. This is one of the most important paintings and it touches me greatly."[18]

The Molnars returned to Hungary several times, the last trip just before Frank's mother died in 1993, three years after his father's death.

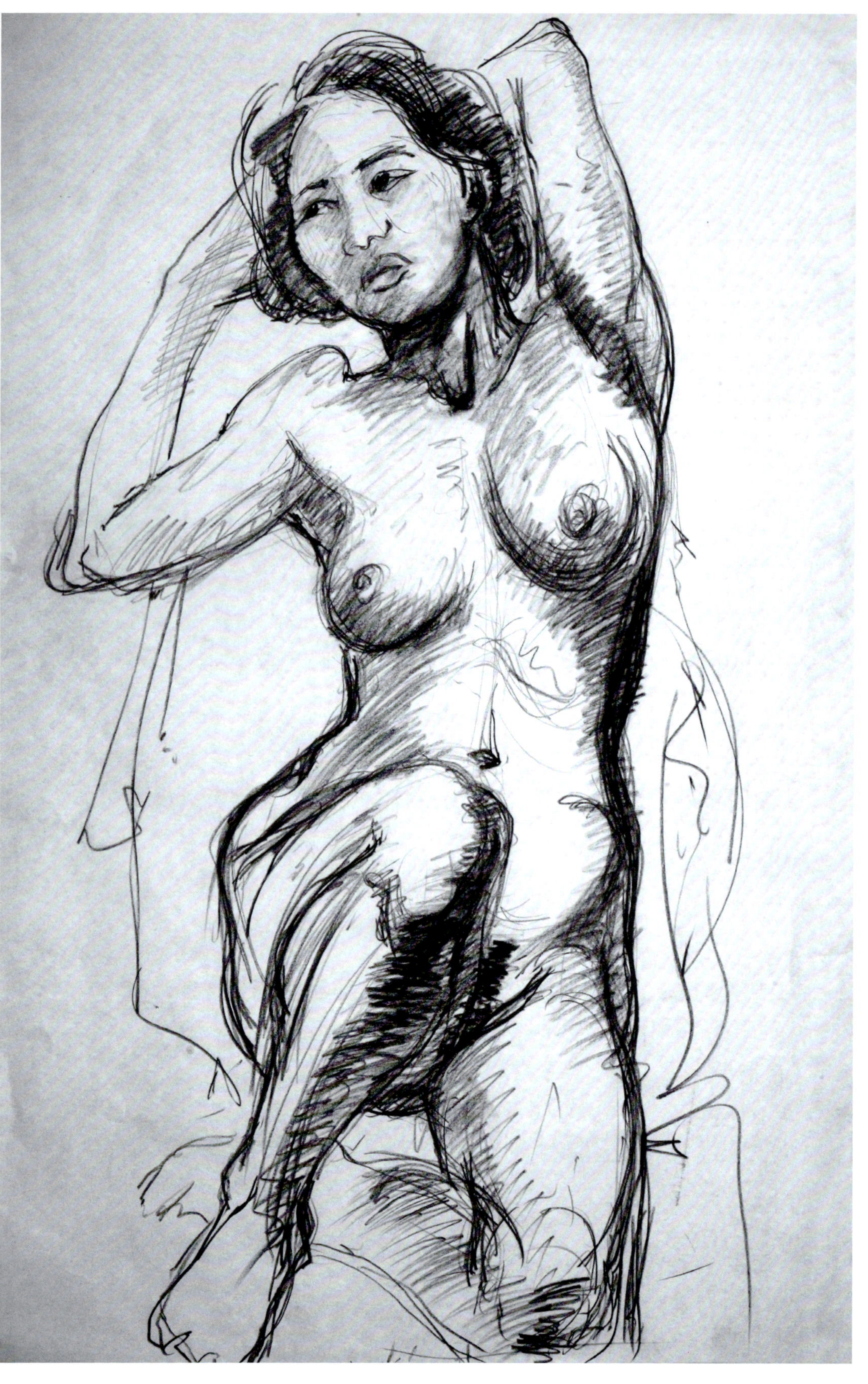

Capilano College

FROM THE MOMENT FRANK STARTED at Capilano College, teaching quickly became less of a way to put food on the table and more of a vocation.

Initially the College was scattered about the North Shore, and the art department comprised one room and a couple of portables on Mathers Street in West Vancouver. Gradually it grew to include two art studios, a pottery and a sculpture department, and the search began for a permanent campus.

Frank became a teacher in both the fine arts and the commercial design programs. The problem was that the two departments had very different philosophies. "Fine arts wanted it to be another Vancouver School of Art—everything was just *express* yourself. We don't teach basics, we don't teach drawing," he said.[19] At that time, commercial design was a three-year program; fine arts was two years. His job was to teach the foundation program and instill the fundamentals of art, no matter if the students were painters, sculptors or headed for the commercial world.

‹ Charcoal on paper, 2004, 18" x 24"
DAN FAIRCHILD PHOTOGRAPHY

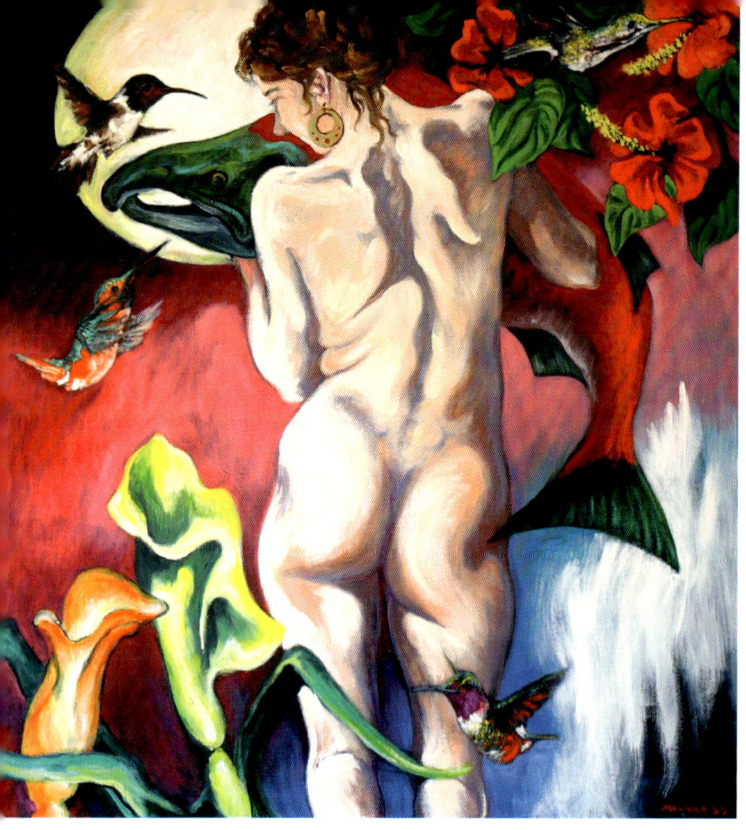

David Marshall joined the college sculpture department and foundry, and he and Frank were colleagues and friends for almost 20 years. He would often give Marshall a ride home after classes. Marshall, he said, was "an artist's artist… He was underrated by the public, by the art experts and all these institutions like the Vancouver Art Gallery. But he was admired and respected by all the other artists and sculptors. He was a perfectionist, and he paid tremendous attention to the last detail of the finish whether it was marble, bronze or wood."

Frank taught artistic anatomy and life drawing. Not everyone loved his style. His insistence that students mastered the technical skills grated on those who were used to a conceptual approach where the idea is more important than the art. "I tried to teach them to be an artist, to have the eye of an artist, to look at things and see things as an artist," he said, adding that many of his students got jobs instantly and went on to be well-known illustrators and commercial artists.[20]

Untitled, 1999, oil on canvas, 40" x 48"
DAN FAIRCHILD PHOTOGRAPHY

Charles van Sandwyk, now one of Canada's most important and best-selling illustrators, said Frank is the "single largest influence in his career." He studied with him from 1984 to 1986, and nearly 25 years later, he still turns to his former teacher and mentor for help and advice. In 2005, the Folio Society commissioned van Sandwyk to draw a picture of an artist painting a flower for *Which Was the Happiest?* from Hans Christian Andersen's *The Complete Tales.* Although far more comfortable drawing animals than people, he decided to submit a self-portrait dressed in full eighteenth-century garb, before coming down with a severe case of artistic block.

›› *Portrait of Elizabeth Mihalik* 1980, oil on canvas, life size
PRIVATE COLLECTION

"I was having so much trouble doodling away, and my anatomy is not good that I took it over to Frank, and he said, 'What is this? The legs are so short that if you stood up you would fall right over on your keester!'" He told him to start again and, this time, try a little subtlety. "Make a suggestion that it looks like you," Frank told him. "Think of it as if it's a prayer and you are bending over the rose." van Sandwyk said, "I went there with a piece of crap, and I came home so inspired."

› *Untitled,* 2003, oil on canvas, 10" x 14"
PRIVATE COLLECTION
DAN FAIRCHILD PHOTOGRAPHY

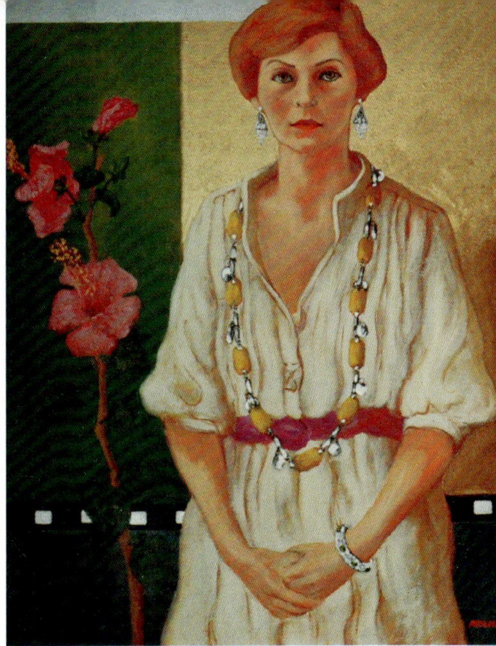

At art school, Frank was gruff, but the students loved him, according to van Sandwyk: "He'd say, 'I'm trying to draw you out of mediocrity; that's what I want to do.' And I swallowed that message whole. I was always doing the kind of work that I do, I just wasn't doing it very well. Frank was the best art teacher you could ever have." [21]

Pastel artist Andrew McDermott took life drawing with Frank in the late 1980s. "He was old school, and I needed that at the time; I just wanted the traditional way of drawing," says McDermott. Frank taught him to draw big and bold. "You know—classical—which all the schools really should be teaching," he said. "We have to get back to basics here. You get these graduating students that are doing all this weird stuff, but they have not been taught how to draw and paint the old way."

According to McDermott, Frank is an enigma who avoided marketing and refused to bend with the fads of the time: "He didn't cave into all the BS; if he did he'd probably make money at it, but he didn't and all the power to him. [22]

Now a successful North Shore-based artist, Cori Creed took classes with Frank in the mid 1990s at Capilano College. She remembered him stomping through life drawing classes yelling, "Volume! You've got to have more volume!" she said in a very passable knock-off of his Hungarian accent. [23]

Volume, among other things, is a lesson that has stuck. As Frank explained it to me later, volume is the process of creating space. A still life of fruit on a table has a dark corner and coloured shadows to give you the feeling that you can walk behind the table and pick up the fruit. The shadows, he told me, create the feeling that objects have volume, or three-dimensionality, and he's right, the table does give the perception of depth.

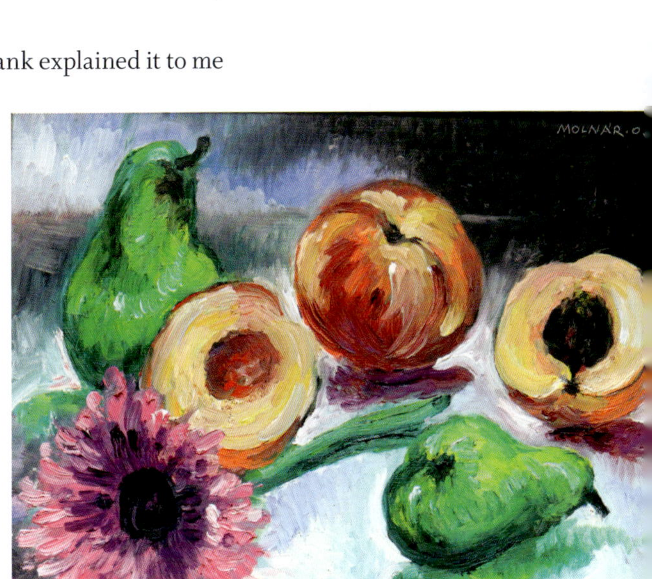

While Creed now mostly does large landscapes, she's starting to do a little more figurative work. "When I do go to life drawing, I still think about some different pointers that he gave. He taught me different classical techniques that were like tools for my tool box," she said. "He really cared that you were getting his lessons. You definitely felt that he was invested in his student's success." [24]

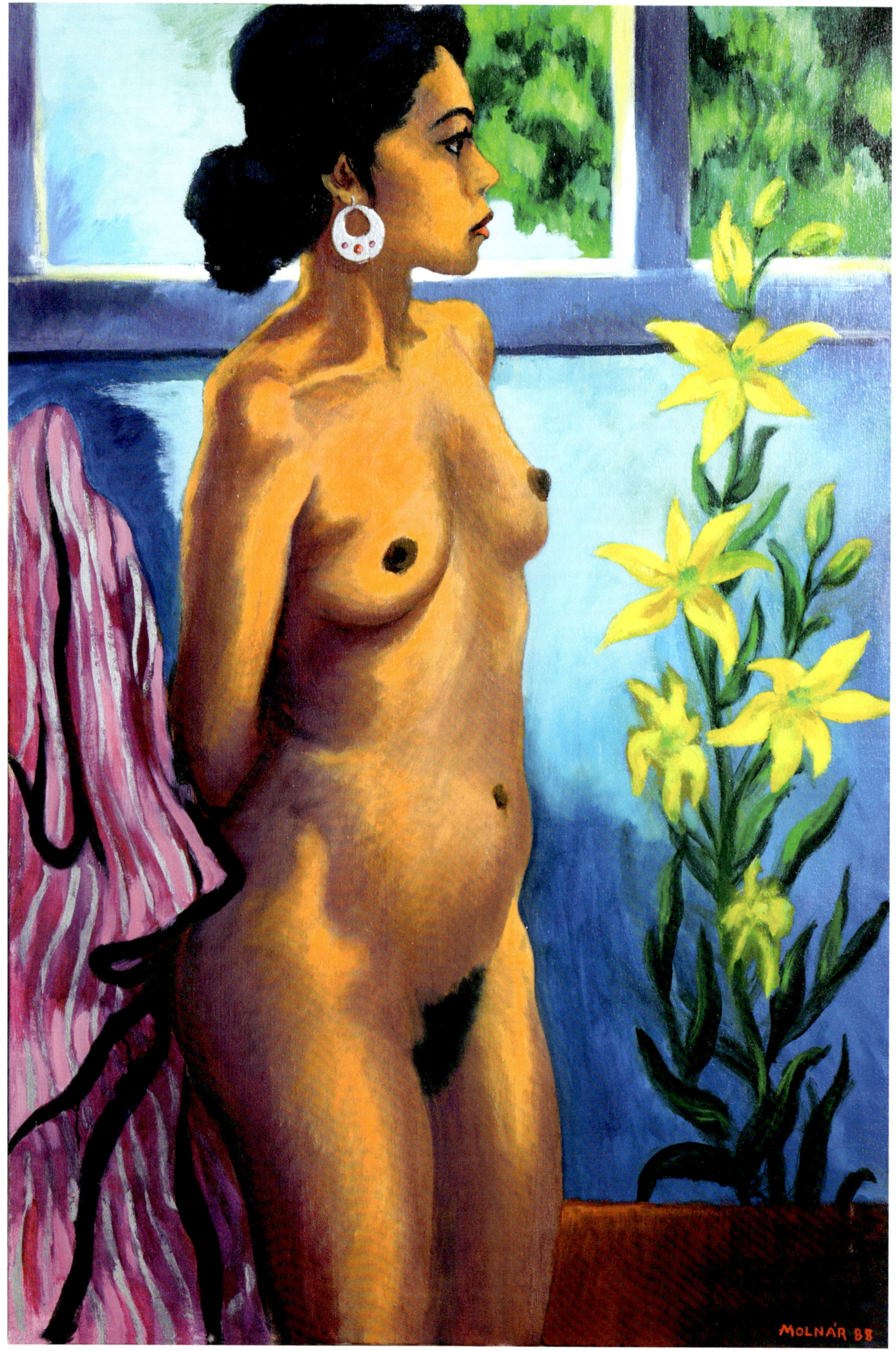
MOLNÁR 88

Canadians and the Nude

"Frank," said David Maclagan, a former colleague at Capilano College, "was a real artist. He was that old school of painter where you really lived and breathed your art."[25] Maclagan added that Frank, like other traditional artists of the '60s and '70s was largely ignored in the public and gallery rush to embrace change. He also remembered that when the instructors had shows in the North Shore galleries, Frank was usually excluded: "In those days, you just didn't hang nudes."

According to Frank, Canadians simply cannot handle nudes: "They think my art is disturbing for the children. They say they wouldn't have it in their living room, wouldn't have it in their home."

In *The Nude in Canadian Painting*, Jerrold Morris stated that numerous paintings of the nude remain secluded and hidden from public view "like the inhabitants of an old-fashioned red-light district."[26] When Morris, a former curator at the Vancouver Art Gallery, wrote the book, he found that even reference mate-

‹ *Mulatto Nude with Yellow Flowers,* 1988, oil on canvas, 44" x 31"
DAN FAIRCHILD PHOTOGRAPHY

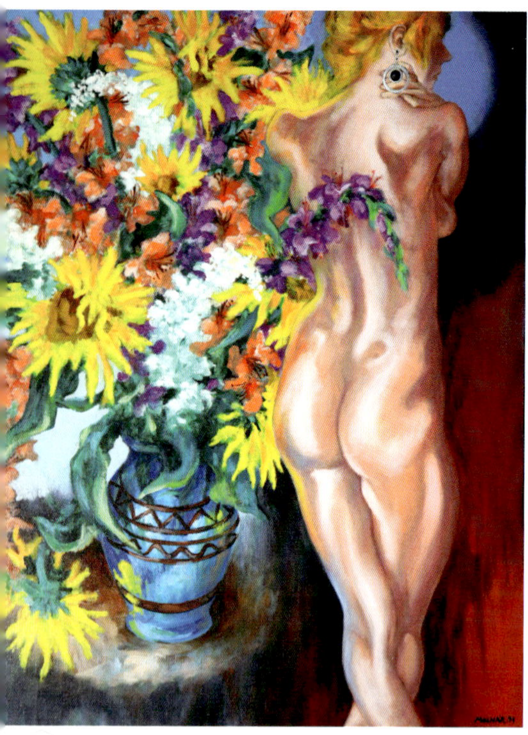

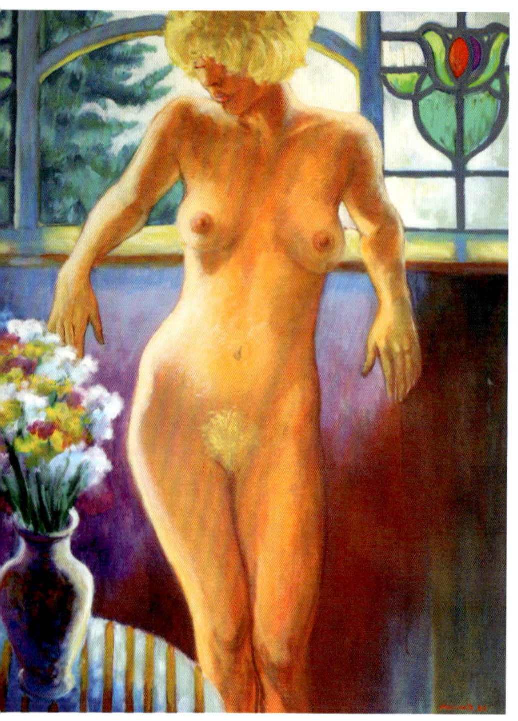

rial about the nude in art was almost non-existent. He mentioned several examples of what he calls Canadians' "depressingly prudish attitude to art," pointing out that when the National Gallery of Canada mounted a Centennial exhibition called Three Hundred Years of Canadian Art only one nude was included among the 375 works. Another bizarre example was the trial of Toronto gallery owner Dorothy Cameron who was charged with exhibiting obscene material after she mounted an exhibition called Eros in 1965. In 1966, a Vancouver gallery owner was acquitted of a similar charge.

Frank had his own brush with the law. In the mid-1960s, the police were called to the Danish Art Gallery over the exhibition of one of his full-frontal nudes. The gallery owner refused to take it down. More recently—this century in fact—a Calgary gallery owner came to the Molnars' home on the recommendation of a gallery owner in Vancouver.[27] "He walked through here and walked out," said Frank. "He was as mad as hell that I dared to paint nudes and pubic hair, and he said 'My gallery doesn't deal with it!'"[28]

But while Frank may have hoped that Canadians would eventually have a European sensibility toward the nude, it didn't deter him from painting them. "If we were in Montreal or Toronto or New York or Europe, it would be a different story because people there do not have this problem that we have here in Vancouver with the nude," said Sylvia Molnar. "I get so furious. You have to accept the human body as being something rather wonderful."[29]

The frustrating thing for a Molnar fan is that few of his hundreds of paintings and drawings are accessible to the public. Most are in the hands of more than a hundred private collectors in Europe, New York and across Canada and the U.S. A few of his watercolours and still lifes hang in corporate offices.

Karen Gruninger Shu, a life drawing student, first met Frank in 1971. Years later, as a wife and mother, she attended a friend's birthday party and spotted a magnificent painting hanging over the fireplace of a nude coming out of a bathtub. She immediately recognized Frank's work and bought the 1968 nude, as well as an oil painting of an orchard in the Okanagan, from her friend.

Over the years, Gruninger Shu and her husband, Maurice Shu, added other nudes from Frank's *Leda and the Swan* series, watercolours of the West Coast of Vancouver Island and various charcoal drawings. "There is not a day that I don't look at my paintings. I love them so much," said Gruninger Shu. "It's timeless. I've never grown tired of looking at his work."[30] They became one of Frank's largest collectors.

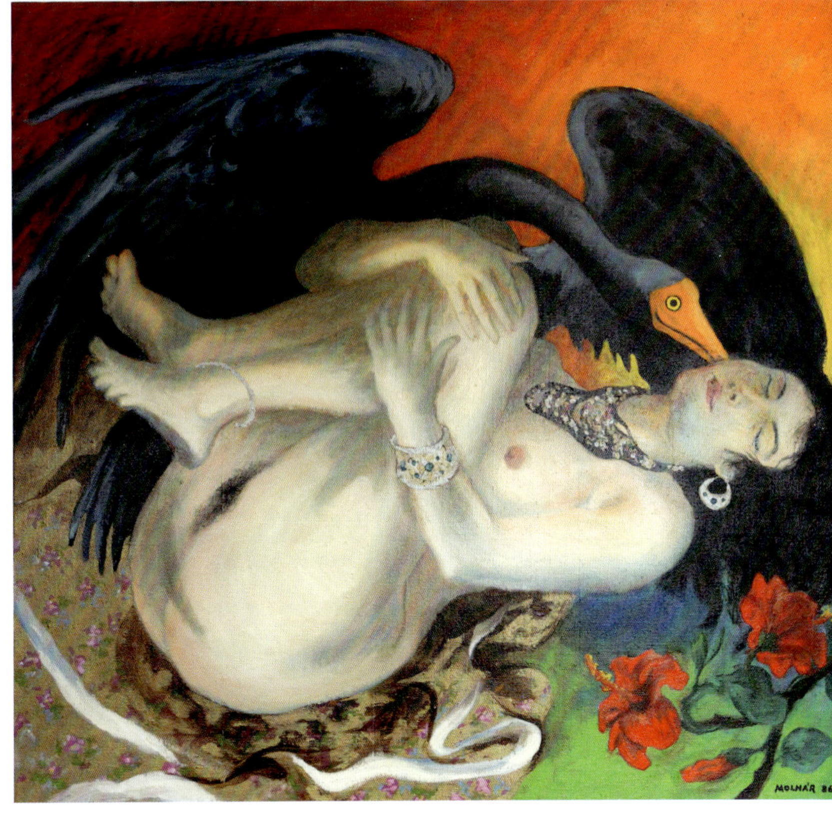

When the South African-born Charles van Sandwyk is not spending half the year in Fiji, he lives in a tiny Deep Cove cottage filled with his wonderful illustrations, as well as a 1984 Molnar painting of *Leda and the Swan* and a series of his mentor's still lifes. "His pictures were softer in those days," explained van Sandwyk. "He played with two very different and interesting themes. He'd often do very soft-skinned ladies and a black swan, and other times, a mulatto or Polynesian with a white swan, so he's playing with the yin-yang balance."[31]

Untitled, 1986, oil on canvas, 42" x 50"
PRIVATE COLLECTION OF KAREN AND MAURICE SHU
DAN FAIRCHILD PHOTOGRAPHY

With the eye of both a gifted artist and a long-time friend, he pointed to the repeated themes of gladioli—Frank and Sylvia's birth flower: "I like the pose; it's soft but it's vibrant, and it's also a form of chaos when you think about it." According to him, Frank's paintings challenge the viewer: "They are not subtle little things that you can put in the corner. Frank's paintings say a lot, and he's a classic example of a fabulous artist operating in the wrong place."

‹ *Untitled,* 1991, oil on canvas, 51" x 41"
PRIVATE COLLECTION OF EVE LAZARUS
DAN FAIRCHILD PHOTOGRAPHY

I follow van Sandwyk to another of the cottage walls, as he points to a series of still lifes by Frank. "Even these little ones are sensual. Look at the fillet of salmon with the scallion and the lemons. That's a fabulous little painting; it's nicely handled, it's soft, it's suggestive and it's juicy."[32]

Frank, he explained, has always been able to see beyond the skin.

‹ *Nude Against the Light,* 1986, oil on canvas, 54" x 38"
PRIVATE COLLECTION OF KAREN AND MAURICE SHU
DAN FAIRCHILD PHOTOGRAPHY

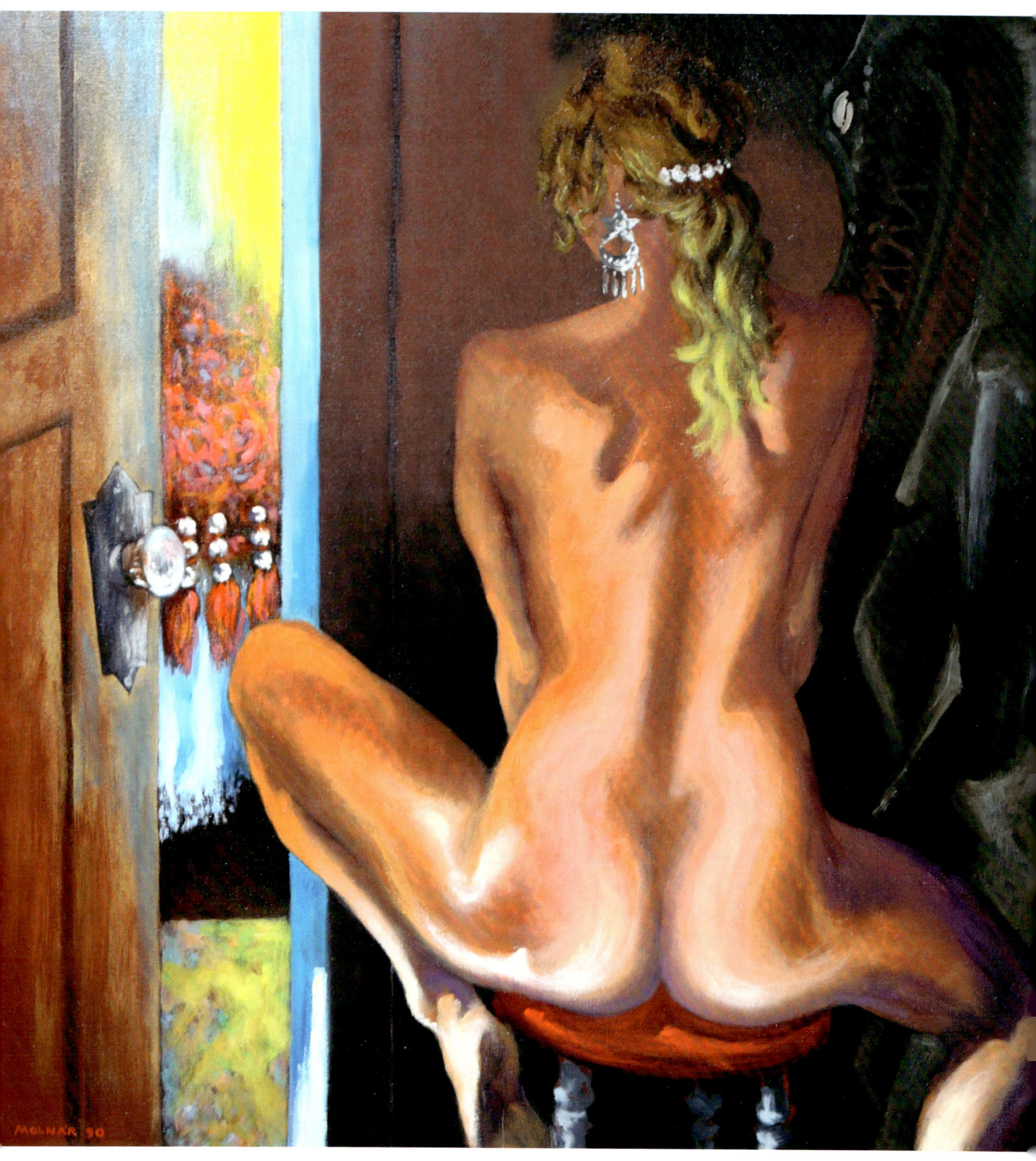
MOLNÁR 90

Point Grey

If you sit in the Molnars' kitchen long enough, you'll likely meet Knocker, the resident seagull, named because he pecks loudly at the back window demanding food two or three times every day. In summer, ruby-throated hummingbirds hover in the garden, sharing a riot of colour with squirrels, raccoons and human visitors. Hoppy, the disabled crow, also visits the house several times a day. He appears in some of the paintings. "The crow," Frank said, pointing to a huge oil of Persephone, "just happens to be there because he's a wise one; he's the only one aware of what's happening."

‹ *Untitled,* 1990,
oil on canvas, 44" x 44"
DAN FAIRCHILD PHOTOGRAPHY

The fact that Frank loves nature is evident in every one of his paintings, dozens of which hang in his Point Grey home and span more than half a century. In his collection, his work shares space with paintings from contemporaries such as Jack Akroyd, sculptures from Georg Schmerholz and Elek Imredy, as well as African masks, wood and soapstone carvings and ceramics from all over the world.

The heritage house that the Molnars bought in 1974 is just blocks from where Sylvia grew up. The touches throughout this living gallery smack of European

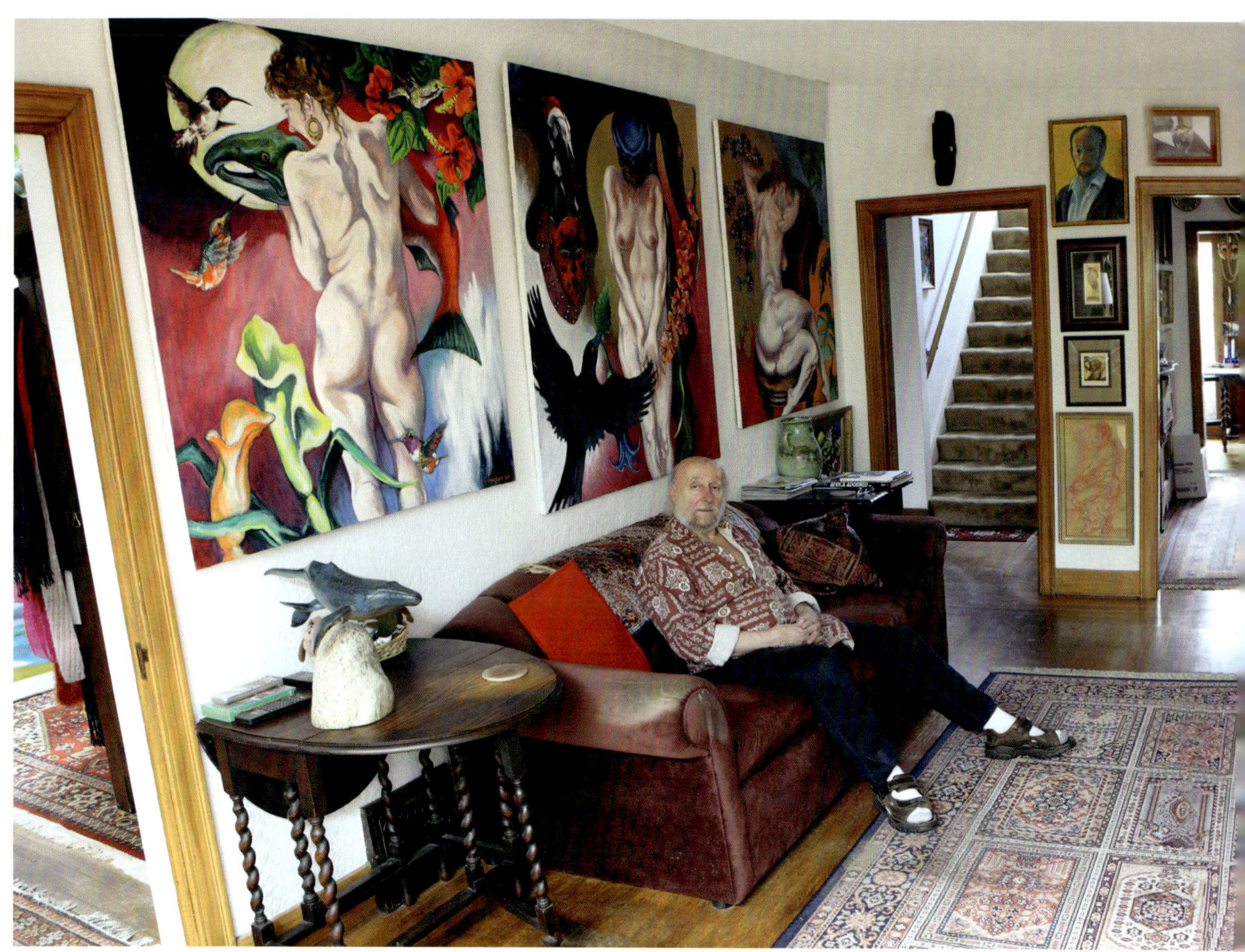

Frank and Sylvia, 2009
DAN FAIRCHILD PHOTOGRAPHY

sophistication, texture and colour. Except for the two bathrooms, there are no inside doors, and everywhere you turn, there are bright vivacious paintings filling white walls, warm woodwork, stained glass, plants and elegant antique furniture.

Then there are Frank's self-portraits. In them you can see the intensity of the young artist, as his eyes gaze out and challenge the viewer, and of the vibrant colours that are characteristic of all of his work.

While Frank's still lifes, landscapes and figurative drawings are all over the house, the most visually stimulating are his nudes. From his interpretation of Leda and the Swan to Persephone, mythology entwines with a waterfall of yellow forsythia, cherry blossoms, fuchsias and angel trumpets from his own garden, so real you can

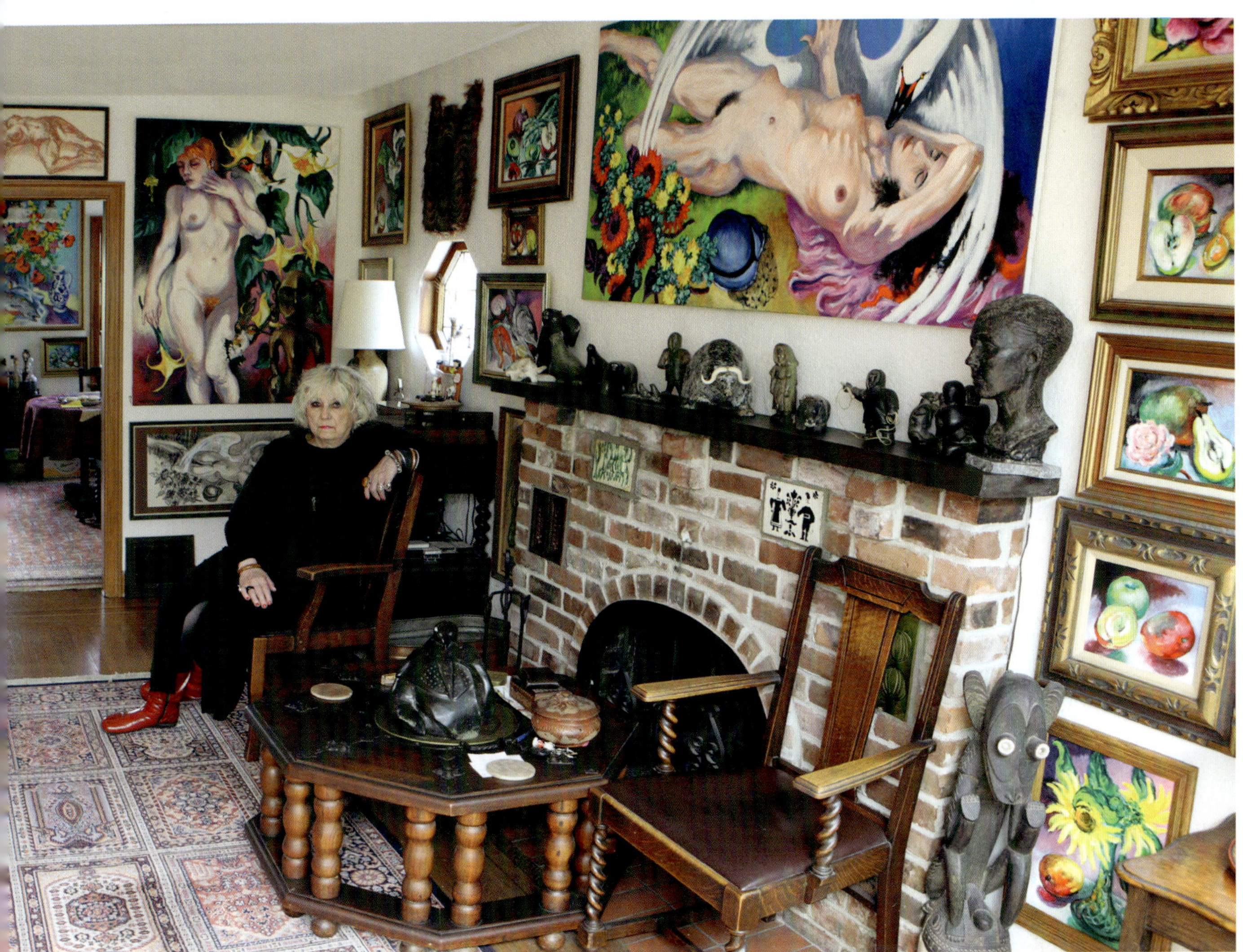

almost smell their heavy fragrance. He revels in the erotic content of ancient mythology. The sensuality of the stories Leda and the Swan and Persephone, both involving beautiful young women, allows him to rework the myths on his own terms and in his own colours.

"I love the human figure, I love the feminine figure, I love the sensuality of it," Frank explained. "Colour to me is a manifestation of sensuous painting. You can paint an apple and make it sensuous and romantic by the use of colour; it's a much more European concept of colour."

Frank considers himself a colourist in the same tradition as French romantic painter Eugene Delacroix, and later Georges Seurat, Paul Gauguin and Pierre Bon-

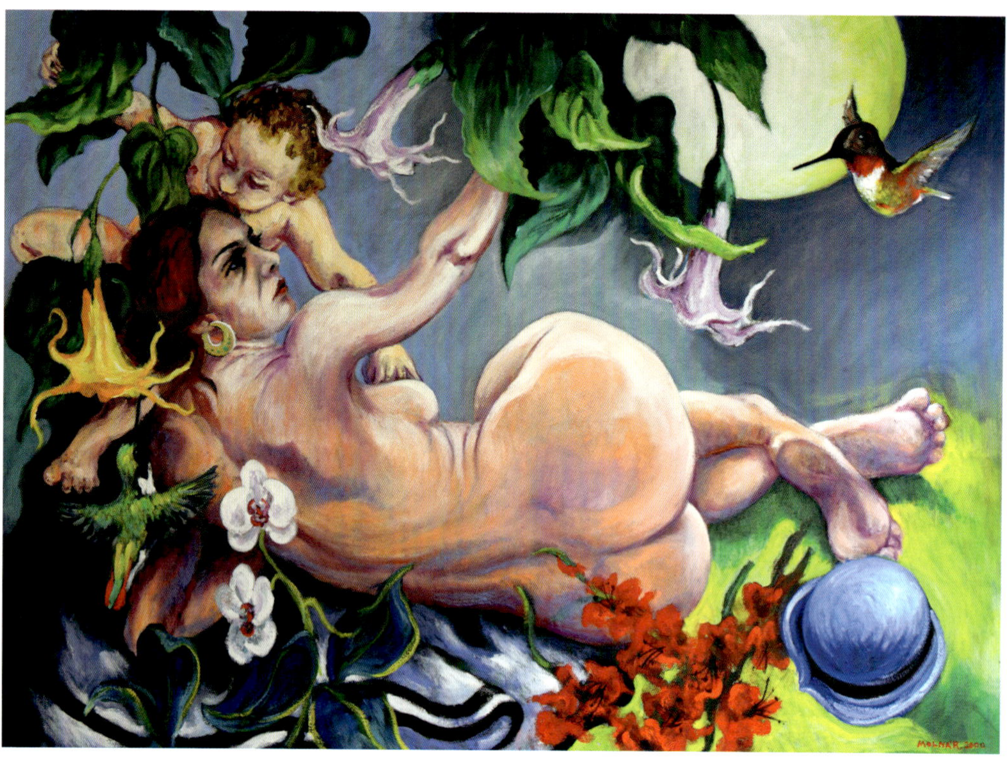

Valentine, 2000,
oil on canvas, 41" x 57"
PRIVATE COLLECTION
DAN FAIRCHILD PHOTOGRAPHY

nard. "I consider the sensuality of different colours more important than just a figure itself or the sexual content of a nude," he explained. "I think sensuality comes through a combination of different colours that create a mood."[33]

He deeply admires Delacroix and is a devotee of the work of the post-impressionist painter Gauguin, ever since seeing his work at the Museum of Modern Art in 1959. He pointed to a huge nude painted in a surrealist style. In it there's a woman lying down with her arm outstretched, a child, angel trumpets, a hummingbird and the moon. It was Frank's valentine present to Sylvia in 2000. He hired a model for the body so she would not know and painted her face from a photograph.

Frank finds that if he looks at something too closely he gets carried away by the reality of it. Instead of painting from the model, he'll sketch first and paint from the sketches. He mostly chooses blonde or red-headed models because they have the whitest skin and can both absorb the colour of the flowers and reflect them.[34]

Frank paints on expensive Irish or Belgium linen that he sizes and stretches. Using acid-free canvasses that stand the test of time, he applies top-quality paints imported from Japan and Holland.

Another massive nude is propped up on his studio easel. *Persephone*, the daughter of Zeus, is a challenging painting to absorb. As in others in this series, Frank has painted himself into the picture as Hades, her abductor, brother of Zeus and ruler of the underworld. The myth symbolizes the budding and dying of nature. The colours are darker in this painting, making it seem less surrealistic and more foreboding. It looks finished but remains unsigned.

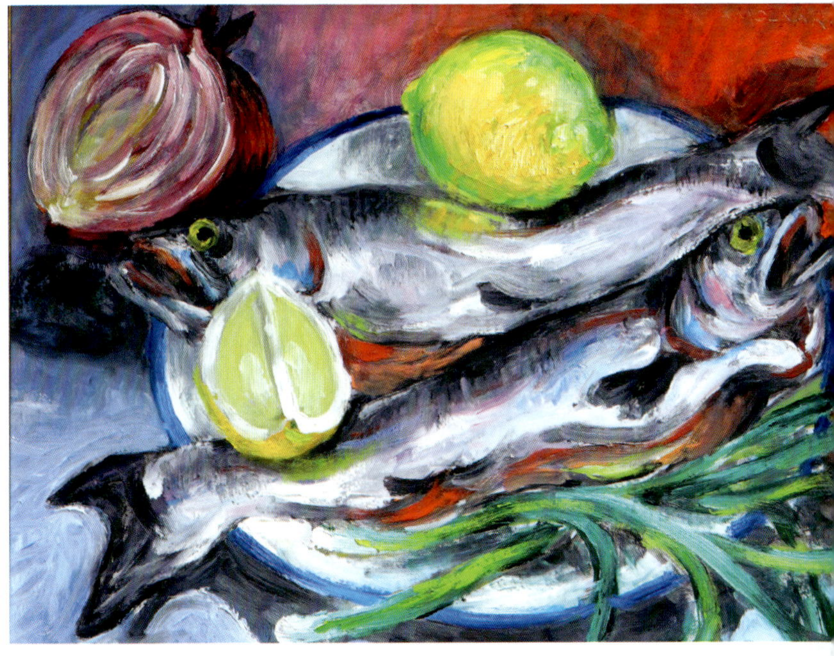

Untitled, 2006,
oil on canvas, 12" x 16"
DAN FAIRCHILD PHOTOGRAPHY

He pauses to run his hand over the layers of paint making up the curves of Persephone's body and invites me to do the same. It's more textured than his other paintings. "I enjoy the texture; I think it makes it more alive or organic, and I keep doing the face. It's almost like my farewell to some of these big paintings. I don't know if I can do more unless my health improves."[35]

A wooden statue from Papua New Guinea, with the head of a saltwater crocodile and a large penis, stands in the Molnars' living room and also appears in several of his paintings. "I used him as a counterpoint to the women I have painted. Very often they cover their faces. Westerners have a guilt-ridden sensuality," explained Frank, adding that most native art has a sensuality and eroticism about it. He described native art as fresh and direct in its execution: "It has tremendous power."

With his hypnotic accent, Frank likes to take his time to talk about his painting and his life, using his hands to punctuate his speech. He laughs impatiently as I pepper him with questions.

Frank admitted that he hasn't painted for over a year. He told me he is hoping for inspiration when the weather is warmer and he can throw open all the windows to get rid of the pungent smell of turpentine. His lack of painting clearly worries his wife, who said, "He's emotional and highly sensitive; my goodness, that's okay, I like that. I like a person with a pulse. When he doesn't paint, I can feel it. You can be sure he's depressed and not feeling well. He's happiest when he's painting."[36]

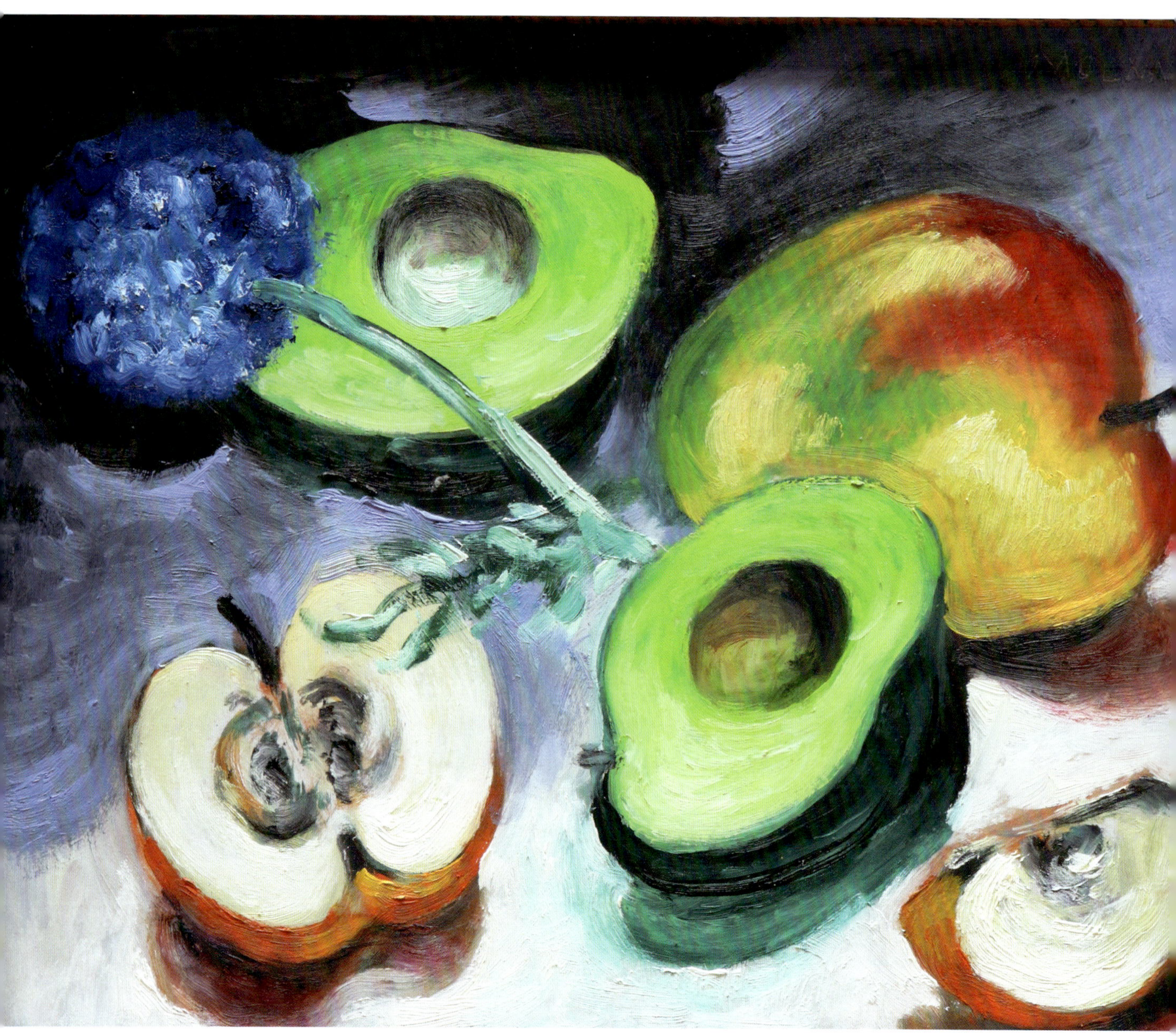

Frank's Legacy

FRANK'S WORK during his lifetime was rooted in a timeless tradition, yet never part of the current fashion. He distrusted gallery owners, refused to curry favour with art dealers or curators and had absolutely no interest in self-promotion or in marketing his work, preferring to spend his energy painting and teaching.

‹ *Untitled,* 2005,
oil on canvas, 11" x 14"
DAN FAIRCHILD PHOTOGRAPHY

Before moving to California in 2001, Georg Schmerholz lived in Vancouver for almost 30 years. He and Frank remain good friends. Schmerholz described him as a very moody and emotional man. "All you have to do is look at his work to understand that you are dealing with a person of emotional depth and volatility." In Eastern Europe, if you were an artist or a musician, you were expected to be humble and modest and let your work speak for itself and for you. But in Canada and the United States, it's not what your work is, or what you know you can produce, it's how well you can sell yourself.

And that, he claimed, is the root of Frank's problem: "In spite of Frank's incredible talent and sense of colour and composition, he just couldn't quite

Sylvia and Frank at home, 2009

DAN FAIRCHILD PHOTOGRAPHY

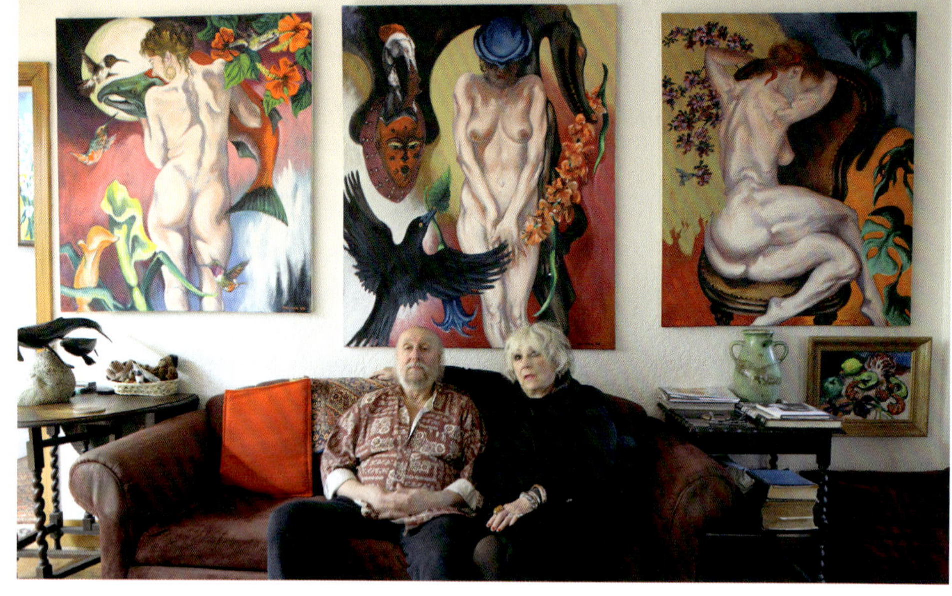

Untitled, 2001, oil on canvas, 41" x 56"

DAN FAIRCHILD PHOTOGRAPHY

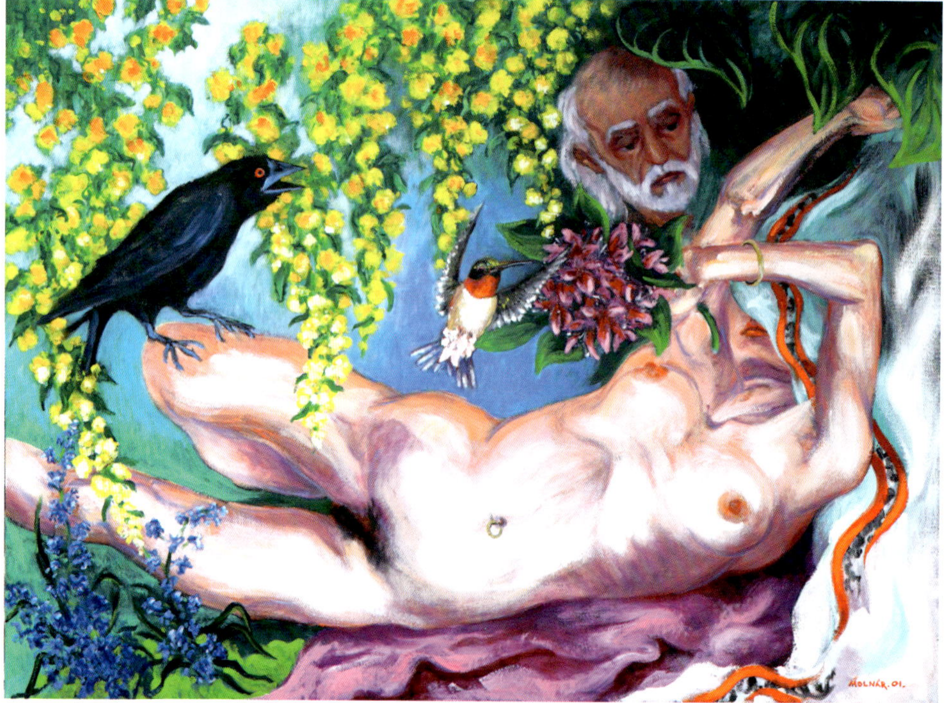

break into the inner circle of the Vancouver arts scene. Just as David Marshall couldn't break in and just as I couldn't break in."[37]

Charles van Sandwyk thinks of Frank as an Ernest Hemingway kind of character: "He's larger than life; he'd tackle a bull with his bare hands, if the bull so much as looked at him the wrong way." Frank, he said, is a blindingly intelligent man with incredible wit. "He wasn't going to be the flavour of the month. He's a rebel and rebels don't work well with the establishment," he continued. "I don't think there has ever really been a gallery in Vancouver that could handle his work."

Van Sandwyk believes that Frank will be remembered as one of the great sensualists of this province: "I think he'll be remembered in the same tones as painters like Varley who were fabulous painters that did their own thing. They all struggled. Look at what happened with Gauguin. He sold a few paintings here and there, but after his death, his paintings were selling for thousands of pounds."[38]

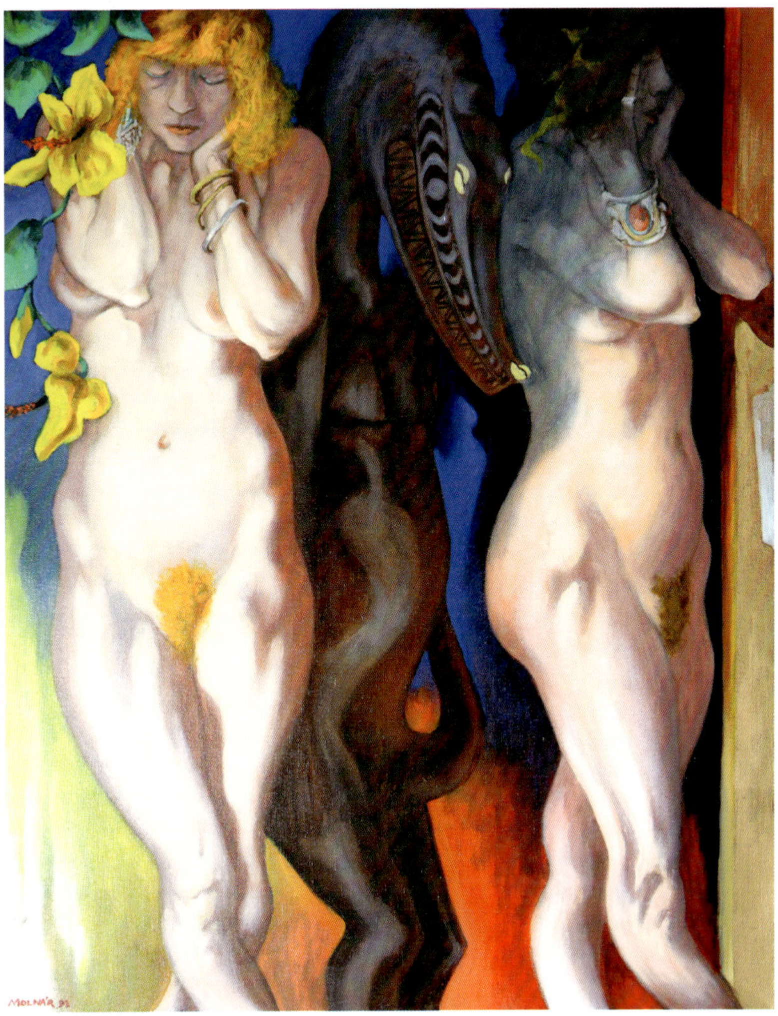

Two Women & Ralph, 1991, oil on canvas, 51" x 41"
DAN FAIRCHILD PHOTOGRAPHY

Frank does not paint to suit the market, or as Sylvia once said, he refuses to paint to match the chesterfield. But, as one of the unheralded artists of B.C., he is a true artist and maverick. His personal vision is part of his magic, and also his bane. His refusal to compromise his art kept him out of the galleries, his work out of the public eye and propelled him into a 30-year teaching career. And, while Frank continues to paint, perhaps his real legacy will be his hundreds of students, many who have gone on to international acclaim and success.

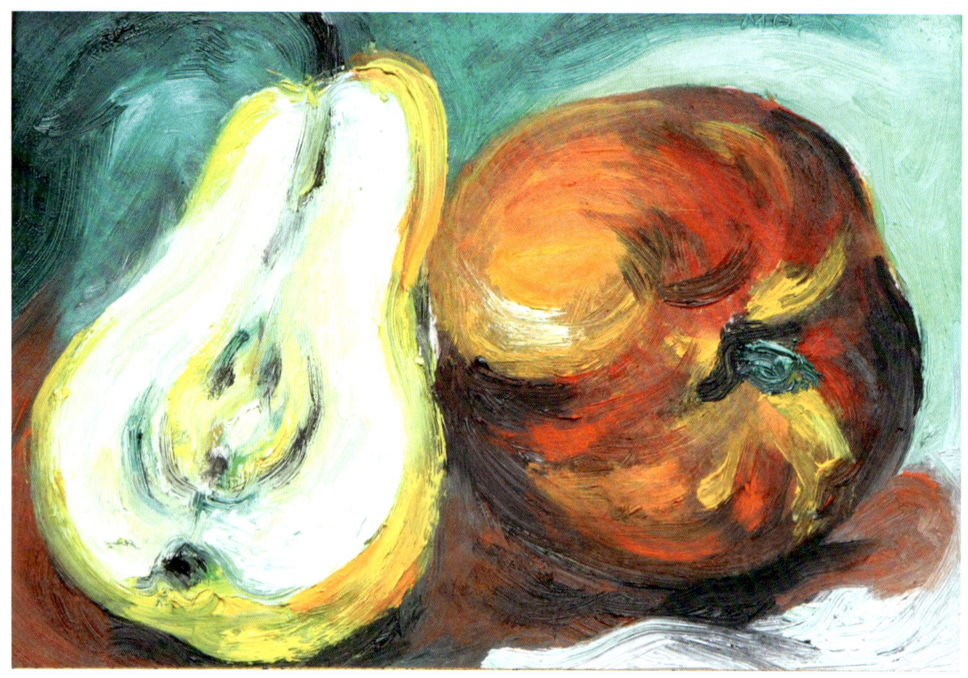

Untitled, 2007,
oil on canvas, 4.5" x 7"
DAN FAIRCHILD PHOTOGRAPHY

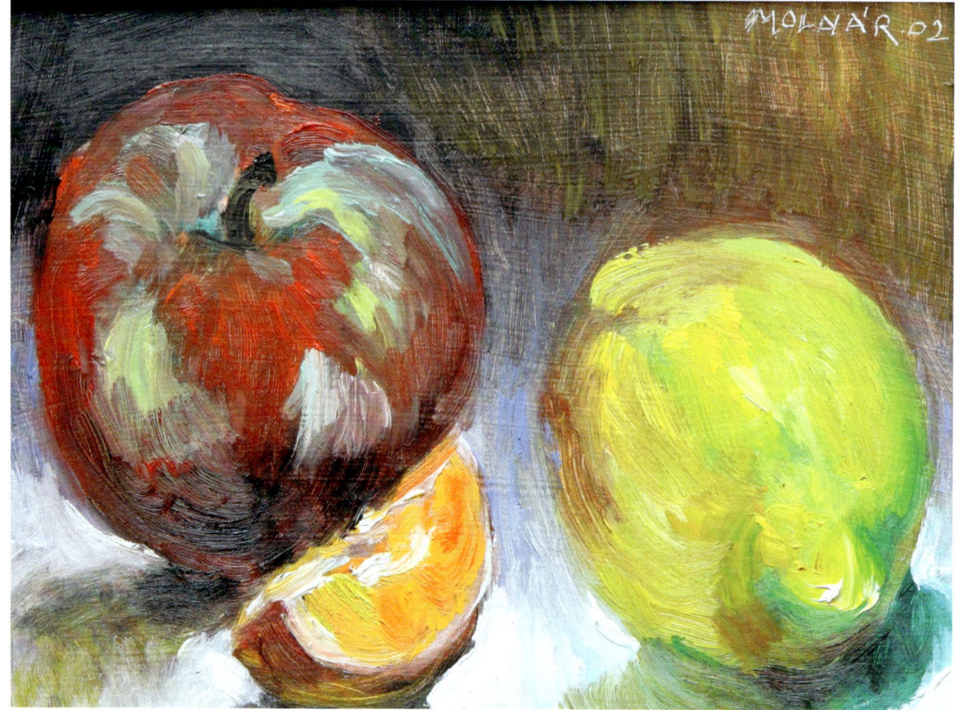

Untitled, 2002,
oil on canvas, 6" x 8"
DAN FAIRCHILD PHOTOGRAPHY

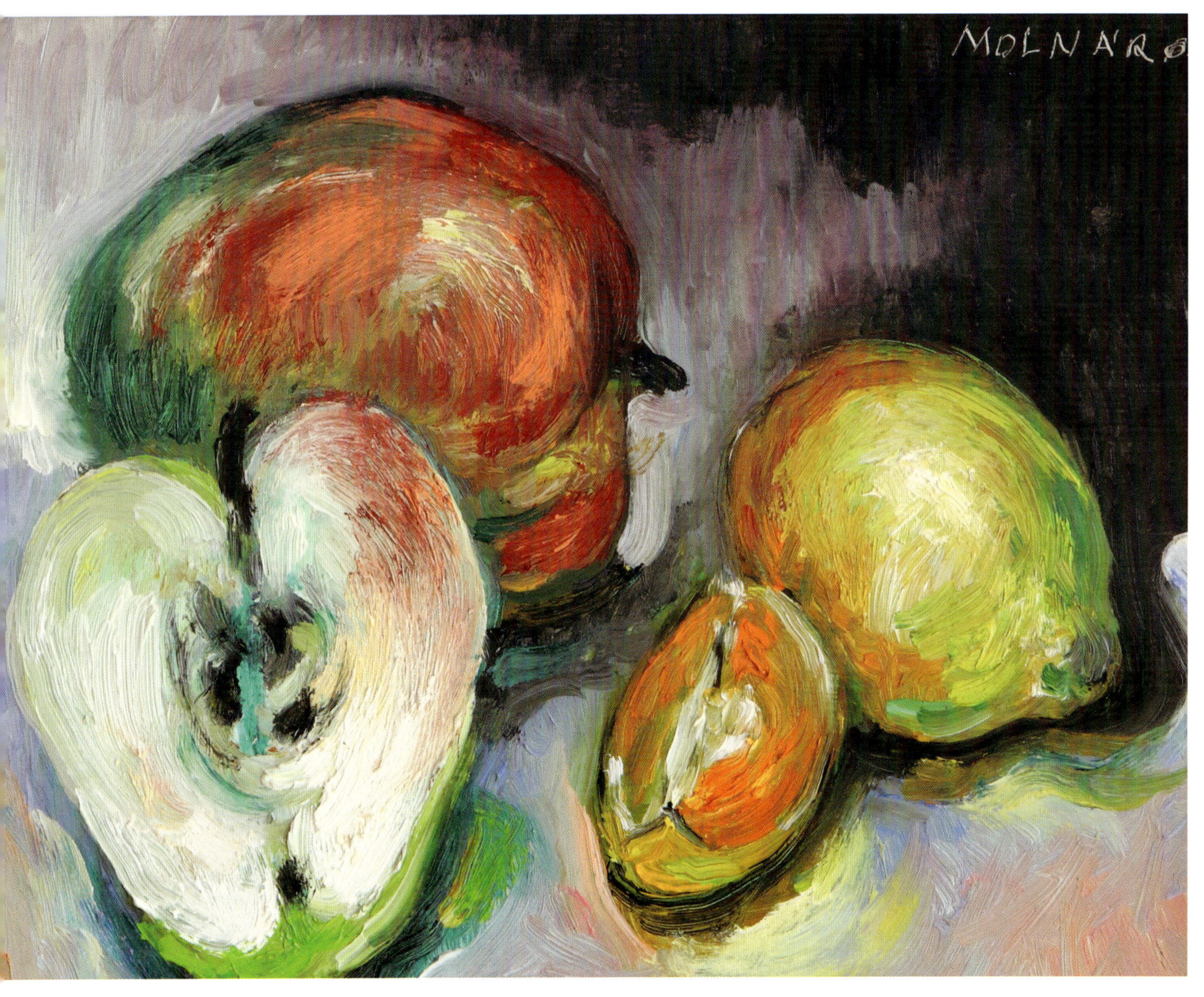

Untitled, 2004,
oil on canvas, 8" x 10"

DAN FAIRCHILD PHOTOGRAPHY

FRANK MOLNAR
EXHIBITIONS

1963	Gallery of B.C. Arts, group show
1964	University of British Columbia Faculty Club Danish Art Gallery, two shows
1965	Danish Art Gallery, two-man show with Jack Akroyd. Molnar exhibited figure paintings, November 14.
1966	Danish Art Gallery
1967	Danish Art Gallery. Two-man show with Jack Akroyd, October 11–25
1968	Gallery of B.C. Arts
1970	*Survey 70: Realism(e)s:* Montreal Museum of Fine Arts, May 8–June 7. The Art Gallery of Ontario, August 7–September 6. Forty-six artists, Molnar exhibited three oil paintings.
1972	Artist's home, Vancouver, exhibition of paintings, watercolours, drawings, December 14–17
1973	Artist's home, Vancouver, November 23.
1974 to 1989	The Molnars held a show once every three years in their home
1985	Ohler Gallery, Vancouver, exhibition of nudes, landscapes and figure paintings, July 25–31
1989	Artist's home, Vancouver, June 10–12
1990, 1991	University of British Columbia Faculty Club, Vancouver Tom Lee Music, Vancouver, Recital Hall and Grand Piano Salon Capilano College, North Vancouver, faculty show Delta Place Hotel, Vancouver

1990, 1991	Georg Schmerholz Studio Gallery, Vancouver Artist's home, Vancouver
1992	Georg Schmerholz Studio Gallery Vancouver, three separate exhibitions Artist's home, Vancouver University of British Columbia Faculty Club, Vancouver Georgia's Gallery, West Vancouver Raintree Restaurant, Vancouver Waterfront Centre Hotel, Vancouver Hungarian Festival '92, Plaza of Nations, Discovery Building, Vancouver
1993	Several watercolours were accepted into the Richmond Art Gallery's art rental program, which ran for a number of years. In November 1993, Frank donated a seascape from the West Coast of Vancouver Island to an event put on by the Marquis Wine Cellars. It was a fundraiser, wine tasting and art auction with the proceeds going to the B.C. Lions Society for Children with Disabilities. Other artists who donated work were Joe Average, Tiko Kerr, Alix Hirabayashi and Roberta Nadeau.
1994	Artist's home, Vancouver, November 6
1996	Octavia Gallery, South Granville, Vancouver. Group show called Eros
After 1996	Artist studio visitation by appointment

PRIVATE AND CORPORATE COLLECTIONS

Europe, United States, Canada

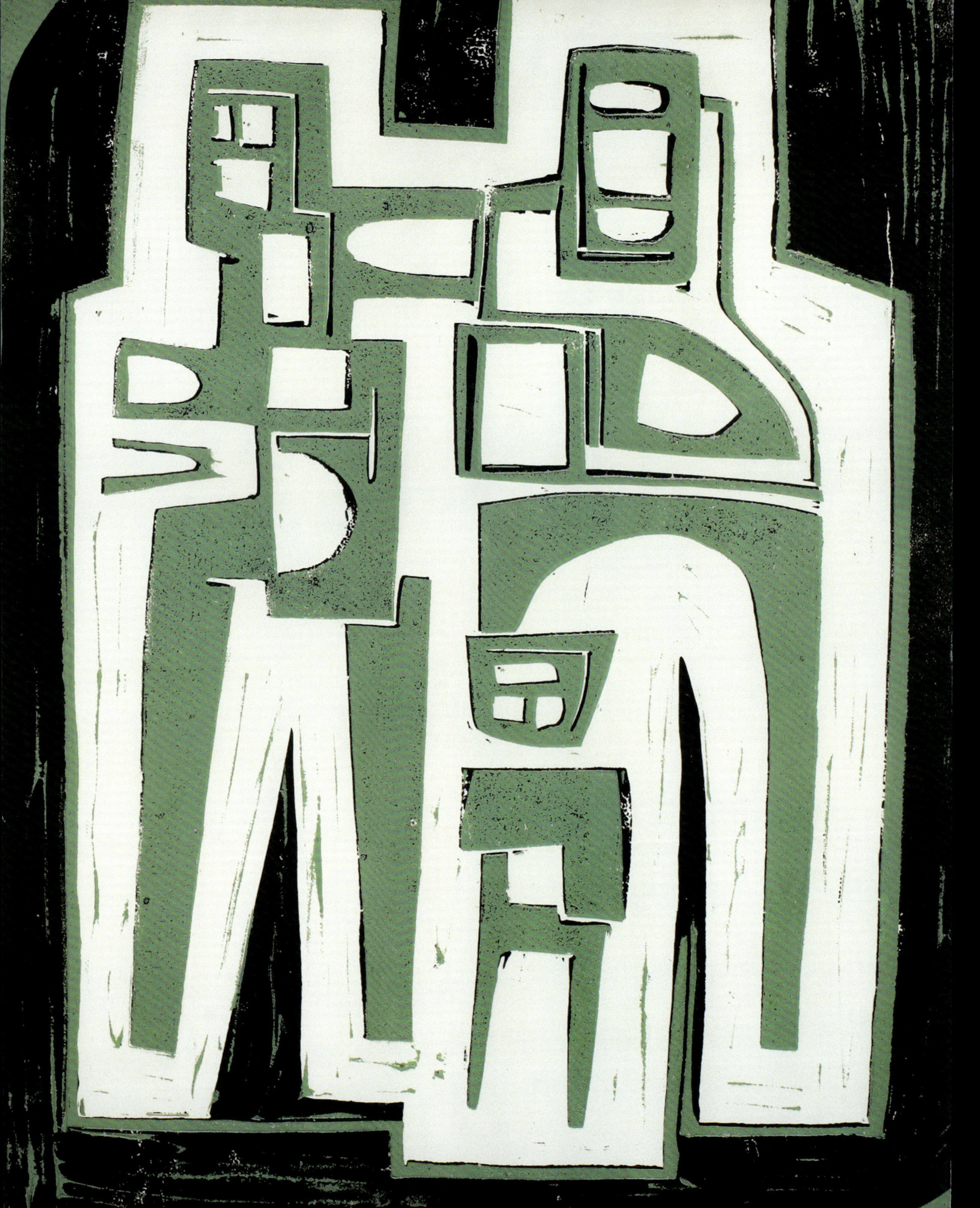

JACK HARDMAN

—CLAUDIA CORNWALL

preface by JEAN FRANÇOIS GUIMOND

Preface

‹‹ *Linocut,* early 1960s, 18" x 15", FROM THE CITY OF BURNABY PERMANENT ART COLLECTION, PHOTO BY INGEBORG HARDMAN

DURING THE '60S AND EARLY '70S, Jack's art was acclaimed, locally and nationally. He ploughed his own furrow, in B.C.'s cultural terrain, creating original prints and sculpture, some small and intimate, others totemic, occasionally experimenting with new media, techniques and forms, all reflecting his unique vision. He did so until confronted by monumental health challenges. Regrettably, this setback coincided with a shift in the local art establishment. As this hierarchy became, in my opinion, increasingly incestuous and infatuated with foreign trends, exceptional indigenous talent, like Jack's, suffered neglect.

I met Jack in the late '70s via our mutual friend, Joe Plaskett, after Jack succeeded Sheila Kincaid as director of the Burnaby Art Gallery (B.A.G.), which he helped found. Unfortunately, while in his prime as its second director, he suffered a major stroke.

Undaunted by partial paralysis, Jack regularly visited Vancouver's commercial galleries, although walking was awkward and tiring. I shall never forget Jack, one arm limp and the other wielding a cane, hobbling with his lame leg into the gallery where I worked. On each occasion, he insisted on laboriously climbing the long flight of stairs to the second floor to examine everything new in stock since his previous visit. His insightful remarks revealed an impressive knowledge of art history and techniques.

On another occasion, while visiting a Vancouver dealer of historic art, I expressed interest in a fine early nineteenth-century Canadian topographical watercolour by George Heriot. Alas, Jack had already beaten me to it, having placed his name on the piece! Years later, as the Burnaby Art Gallery's chief curator and beneficiary of Jack's legacy and connoisseurship, I was further privileged to oversee the many gems his foresight had acquired for its nascent permanent collection that he helped establish.

I further remember Jack selecting exceptional exhibitions for the Burnaby Art Gallery. Perhaps his professions of artist and art teacher groomed his curatorial acumen, enabling him to appreciate distinctive creativity. These exhibitions demonstrated that he had the courage, reflected in his own art, to stand apart from the mainstream, and expressed a singular vision. His refined eye eschewed the mundane, choosing unparalleled quality and remarkable originality over prevalent trends. Without the benefit of his exhibition schedule, I rely on memory, but immediately recall him featuring talent such as David Marshall, Myfanwy Spencer Pavelić and George Rammel. His roster was impressive and, in my view, unmatched.

I also recall Jack organising a B.A.G. exhibition of animation artists from the local National Film Board office. Although Vancouver had developed an international reputation in this genre, it was largely unknown to the local public. He felt it deserved their attention.

Jack weathered his challenges. Through commitment, perseverance and the support of family, friends and colleagues, he made a significant and lasting contribution to his community. He remains largely unrecognized among the province's cultural functionaries, except for a discerning circle. Thankfully, this volume begins to redress that shameful lacuna.

Jean François Guimond, formerly chief curator of the Burnaby Art Gallery, is a retired lawyer residing in Vancouver.

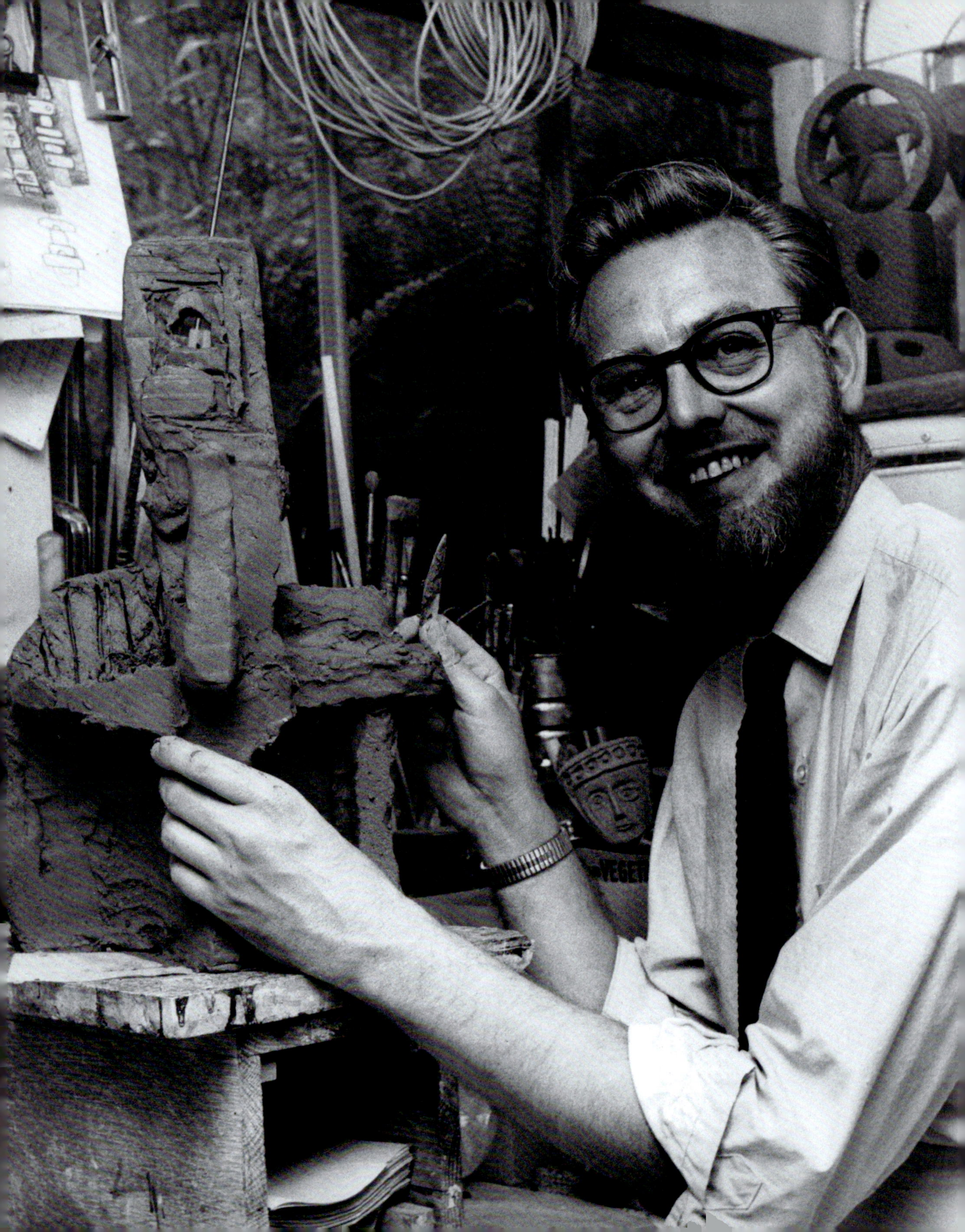

Artist, Mentor, Enfant Terrible

"WHO ARE YOU and where do you come from?"

Jack Nelson Hardman drew himself up to his full 6 feet 4 inches. A handsome man with an elegant sweep of blond hair, a Vandyke beard and blazing blue eyes, he cut an imposing figure. As the noise and sights of the Royal Academy soiree swirled around, Jack looked down at the small Englishman who had spoken to him.

‹ Jack Hardman, 1964, studio, Burnaby, BC
PHOTO BY BASIL KING

"Actually," he said, "I'm an Eskimo."

"But I thought they were short and dark."

"Not at all," demurred Jack.

Jack was *méchant*, as the French say—"naughty." He had no hesitation about speaking his mind. He liked to surprise and shock people—*épater les bourgeois.*[1]

Jack, of course, was not an Eskimo. He was born on October 2, 1923, in New Westminster, B.C., where his family had lived for a long time. His grandfather, Alfred Hardman, originally from London, England, had ridden the rails across

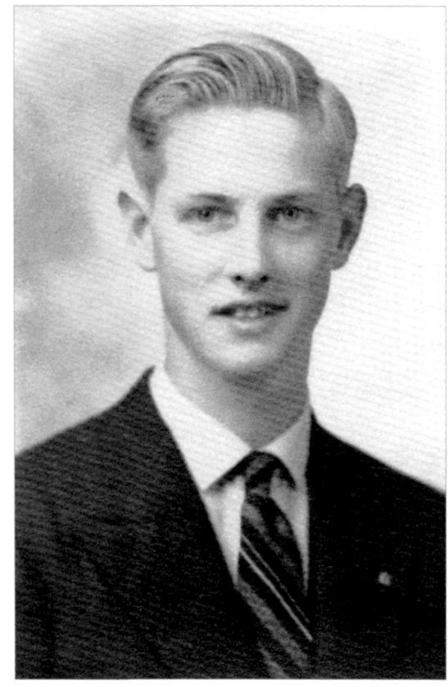

Jack Hardman, 1941, 18 yrs, at graduation

Canada and arrived in New Westminster in 1883.[2] This was just 25 years after British Columbia was made a crown colony. Alfred became a wealthy businessman with significant real estate holdings, including at one time, part of what is now Queen's Park (which he traded for a grand piano).[3] Alfred married a Scottish woman, Annie, and they had four children. Jack's father was the youngest, Gordon Clarkson Hardman.[4] In 1918, Gordon lied about his age to get into the Canadian Army, then fighting in Europe.[5] After returning, he became a fireman and married Irene Nelson, a woman whose family had emigrated from Sweden and established a farm in Blaine, Washington.[6]

Gordon was nervous, erratic, a martinet. Both Jack and his younger sister, Elizabeth, suffered from his harsh and unreasonable discipline. For several years, Jack didn't live with his family but stayed with the Rutherfords up the street. When his father was working, he'd come home to visit his mother with whom he was very close. In an interview from her home in North Vancouver, Jack's sister, Elizabeth Swartz, recalled asking her mother why her brother didn't live with them. Her mother said it was because one of the Rutherford daughters, Thelma, had a club foot and Jack had to protect her when she went to school. Elizabeth never felt it was the whole story.[7] At the very end of his life, Jack said to his old friend Abraham Rogatnik, "I was an abused child. My father hated me."[8]

Elizabeth and Jack were happiest when they could visit their grandmother, Emma Nelson, on her farm in Blaine. Elizabeth remembered, "She was a lovely woman. She'd wear two or three petticoats and a gingham hat. She had milk cows, two pigs, a brooder house for chickens. For miles you couldn't see any houses. It was such a treat to go there."[9]

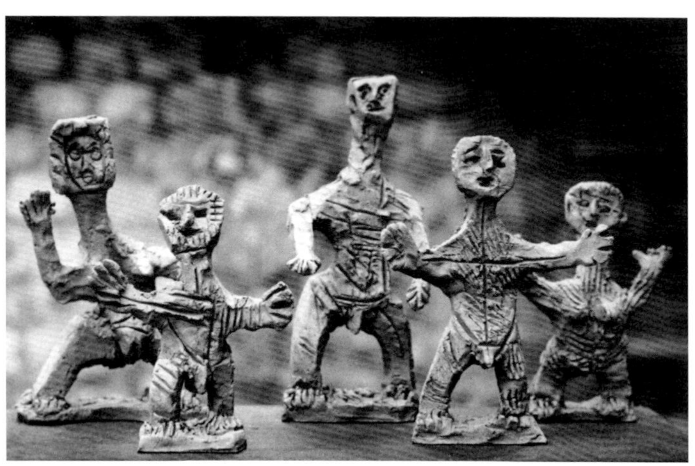

Damaged Family, mid '50s, glazed ceramic, 24" x 9" x 12"
PRIVATE COLLECTION
PHOTO BY JACK V. LONG

Gordon Hardman had suffered from two bouts with tuberculosis, and in 1945, Jack came down with the illness too.[10] He was sent to Tranquille, a sanatorium near Kamloops. At that time, the treatment was basically rest, fresh air and sunshine. After two years in the sage-scented dry hills, Jack was cured. But his health was permanently affected. As a result of the illness, one lung had to be removed, leaving him subject to

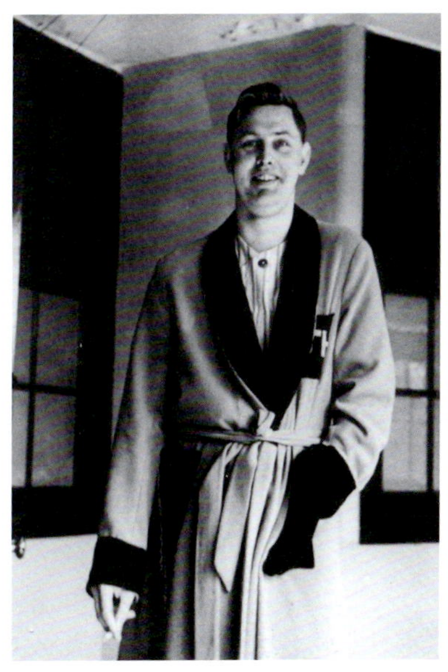

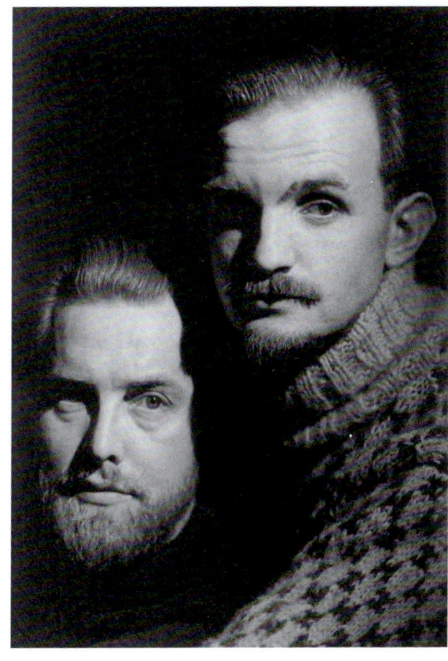

Jack Hardman and Joe Plaskett, 1968
PHOTO BY BURLIN, FOR *THE BRITISH COLUMBIAN*, COURTESY OF NEW WESTMINSTER MUSEUM AND ARCHIVES AND BURLIN STUDIOS

‹‹ Jack Hardman, at Tranquille, late '40s

bad colds and sinus infections all his life.[11] However, on the positive side, as a result of being at Tranquille, Jack started to forge important connections to the art community. Joy Zemel Long, who also became an artist, recollected, "We were in Tranquille at the same time. We corresponded with each other in a way. We wrote notes, dropped them out of a window and hauled them up."[12]

After Jack left Tranquille, he met another young artist, Joe Plaskett. In an email from England, where he now lives, Joe explained how they met.

> Though we were both artists in New Westminster, there was an age difference of several years, which perhaps prevented early contact. When in 1945 I studied at the summer school in Banff (School of Fine Arts), I became friends with Dorothy Williams, who taught art at the Kamloops High School. She told me about Jack, whom she often visited when he was at the TB clinic in nearby Tranquille. It was her ambition to bring us together. So it could not have been earlier than the autumn of 1945. I have no recollection of our first meeting, but it began a lifetime friendship.[13v]

Joe and Jack were very different artists—Joe was romantic, and impressionistic, favouring vibrant colours. Jack was modern, abstract and used a much more subdued palette. But the two enjoyed each other's company, nonetheless. In an email, Joe wrote:

> Jack had a very singular character. He was always doing or saying naughty things. He had a wicked sense of humour. He was a wonderful friend to have. One heard

Woman & Child,
mid '50s - '60s, ceramic, 14" x 6" x 6"
COLLECTION OF ROBIN & ESTHER MATHEWS
PHOTO BY INGEBORG HARDMAN

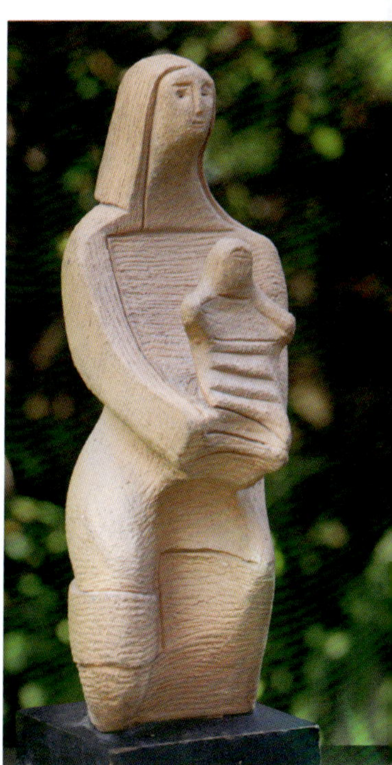

and learned gossip and scandals about any number of eminent persons, an education in itself. He was always an ardent fan of my work, much more than I was of his, which is not to disparage the quality of his sculpture and work in other media.[14]

›~At home, n.d. linocut, 20" x 18"
PHOTO BY INGEBORG HARDMAN

› Jack & Marya, 1953-4, London, England

Untitled, ceramic, mid '50s, 9.25" x 11" x 7"
PHOTO BY INGEBORG HARDMAN

In 1947, Jack first publicly showed his sculpture, two titled *Susan* and *Abstract*, as part of the annual B.C. Artists Exhibition at the Vancouver Art Gallery. It was a time of great ferment in the arts in Vancouver. Ian McNairn, an associate professor of art at the University of BC, wrote in *100 Years of B.C. Art* that the years after the war were "exceptionally fruitful for art" in British Columbia. He mentioned several reasons for this, including "the social acceptance of the artist... In the last fifteen years the artist and society, or the public, have grown closer together. Economic conditions have a bearing on this. Certainly financial security for the artist is one result."[15] While Vancouver prided itself on the achievements of its artists, McNairn was probably too optimistic about the possibilities of economic security for an artist there. As Scott

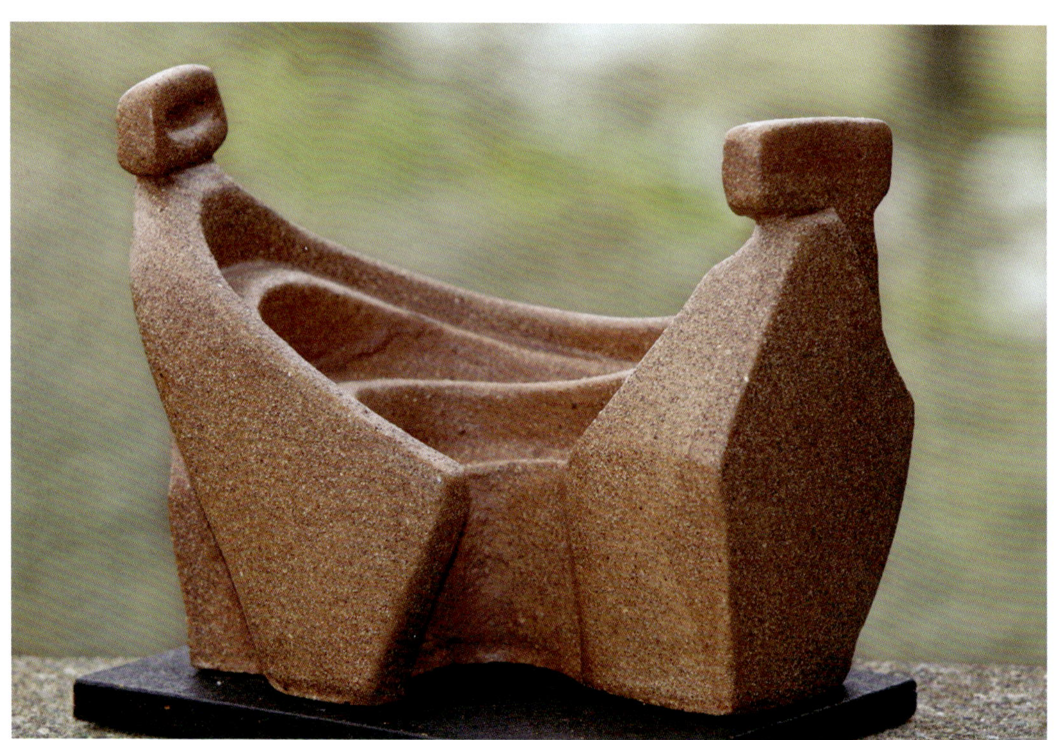

Watson pointed out in *Vancouver Art and Artists: 1931–1983*, although there were some private collectors of art, "this group was not large enough to allow painting as a self-sustaining career for local artists." There were public patrons, the Vancouver Art Gallery and the National Gallery of Canada.

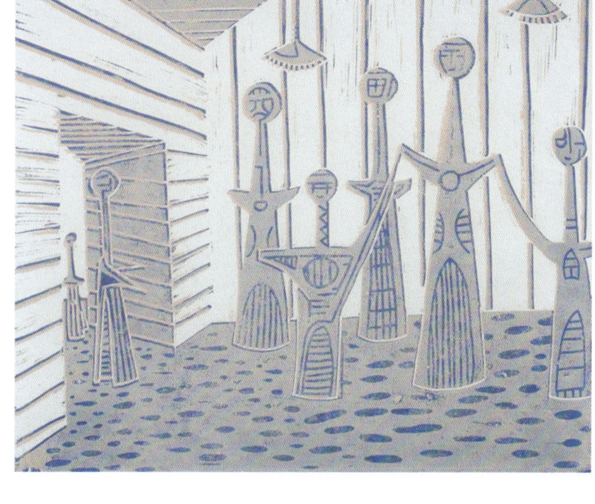

> [But] although the Vancouver Art Gallery promoted regional art in its exhibition program, it did not follow through with an acquisition policy. There were no funds to encourage such a policy, and the amount of work the Gallery acquired from local artists was, by any standard, appallingly small. The National Gallery acquired the work of fifties' painters but sporadically and superficially. Acquisitions by either institution no doubt conferred prestige but did not constitute material support or signify serious interest.[16]

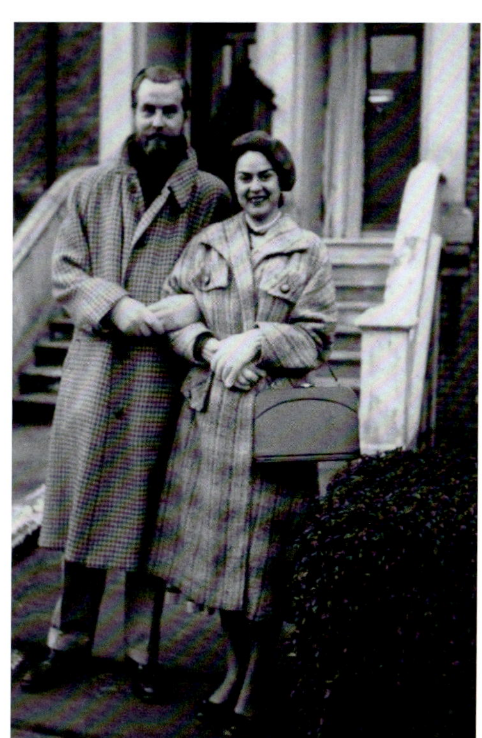

In other words, for a young artist like Jack to make his living by selling paintings or sculptures was still chancy. After attending Vancouver Normal School,[17] Jack began teaching art in 1949 at Edmonds Junior High School in Burnaby.[18] The students loved him, although he did not always get on so well with the administration. His sister Elizabeth recalled, "On sunny days, he'd take the kids to the beach to fly kites. In those days, you didn't do that. He almost got fired over it."[19]

In 1953, Joe Plaskett introduced Jack to a friend of his sister's, Marya Fiamengo, a young poet and librarian. Marya's parents were Yugoslavians from what is now Croatia. She was dark-eyed, passionate, emotional, a sultry beauty. Jack was instantly smitten. He was engaged to someone else but he broke off the engagement. Two months later, Jack and Marya were married. Both taught for a year, and the next summer, they embarked on a grand European tour. In an interview from her present home in Gibson's, Marya said, "We did brilliant things in Europe."[20]

First, they visited Yugoslavia—Tito's Yugoslavia. Marya wanted to see her mother's birthplace, the island of Vis near Split. When Jack and Marya got to the gangplank of the ferry to the island, they found it guarded by soldiers with fixed bayonets. When one asked to see their

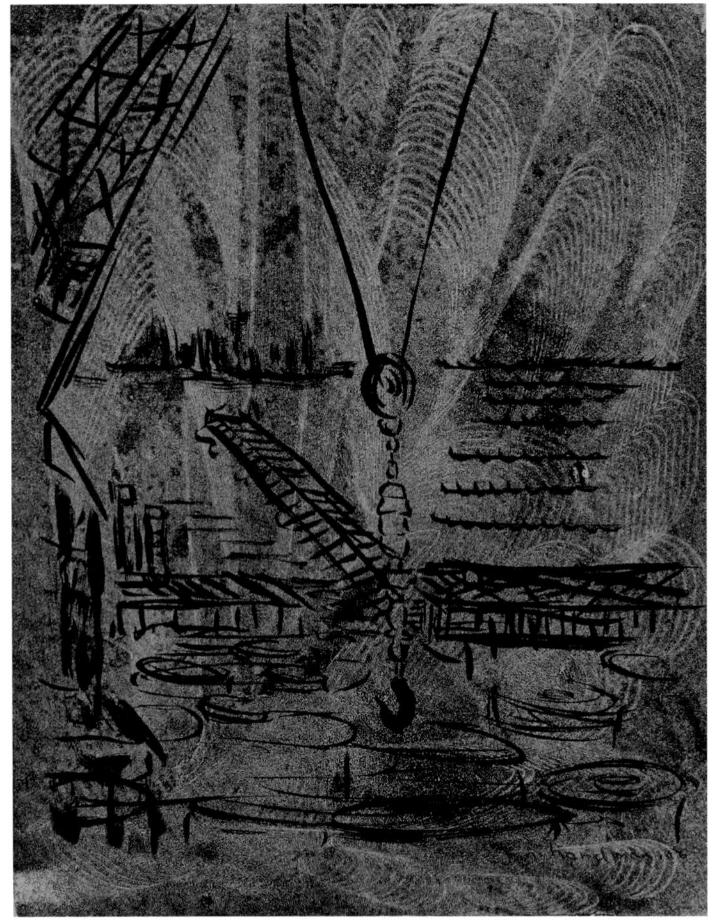

passes, they produced their Canadian passports. But he wasn't satisfied. Vis was a military frontier, he said, and they needed special permits. Marya recalled:

> Being Canadian, I thought this was all rubbish. I said, "Get lost," and moved in the direction of the ship—whereupon a bayonet was planted in my capacious bosom. Then I said in a loud voice, "There lies my mother's native land and are you going to prevent me from visiting?" Everybody in the boat rose to their feet. They shouted, "Is this a fascist state or a socialist republic? What did we fight for? Let her on." They were ready to pick up clubs and attack the sentry. Then the commanding officer came down and spoke to me. He found out who I was, and the people in the boat began shouting, "Her great-great-grandfather poured oil on the Turks when they stormed the church." I have never been in anything like it. It was like being in film, it really was. We got on.[21]

Harbour Calais, 1956, monoprint, 7.5" x 9.5"
PHOTO BY INGEBORG HARDMAN

By the fall, Marya and Jack were in London. Jack taught art at an East Ham school, and Marya was a substitute teacher. Their flat, rented from Royal Academy painter Steven Spurrier, was so huge that they could put up other Vancouverites who were passing through London on *their* grand tours—friends like Rosamund Bunting and Takao Tanabe. Knowing the Spurriers brought additional perks—like invitations to the Royal Academy soiree where Jack pretended to be an Eskimo. Jack and Marya took the opportunity to soak up everything cultural that London had to offer—the theatre, the ballet, the National Gallery, the Tate and lectures at the Institute of Contemporary Art. On school holidays, they toured Germany and Italy and visited Joe Plaskett who was living in Paris, courtesy of a Canada Council Overseas Scholarship.[22]

› *Father and Son,* 1965, linocut, 12" x 18"
PRIVATE COLLECTION
PHOTO BY INGEBORG HARDMAN

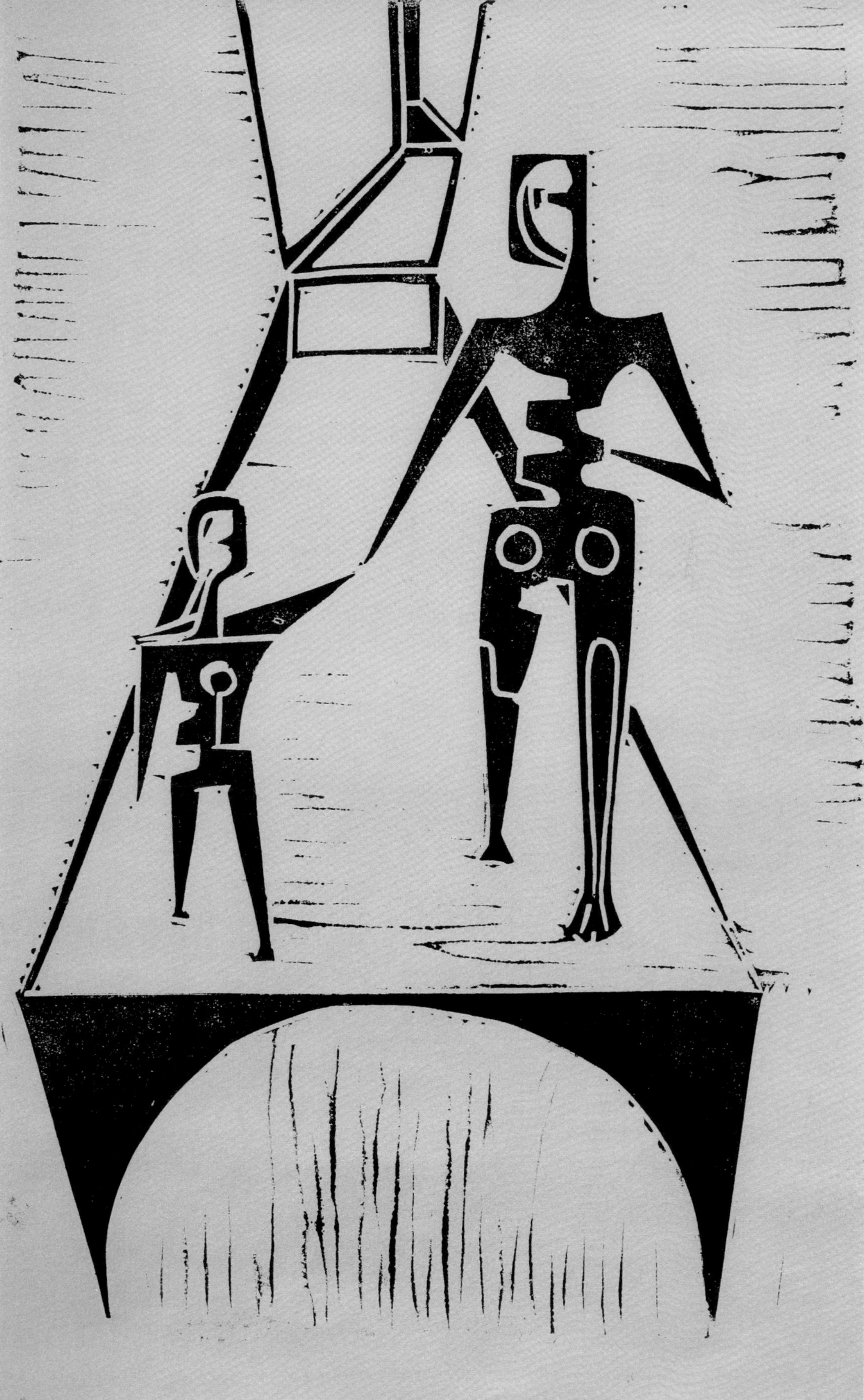

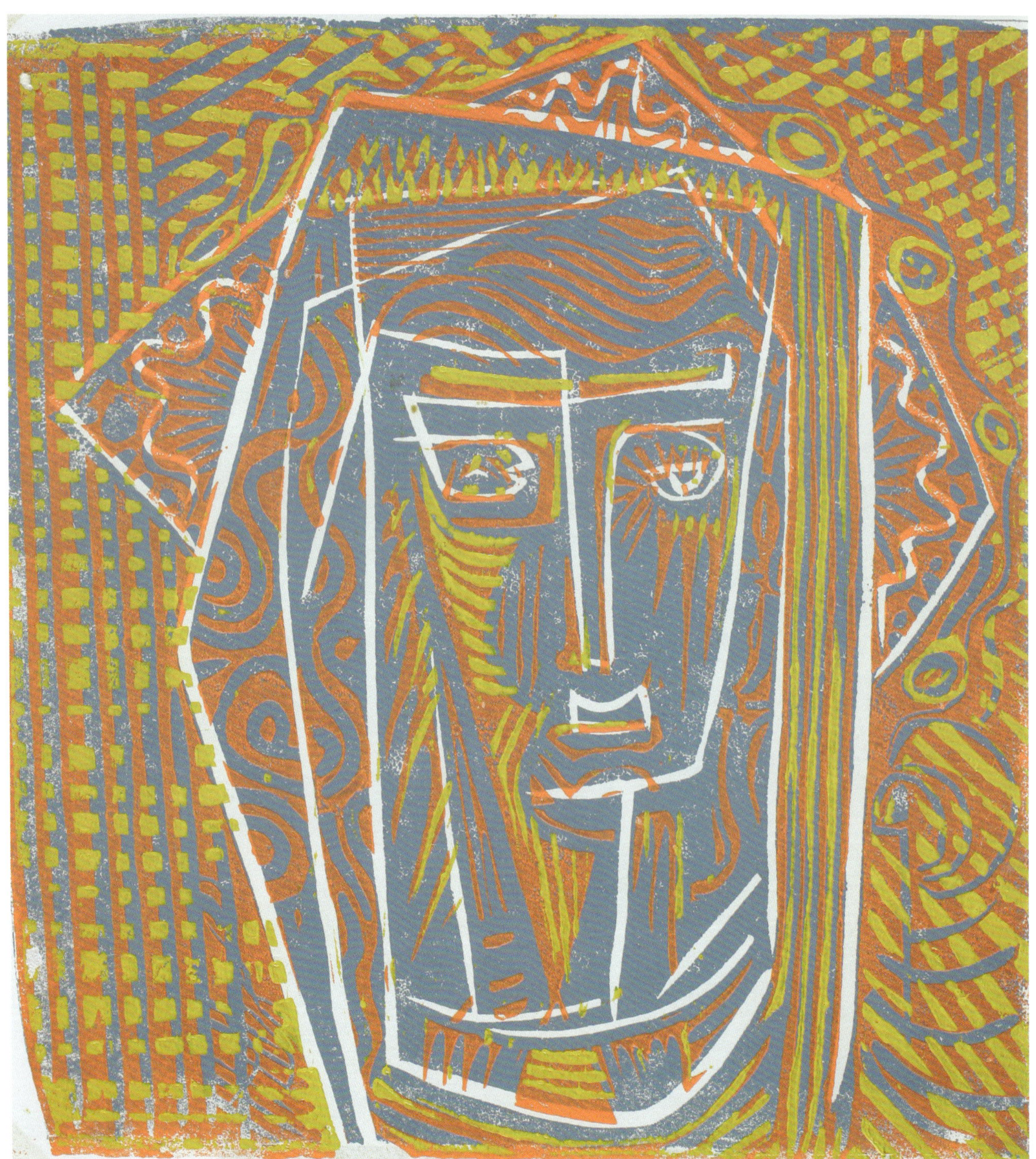

Burnaby: An Artists' Enclave

Jack and Marya returned to Canada in 1955. They had a great argument about where to live. Marya yearned for a house, a picturesque place in a wooded setting with a view, whereas Jack hated the idea of a mortgage and didn't want to own property. However, Marya prevailed and they found a house on Hythe Avenue on Capital Hill in north Burnaby. Small and charming, it had an interesting feature—a beautiful window that came from the bow of a ship. Just as Marya had wanted, the lot was treed—with hemlocks and cedars—and had a terraced garden. It also overlooked the Ironworkers' Memorial Bridge and the sea sparkling in the background.[23] In July 1957, Matthew Dmitri Vincent Hardman was born.[24]

‹ *Untitled,* n.d. collograph, 12" x 12"
PRIVATE COLLECTION
PHOTO BY INGEBORG HARDMAN

Capital Hill was an artists' enclave. Harold Mortimer Lamb, a painter, art critic and collector of Canadian works, lived around the corner from the Hardmans. After teaching, Jack would go over to his house for tea in the afternoons. Lamb was well connected to many Canadian artists. His daughter, Molly

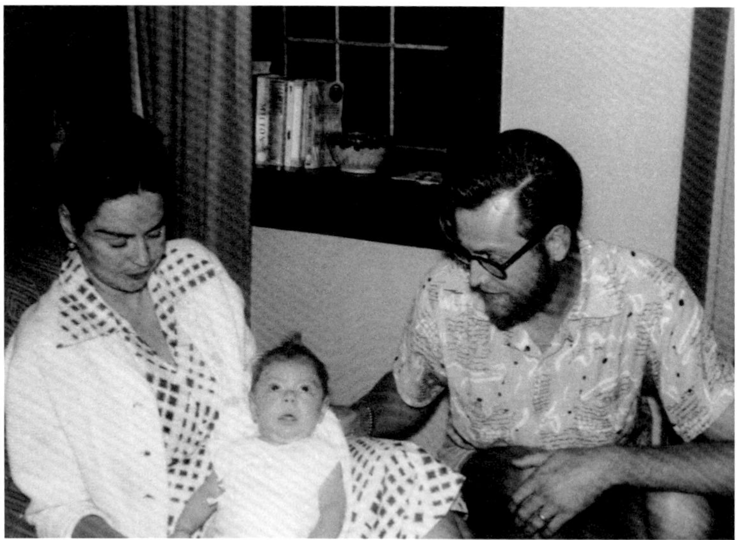

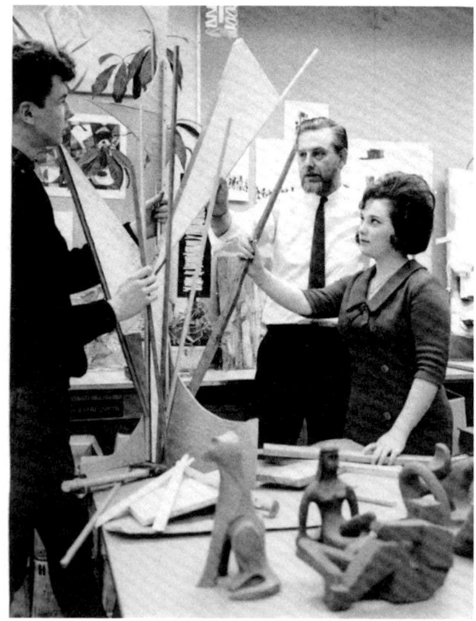

Marya, Dmitri & Jack, 1957, Burnaby

⌒› Jack teaching at Burnaby Central High School, 1960

›› *King and Child,* 1961, collograph, 18" x 15.5"
PRIVATE COLLECTION
PHOTO BY INGEBORG HARDMAN

Lamb Bobak, was the first woman in the Canadian army to be given the title of official war artist. Lamb had also married a famous beauty called Vera Weatherbie, who had once been Fred Varley's mistress.[25] During that time, sculptor David Marshall and his wife Carel were often guests for dinner. They would talk about life, art and politics far into the night. For years Jack and David gave each other great moral support and were the best of friends.

Jack and Doris Shadbolt, who bestrode the artistic world in Vancouver like giants, lived a block away, on Glynde Avenue. From 1950 to 1962, Doris was the docent and director of education at the Vancouver Art Gallery, later becoming the research curator. Jack taught at the Vancouver School of Art. His paintings, which employed avant-garde techniques to make very personal statements, were considered cutting edge and fashionable. Marya recalled, "He was extraordinarily powerful, tall and burly, very articulate. He was also two-sided. If he liked you, he was absolutely fabulous. If he didn't, he wiped the floor with you. He had a killer side; he was ruthlessly competitive. Fortunately, he liked Jack [Hardman] and was kind and supportive."[26]

The Shadbolts threw enormous parties. Through them, Marya said, "we met everybody who was *le dernier cri.* We knew everybody in the art world. We knew the Gordon Smiths. We knew Arthur Erikson. We knew the Masseys and Don Jarvis."[27] Sometimes they met art celebrities from the East. Once the notable American critic Clement Greenberg attended. But Marya wasn't impressed.

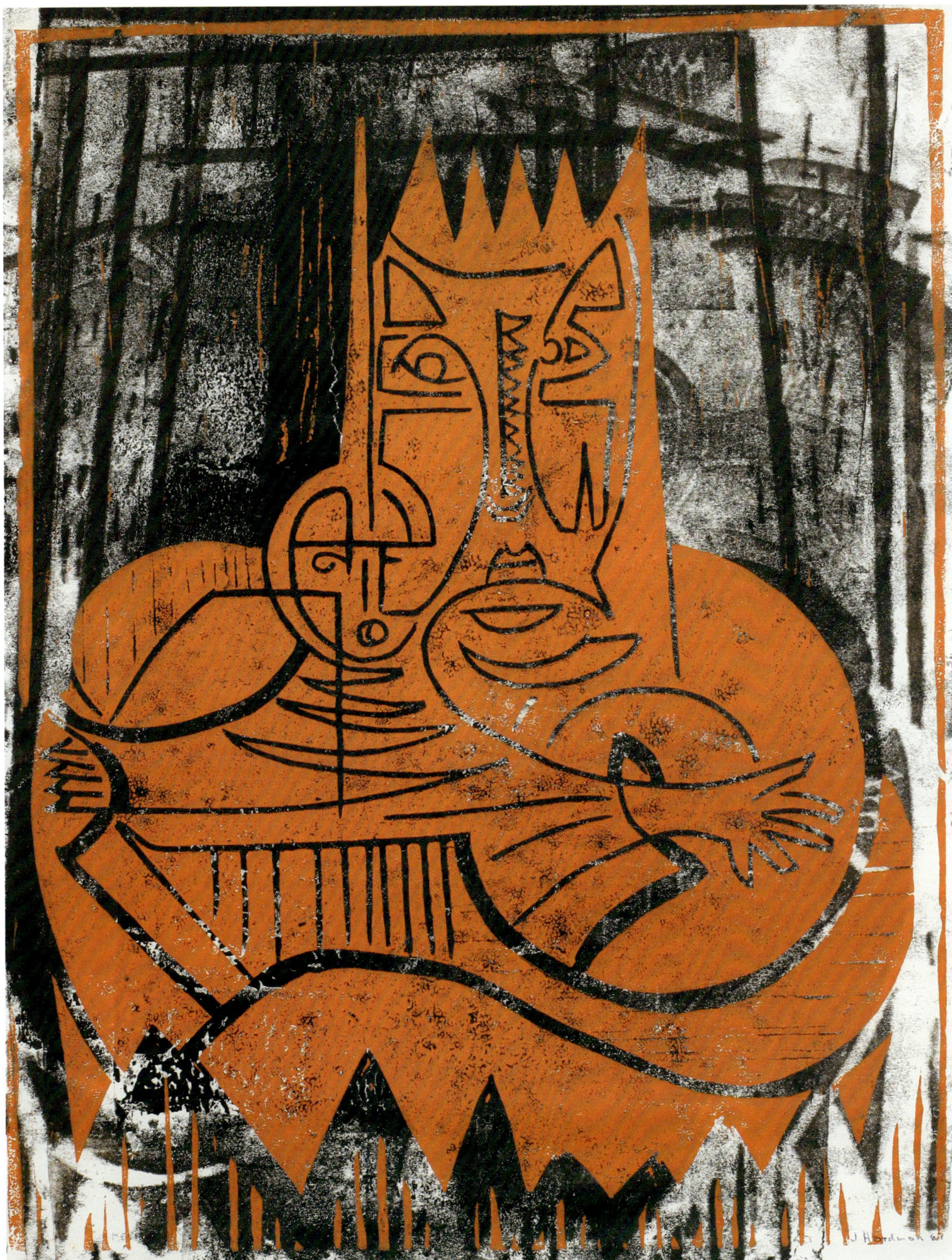

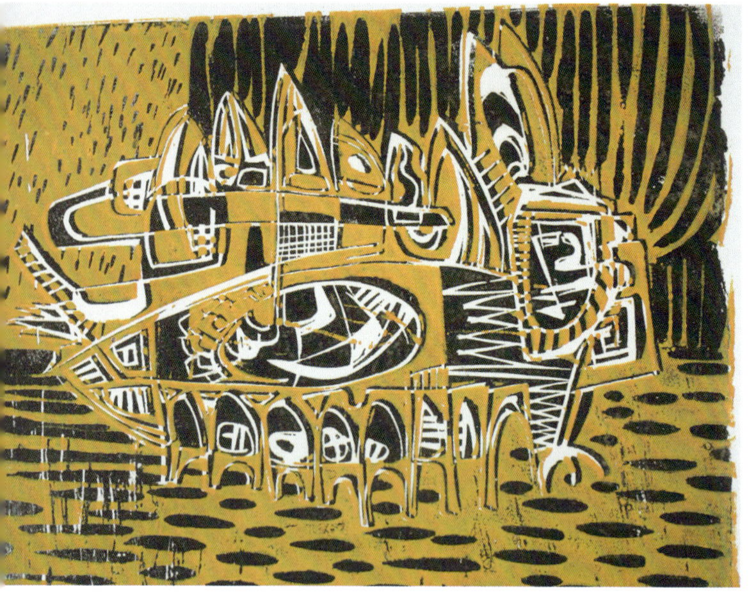

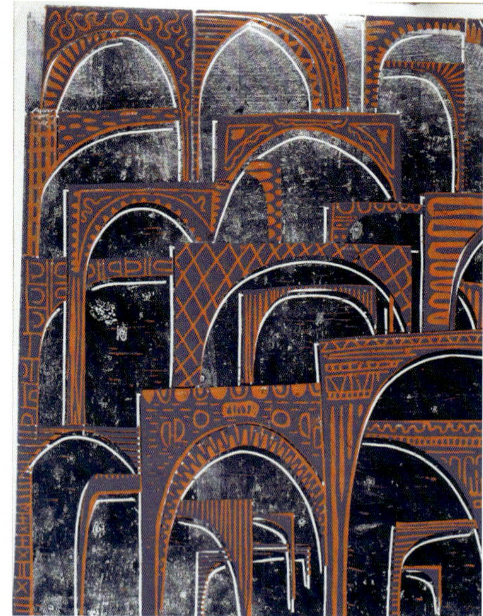

Totemic Insect, n.d. linocut, 13" x 10"
PRIVATE COLLECTION
PHOTO BY INGEBORG HARDMAN

⌒› *Untitled,* 1961, collograph, 13" x 13"
PRIVATE COLLECTION
PHOTO BY INGEBORG HARDMAN

› *The Family,* n.d. linocut, 12" x 18"
PHOTO BY INGEBORG HARDMAN

›› invitation, 2nd National Burnaby Print Show
COURTESY OF THE BURNABY ART GALLERY

> He was boring boring boring. All he did was prose on about Modern Art and the Avant Garde and blah blah blah, while everybody sat at his feet. None of us had the wit to say that it was just one of many styles, for God's sake. We didn't take him on. We were all Canadians. We were too polite. His wife—his third wife—said to me, "This is so boring. Why is everybody listening to him?"[28]

Jack Hardman began teaching at Burnaby Central in 1958, when it first opened. He was charismatic and inspiring. Leonard Brett, who later attended the Vancouver School of Art and became an artist, was his student in grades 11 and 12. He credits Jack with helping him to focus on art.

> I did well at art, but I never would have considered it as a career if it weren't for him. Particularly to a young impressionable student, he seemed like a wild man. He blew my mind. I remember, once, he dropped a piece of chalk and then picked it up and started throwing it all over the classroom. There was chalk flying everywhere. At first, I thought he'd gone mad, but that was typical for him. I thought, if this is what artists can do, this is the life for me.[29]

Ian Lidster, a freelance writer and former newspaper columnist, was another student of Jack's in his two senior years at Burnaby Central. In an interview from

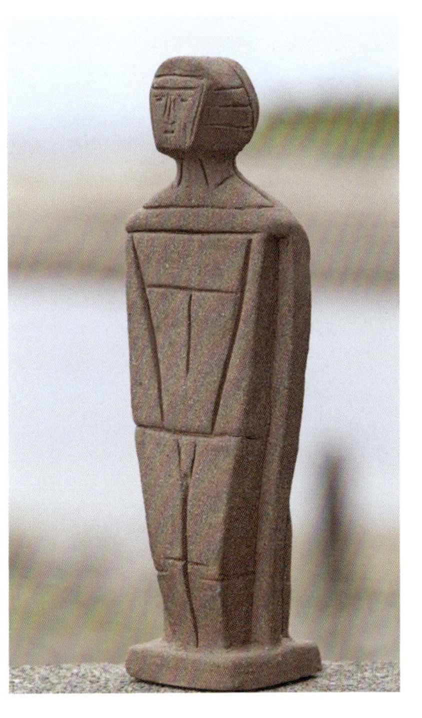

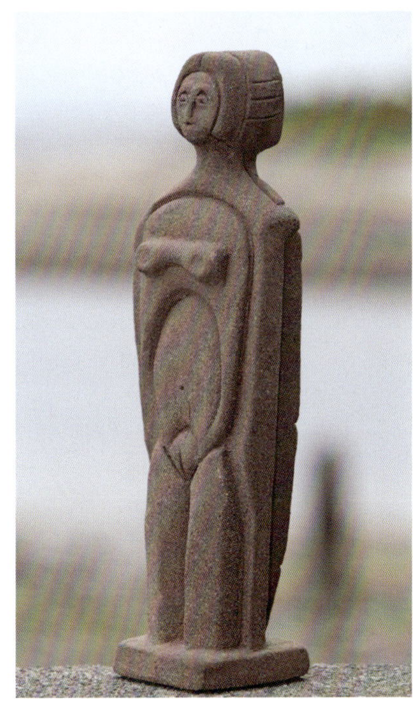

‹ *Untitled Woman,* ceramic, mid '50s/'60s, 15.5" x 5" x 4"
PHOTO BY INGEBORG HARDMAN

‹‹ *Untitled Man,* ceramic, mid '50s/'60s, 15.5" x 5" x 4"
PHOTO BY INGEBORG HARDMAN

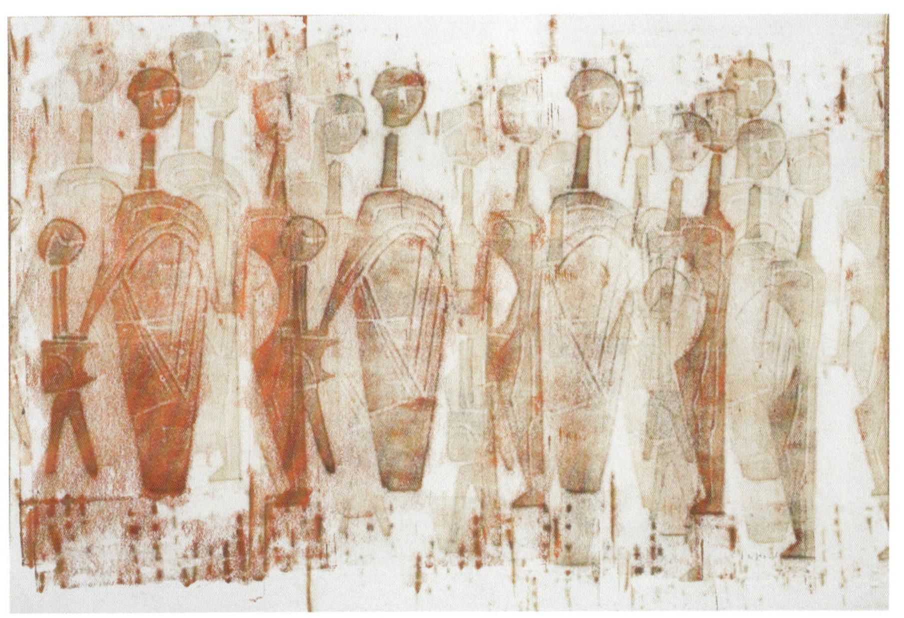

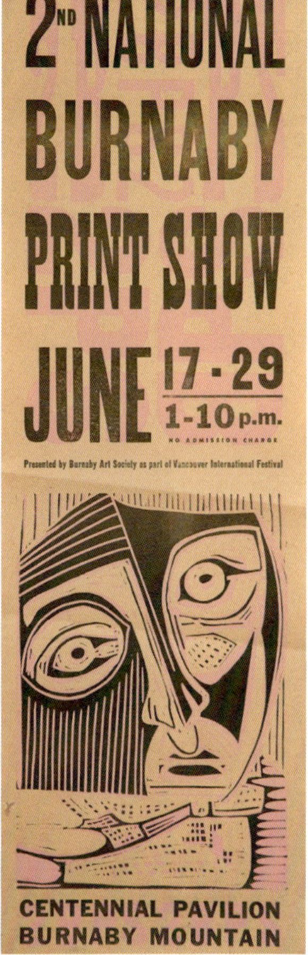

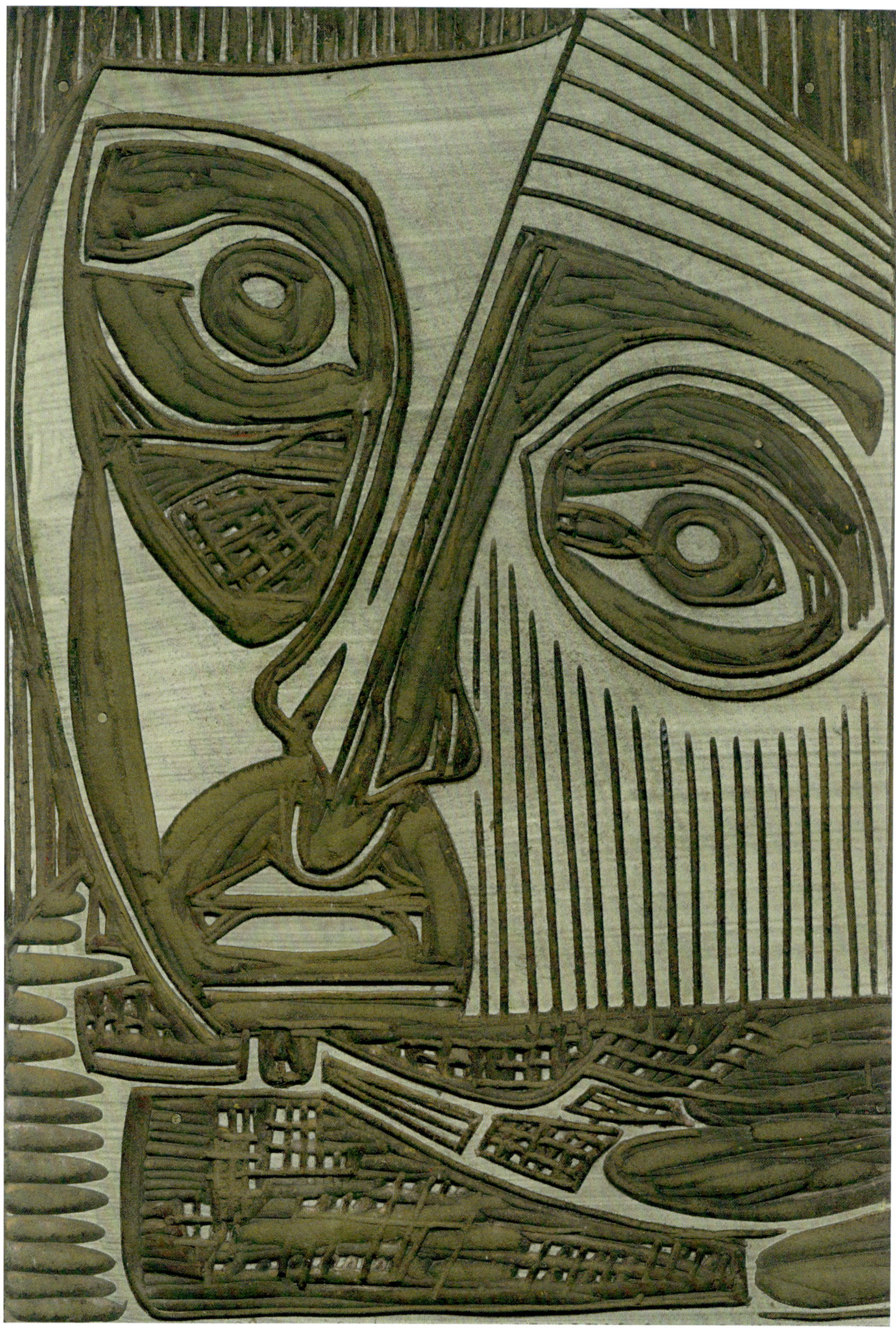

his home in Comox, Ian said that Jack made such an impression on him that a passage about him appears in a memoir he is writing.

> Jack cut a considerable swath back in those days. Bearded like the bard, he was beatnik enough in ambiance that he qualified as cool. He also had a cutting sense of sarcasm that led him to suffer fools not at all. He was adept at verbally slashing any kid to ribbons but even he grew exasperated with us… I wish I'd gotten to know him better because aside from being a remarkably fine artist in his own right, he was also a cultured, sophisticated, and well-travelled man.

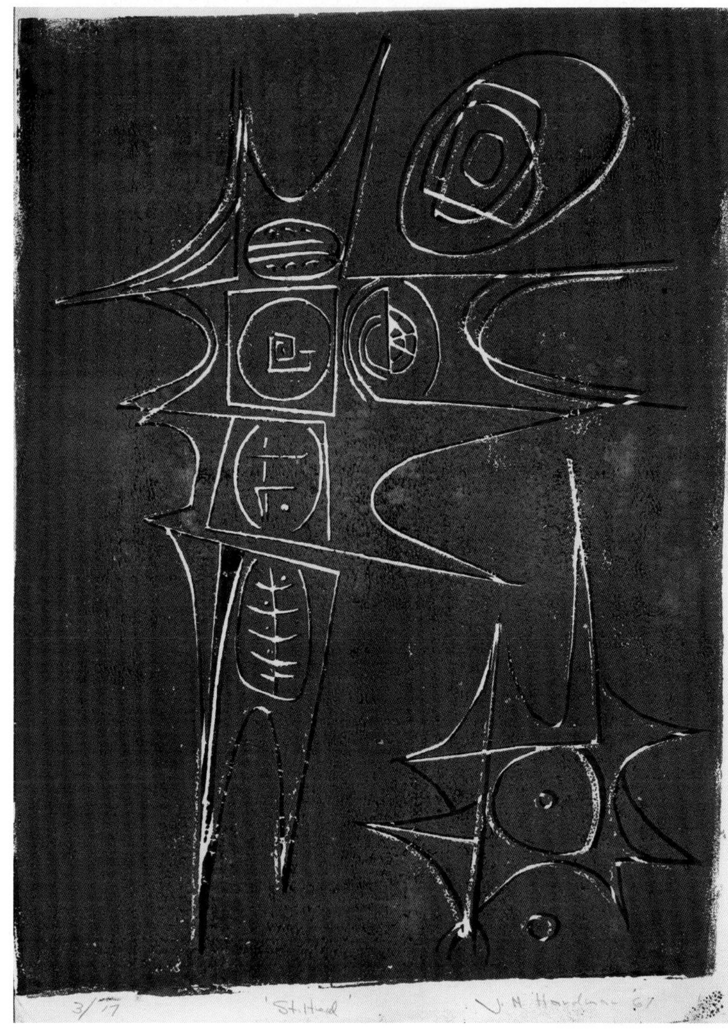

Stilted, 1961, collograph, 13" x 8.5"
PHOTO BY INGEBORG HARDMAN

Lidster remembered one of Jack's assignments vividly: draw pictures of themselves—as they imagined they would be in the future. Lidster drew himself wearing a white tuxedo, standing on a tropical knoll with a manorial structure behind. He thought he was giving the impression of being incredibly wealthy.

When he saw the picture, Jack asked, "Oh, are you planning on being a waiter?"

"No," Lidster said, "I want to be rich and powerful."

"Building looks like a restaurant to me," said Jack. "And you look like a waiter. Maybe that's your destiny. You'll be a waiter serving people who are rich and powerful."

"Asshole," he muttered after Jack was out of earshot.

Thoroughly annoyed at the time, he later realized that Jack's comments were an invitation to think more deeply about his own future.[30]

‹‹ *Untitled,* linocut, 1963, 13" x 8.5" FROM THE ARCHIVES OF THE CITY OF BURNABY PERMANENT ART COLLECTION

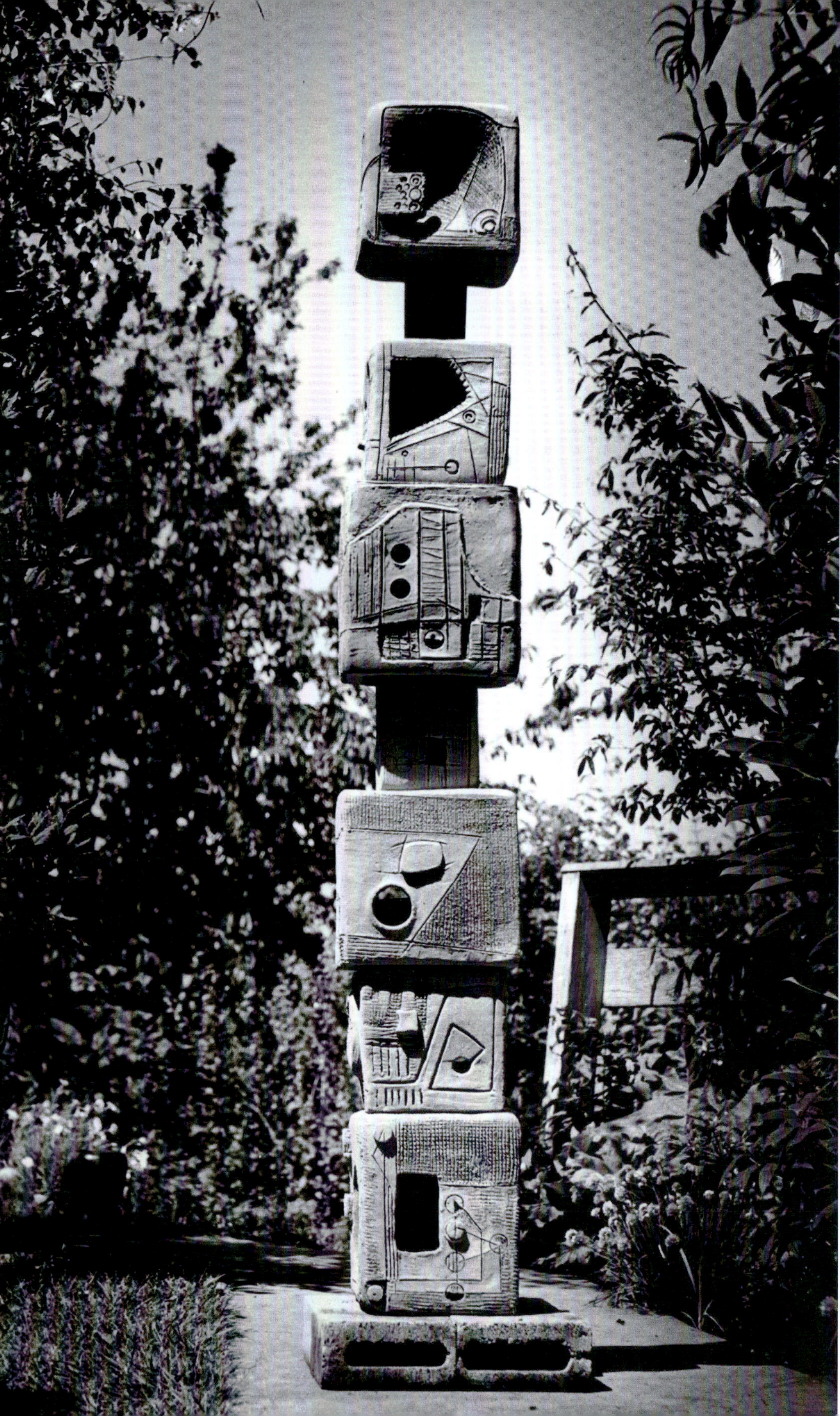

The Professional Sculptor

« *Totemic #2,* 1963, ceramic, 6' high, COLLECTION OF LETHBRIDGE JUNIOR COLLEGE, PHOTO BY BASIL KING

ALL THE WHILE, JACK CONTINUED to develop his art. He took summer courses at the University of Western Washington and graduated with a BA in fine arts in 1960.[31] He converted the utility room into a studio and got up at 5AM to work before going to his school. He punched clay, sculpted, created pottery.[32] He was influenced by cubism, by English sculptors like Henry Moore and Barbara Hepworth, as well as by older traditions—Mayan, Etruscan and Minoan art. Many of his clay sculptures were small in scale—intimate—in order to fit into a kiln. His pieces tended toward the semi-abstract, with some visual references to the real world. He often portrayed poignant family groupings or father-and-son pairs—perhaps reflecting the difficulties he had experienced with his own father. "This went against the prevailing styles," said Jean François Guimond, who sold art at the Bau-Xi Gallery from 1978 to 1982. (He later became a lawyer because he found the politics of the art world "too cutthroat.") Guimond explained that the idea at the time was to get away from the figurative entirely:

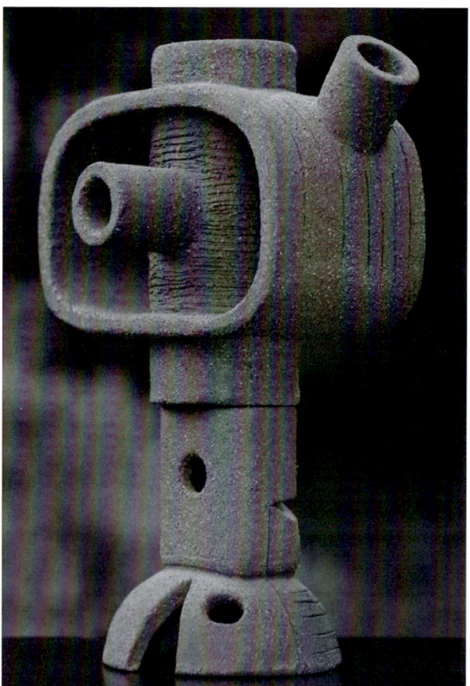

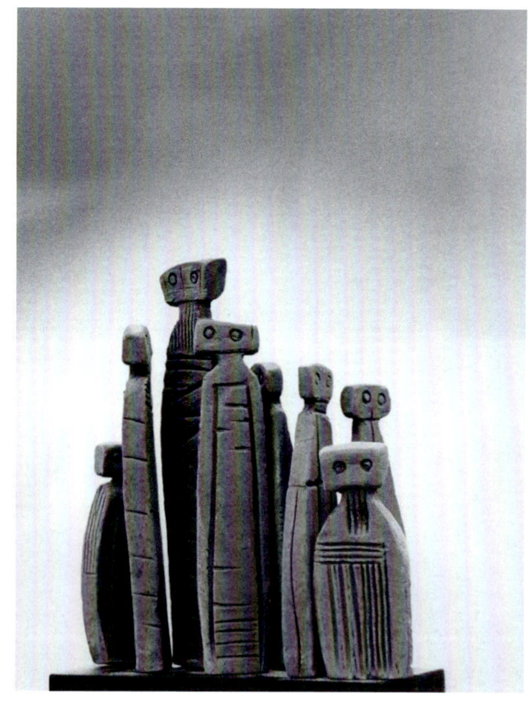

Open and Closed Form, 1960s, ceramic, 19" x 12" x 8"
COLLECTION OF JOSEPH THERRIEN, PHOTO BY INGEBORG HARDMAN

→ *The Group,* mid '60s, clay
PRIVATE COLLECTION
PHOTO BY JACK V. LONG

"Some saw the return to it as a betrayal of everything the modern art movement represented." [33]

In 1953, Jack was part of a group show at the Vancouver Art Gallery. He joined the Northwest Institute of Sculpture and, in 1956, participated in an outdoor show that it organized on the UBC campus. To make his piece, *Two-Fold Astarte,* he used a novel material—concrete. [34] In the summer of 1957, the Ukrainian avant-garde sculptor Alexander Archipenko was teaching in the extension department at UBC, and Jack got a job assisting him.[35] In 1958, Jack's piece *Eleven Saints* won the sculpture prize at the Northwest Craftsman Exhibition in Seattle. [36] That year, he was also part of an invitational exhibition of B.C. painters that the Burnaby Centennial Committee organized. Jack regularly participated in group shows throughout the fifties, with the B.C. Society of Fine Arts and in the Vancouver Art Gallery's annual exhibitions of B.C. artists.

In 1961, Jack was in a show with Doris Shadbolt at the New Design Gallery [37]—an important centre for the leading-edge artistic innovators in Vancouver. Abraham Rogatnik and Alvin Balkind founded the gallery in 1955 with the intention of using it to recognize young talent, as well as show the work of those who were already well-known. "We flourished." said Rogatnik (now 85), in an interview from his home in Vancouver, "because we weren't trying to make money. That made everything easy. We didn't have to sell, sell, sell." The 1961 show with Doris Shadbolt and Jack was "a fun show," Rogatnik recalled. "She was making jewellery. He was doing pottery. I remember the invitation I designed using a nineteenth-century picture of a man who looked something like Jack and a nineteenth-century picture of a lady who looked something like Doris."[38]

Marya doesn't remember it as so much fun:

> It wasn't very successful. Although Jack wasn't disappointed, I cried afterwards, so few people bought anything. I wanted him to make more of a splash. I was so discouraged for poor Jack.[39]... He worked very very hard, enormously hard, but he had little recognition. He was diffident. A more forceful person would have made his way. He expected to be discovered. He wanted to be discovered.[40]

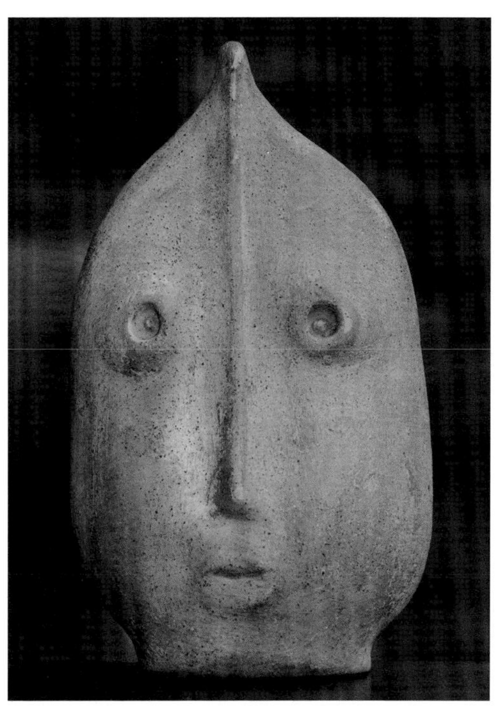

Mask, mid '60s, ceramic, 10.25" x 5.75" x 3"
PRIVATE COLLECTION
PHOTO BY INGEBORG HARDMAN

Guimond said that, for an artist to begin to sell well, "it takes three to five years of steady promotion, one year after another, to show and to market an artist. He explained that, at the Bau-Xi Gallery, one artist was so prolific it was possible to organize four shows in Vancouver over two years. The exposure worked. In the third year, he sold out.[41]

Though the splashy one-man show eluded Jack, there were bursts of media interest as well as various honours. He began making larger works by combining several small kiln-fired pieces. One of these, *Totemic Figure,* graced the November 1963 cover of *Ontario Homes and Living,* as well as the pages of *Western Homes and Gardens.* When the architects for Lethbridge Junior College were looking for a new sculpture to complement the building, they turned to the National Gallery for advice. The Gallery recommended Jack, and the architects chose a six-foot terra cotta sculpture of his. In a February 1964 interview with the *Vancouver Sun* about the piece, Jack said, "My work has vestigial remembrances of other civilizations and peoples plus the contemporary approach for a unique form. The work is not officially titled, but in my

› *Untitled,* ceramic, late '60s, approx. 4.5' high, missing
PHOTO BY JACK V. LONG

›› *Totemic #3,* mid '60s, missing
PHOTO BY BASIL KING

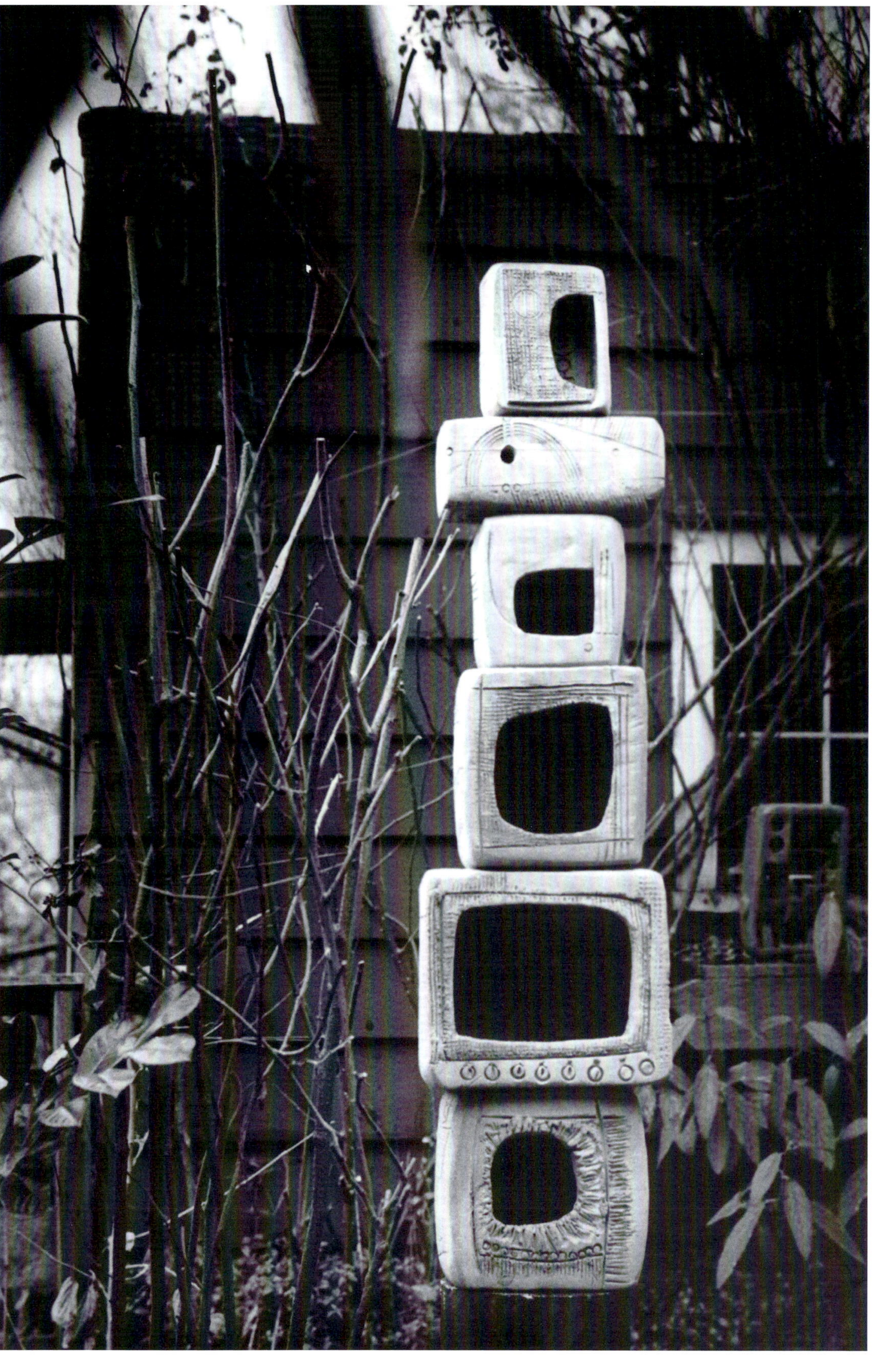

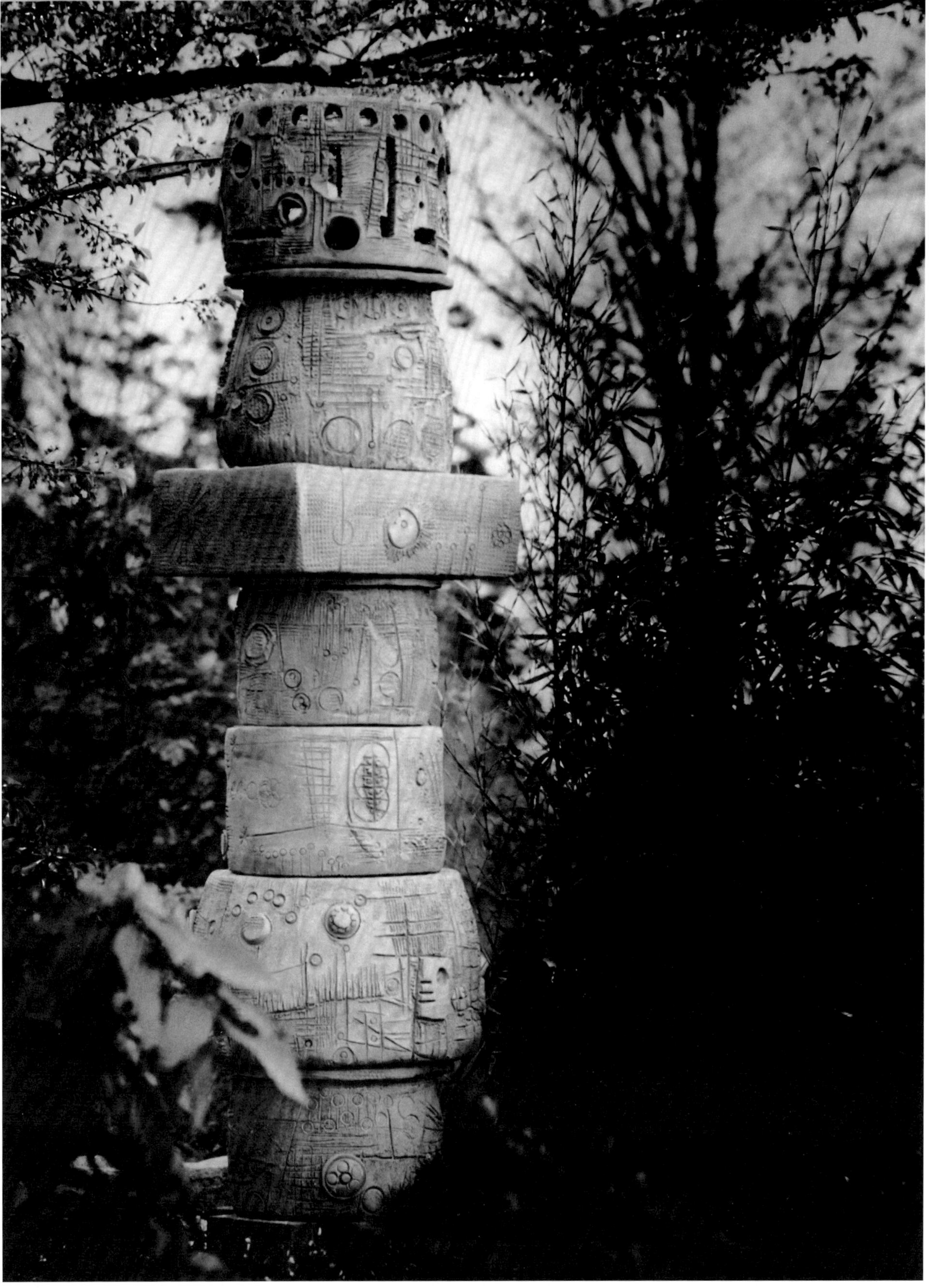

Private Preview: Patrons Dr. & Mrs. E. M. Wilder invite you to a one-man show of work by

j. n. hardman

The Little Gallery, 512 Fifth Avenue, New Westminster, B.C., 3:00 p.m., Sunday, April 4th.

invitation: Jack Hardman exhibition, '50s, Little Gallery
COURTESY OF THE VANCOUVER ART GALLERY LIBRARY

records is referred to as *Totemic Number Two.*"[42] The same year, two of his sculptures, *The Assyrian* and *Familia No. 3*, were chosen to appear with Anne Kahane's and Cecil Richards' work in a three-man traveling Canadian sculpture show organized by the National Gallery. The program accompanying the show had this to say:

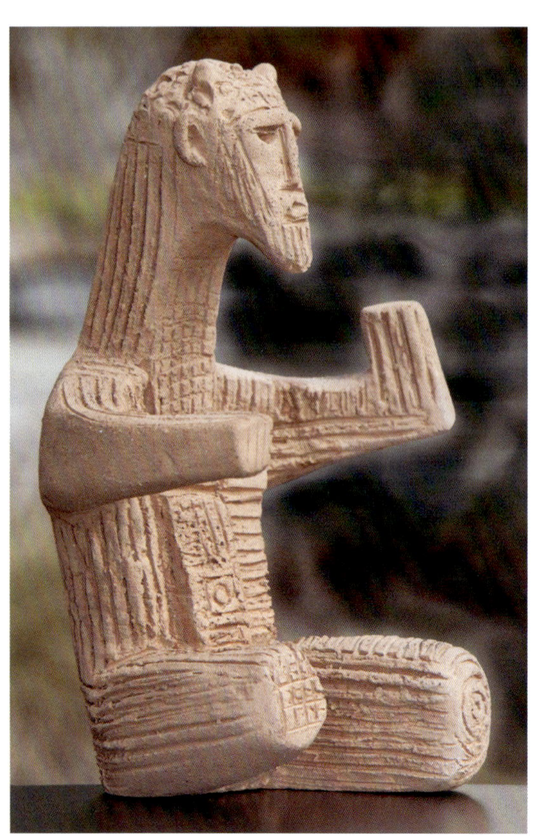

Satyr, mid '60s, ceramic, 9.25" x 7" x 4.75"
PRIVATE COLLECTION
PHOTO BY INGEBORG HARDMAN

> The terra cotta (baked clay) forms by Jack Hardman illustrate still another approach and reveal another kind of artist personality. His works... have certain literary qualities in that a number of them are witty commentaries. Others are definitely aligned to spiritual mysteries, such as are found in the totem pole or in African carvings. The tall columnar forms loom up through the forest as though properly rooted in the ground amid their rightful place with plant life. Sometimes the forms speak of the human comedy, the solidarity of human relations or even of human panic. Hardman's work has the immediacy of today... He is using his medium in a way that suits his sharp perceptions, and his rapid translation from concept to execution successfully conveys the pulse of 20th Century proclivities. On the other hand, there is much spirit, tolerance and humour in his work.

Another piece by Jack, *Totemic Baroque,* was picked for the Second Canadian Sculpture Exhibition the National Gallery, held in Ottawa from June to September of 1964.[43] In June, the *Columbian* also devoted an entire two-page spread to Jack and Marya, headlined "Burnaby Couple Enriches Cultural Life." Reporter Mildred Jeffery wrote:

> Here they work, she curled up in the corner of a chesterfield, surrounded by sculpted forms by her husband and paintings by their close friend and New Westminster artist, Joe Plaskett; he in his off-the-kitchen home studio, wearing a protective apron... When Marya Hardman settles in to compose, first in long hand, there is always a stack of paper close by, and a comforting pot of tea. When Jack Hardman begins to create, it is often in the early hours of the morning, when he finds ideas run vividly. "Terra cotta is my favourite medium," he said. "The clay seems to have a life of its own to which I respond."[44]

Jeffrey was impressed with the amount of sculpture Jack was able to produce, noting that, the previous summer, he had worked through a ton and a half of clay, which he brought home from Abbotsford in a truck. The article included several pictures of Jack's sculptures, small terra cotta pieces with "a large and powerful feeling," Jeffrey captioned. Mentioning Jack's fondness for prints, she quoted him saying, "What I cannot produce in sculpture, I produce in prints," and noted his long-standing interest in the medium.

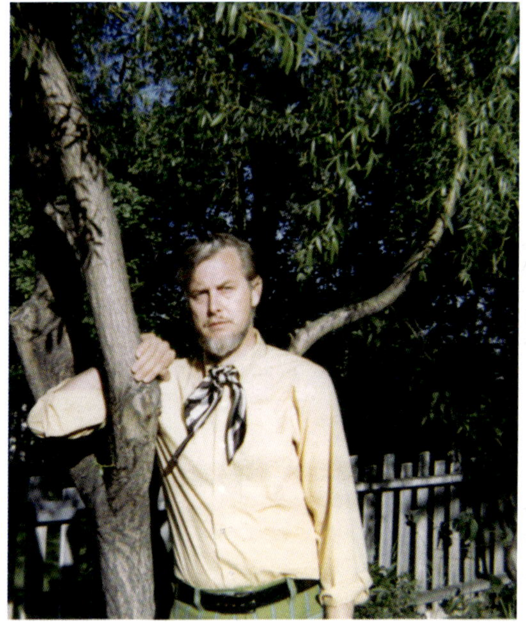

Jack in Toronto, late '60s

Jack visited Toronto in August 1964 and arranged to have his works shown at both the Dorothy Cameron Gallery and the Gallery Pascal. He made a vivid impression on a reporter at the *Toronto Telegram*. "Jack Hardman, 41 and looks 31, hit Toronto Galleries last week: with the force of a six-foot-four Pacific gale—fresh, strong and lively... Vancouver's Hardman, a true westerner, is extremely frank, practical, and articulate. He fears nothing but himself." Jack, who told the reporter, "Teaching is my hobby. Sculpture is my profession," was obviously on a roll. "I recently sold a work for $1,000. I'm a little shocked, to be quite honest. I remember the time when $100 was considered a lot," he said.[45]

In April 1965, an exhibition of Jack's sculptures and prints at the Little Gallery in New Westminster was favourably reviewed in the *Sun* by David Watmough:

> Hardman's art shows a strength of detail and control of his material that is particularly arresting... I liked many of the prints—not least for the rare air of delicate mystery that Hardman has managed to incorporate into several

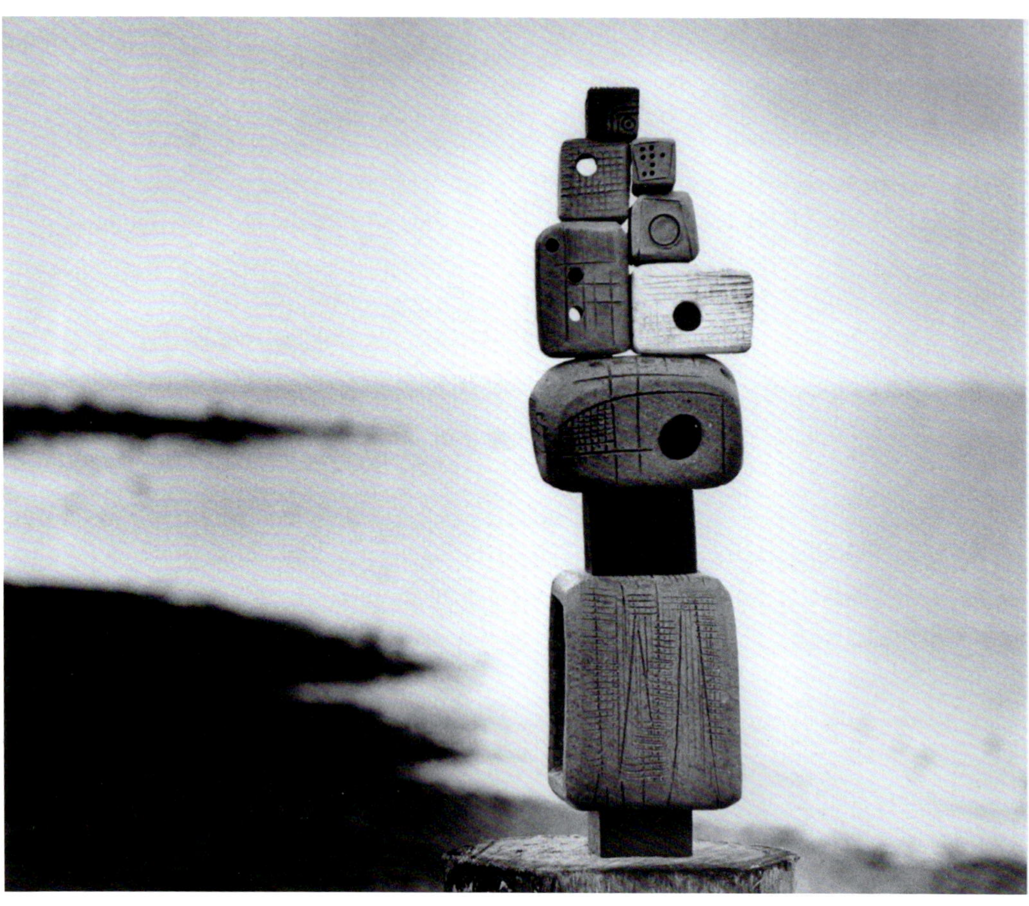

Blocking, mid '60s, clay, 24" x 7" x 7", missing
PHOTO BY JACK V. LONG

of them. But it is in such intense expressions of the family theme as *Familia No. 11* that the major pulse of imagination for this artist palpably lies."[46]

The mid-sixties was a productive period for Jack. However, his family life was beginning to unravel. Not only did Jack have frequent respiratory infections, he also suffered from bouts of mental illness. Marya blamed his father, Gordon: "He suffered from the way he was treated. It was very formative for him." Marya wasn't sure, but she thought that Gordon's time in the army may have had something to do with his attitudes towards Jack. "He came back severely shaken up."[47]

› *Open and Closed Form,* mid '60s, clay, 14" x 12"
PRIVATE COLLECTION
PHOTO BY JACK V. LONG

In any case, Marya said, "I have little patience with illness. I had to look after him, and I'm not good at it. I made him very uncomfortable and unhappy. The fault was more mine than his. But I'm not a nurse. I don't have that kind of patience or detachment." Jack had periods where he would break down entirely and be taken to hospital. "He had horrible depressions where he was suicidal. I remember one time when

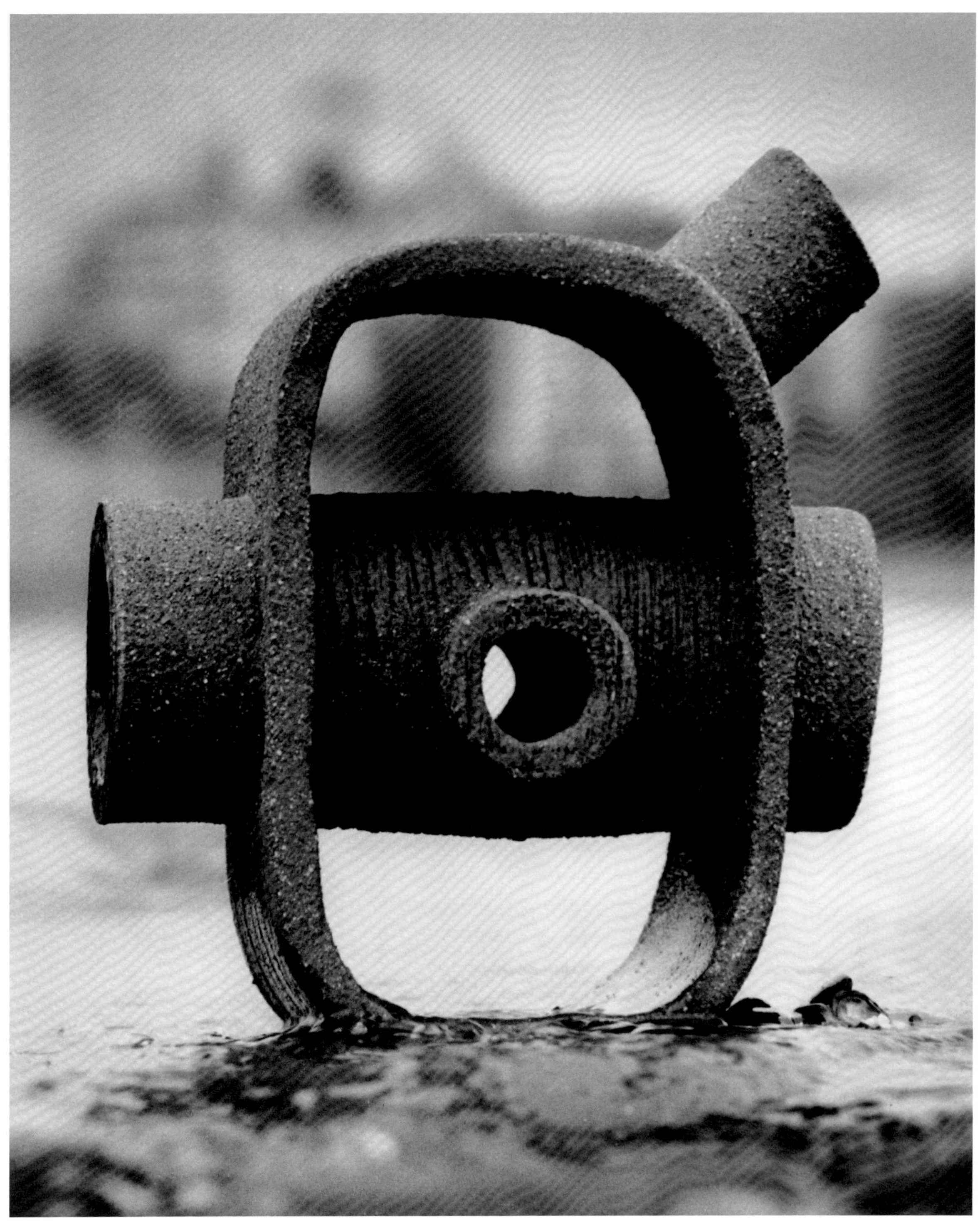

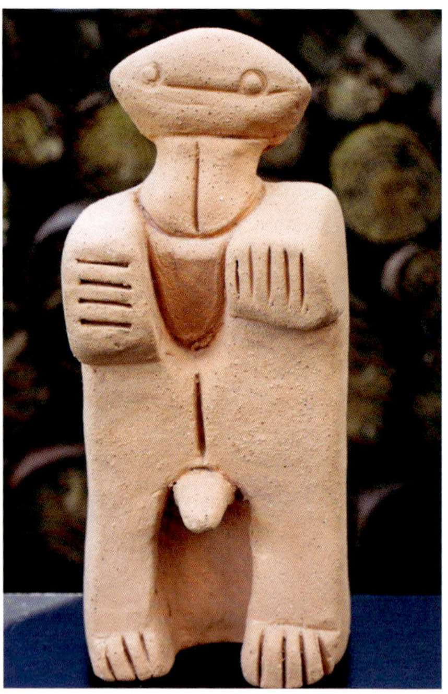

Untitled Man, mid '60s, ceramic, 9.75" x 4.5" x 3.5"
PRIVATE COLLECTION
PHOTO BY INGEBORG HARDMAN

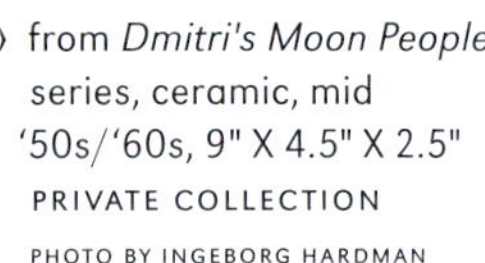

› from *Dmitri's Moon People* series, ceramic, mid '50s/'60s, 9" X 4.5" X 2.5"
PRIVATE COLLECTION
PHOTO BY INGEBORG HARDMAN

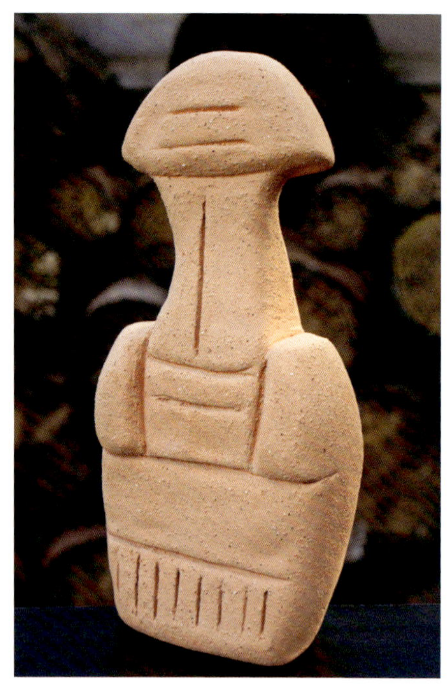

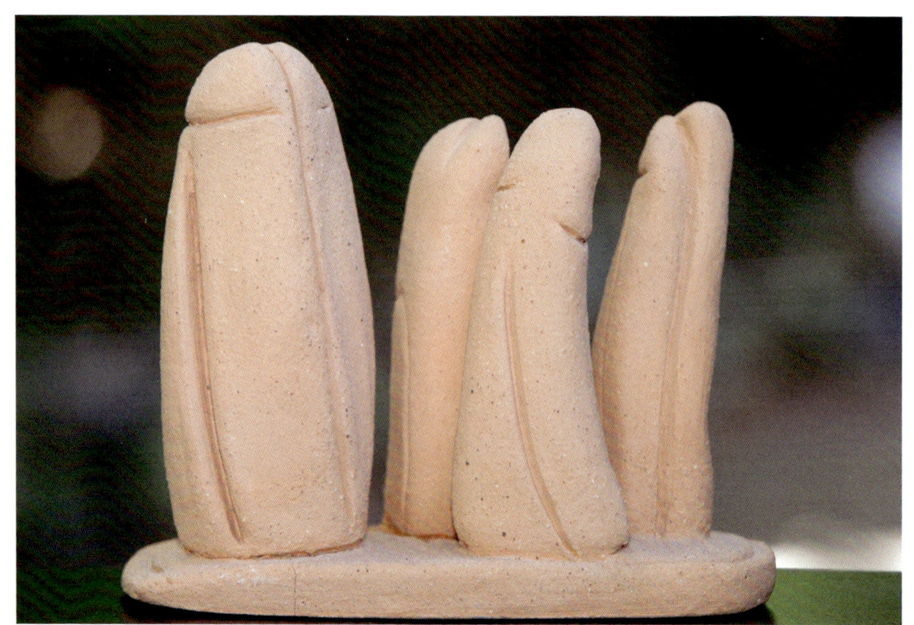

4 Penises, mid '60s, ceramic, 7" x 7.5" x 5"
PRIVATE COLLECTION OF JOY ZEMEL LONG
PHOTO BY INGEBORG HARDMAN

Joe and I visited. We held hands and looked at Jack. We were stricken to see him." Jack's doctor told Marya, "You know, unless he gets more moral support from you, it would be better that you didn't live together." She said, "I felt wrung out. I had no more moral support to give. By this time, we had worn each other out. It was a sad sad thing. Lithium hadn't been discovered then. Once it was discovered, he improved enormously."[48] But it was too late to save the marriage. In January 1966, Marya and Jack were divorced.[49]

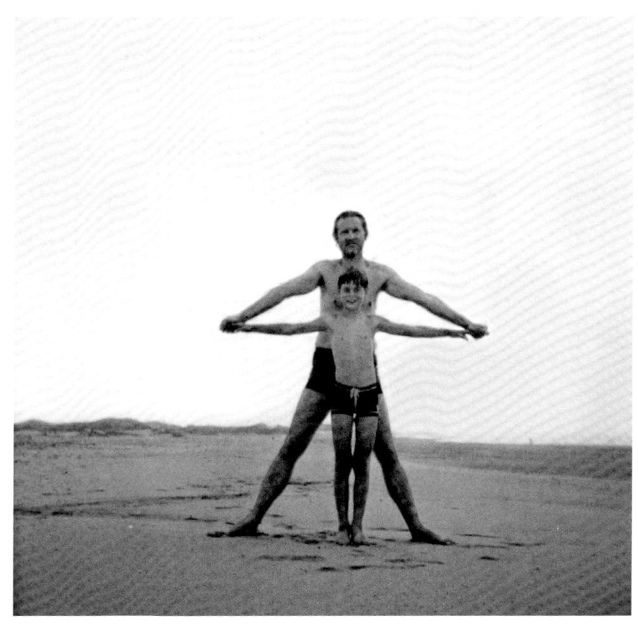

Jack & Dmitri on Prince Edward Island, 1967-68

Two months later, Jack received a $5,000 Canada Council grant to enable him to go to Toronto to observe new sculpture techniques.[50] Marya went back to UBC to complete her MA in English, and Dmitri stayed with her. In Toronto, Jack became good friends with Charles Israel, the novelist, and his wife. Then he befriended the actor Peter Mews, and lived with him.[51] Dmitri came from B.C. to be with his father over the holidays and remembered spending the summers of 1967 and 1968 on Prince Edward Island while Mews acted in the musical of *Anne of Green Gables*. Dmitri wrote in an email:

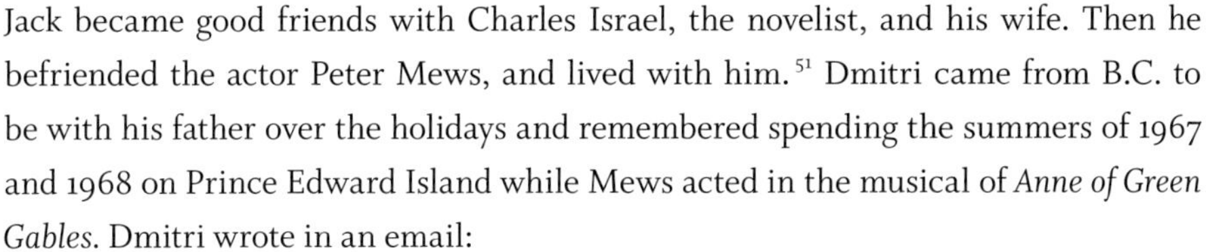

> I would fly to Toronto after I got out of school in June, and after a week or so we'd drive out to PEI for the duration of the summer. Those were the two best summers of my childhood. Jack and I built a hut out of driftwood on an isolated beach on the North Shore of the Island, and it quickly became the changing room for the cast of the theatre company when they had time off from rehearsals. Lots of beach parties and picnics occurred there, often followed by lobster boils at the house Barbara Hamilton rented for the season.[52]

One of Jack's works was included in the display of contemporary Canadian sculptures commissioned for Expo 67.[53] While based in the East, however, he continued to keep a connection with Vancouver. In May of that year, his one-man show, Cybernetic Sculptures, opened at the Douglas Gallery[54] on Davie Street in Vancouver.

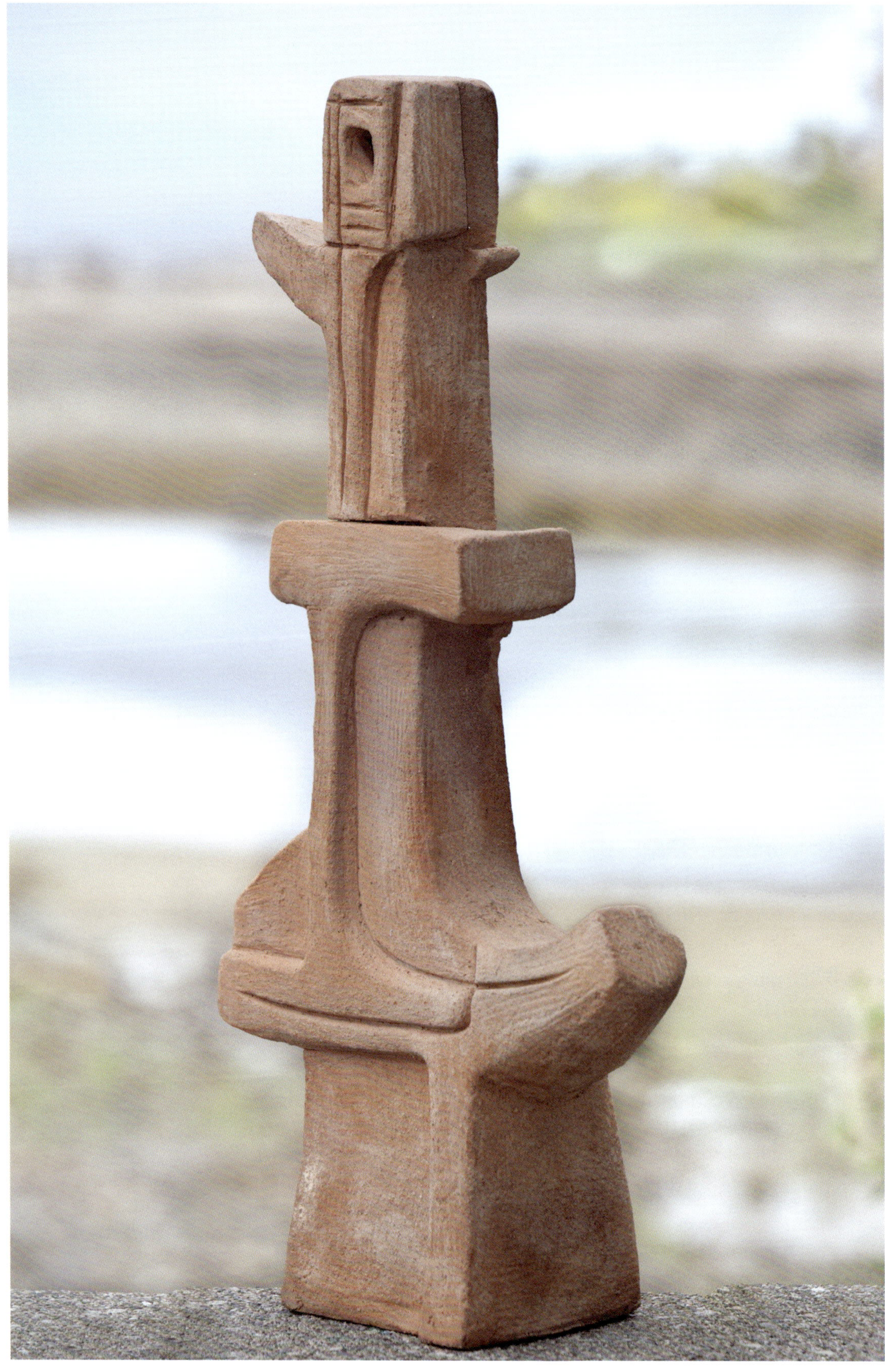

A Mentor's Life

‹ *Untitled,* mid '50s/'60s, ceramic, 15.25" x 9" x 8.5"
PRIVATE COLLECTION
PHOTO BY INGEBORG HARDMAN

In 1969, Jack returned to the Lower Mainland to look after Dmitri because Marya had been hospitalized for what Dmitri called "nervous exhaustion."[55] Jack was haunted by his own demons. When Marya was back in the house they had shared on Hythe Avenue, he visited her there. Marya recalled, "Jack's beautiful totemic pieces were still in the garden." He could no longer see their appeal. He completely destroyed one sculpture and was well on his way to ruining another when Marya remonstrated with him. Horrified, she said, "I told him, 'Don't do that, Jack. Leave them to Dmitri.' That did get to him, and he stopped." But the two pieces were lost. Marya said:

> He was so discouraged. Mona Fertig will tell you that her father, George Fertig, burned some of his paintings. This is what neglect drove them to do. It killed their confidence. They felt they weren't valued by their society or their contemporaries. It made them do rash and impulsive things like burn their works.[56]

Fortunately for Jack, he could fall back on his teaching. He started working at Centennial High School in Coquitlam, which offered an enriched artistic education with four other art teachers on staff: Peter Paul Ochs, another sculptor, a fabric artist, a printmaker and Don Portelance, a fine painter. Joe Therrien, whom Jack taught in 1970 and 1971, became a printmaker and high-school art teacher himself. His first experience working with clay and with printmaking was with Jack. The two hit it off and became good friends.

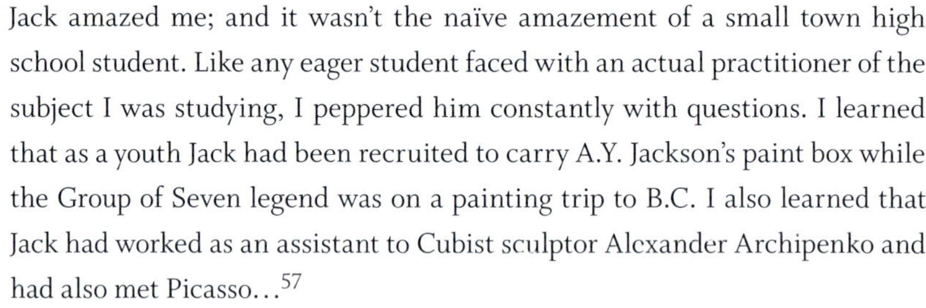

> Jack amazed me; and it wasn't the naïve amazement of a small town high school student. Like any eager student faced with an actual practitioner of the subject I was studying, I peppered him constantly with questions. I learned that as a youth Jack had been recruited to carry A.Y. Jackson's paint box while the Group of Seven legend was on a painting trip to B.C. I also learned that Jack had worked as an assistant to Cubist sculptor Alexander Archipenko and had also met Picasso…[57]

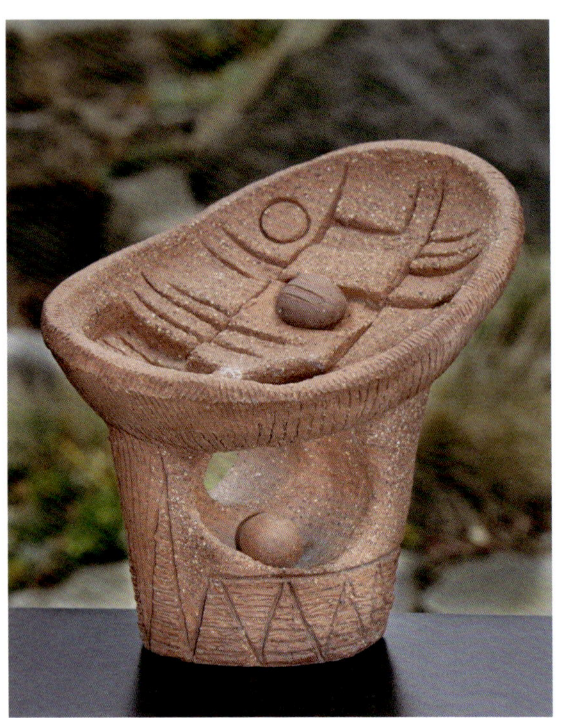

Untitled, mid '50s - '60s, ceramic, 8" x 7.25" x 9.5"
PRIVATE COLLECTION
PHOTO BY INGEBORG HARDMAN

Years after Joe graduated, he travelled several times with Jack to the Davidson Gallery in Seattle to "drool over the Old Masters—Rembrandts, Dürers, Picassos—lots of them." Said Therrien in an interview from his Coquitlam home, "Jack was mad for prints. One of the things that he liked about them was that they were a democratic art form. You could afford to buy Picassos or Rembrandts whereas you couldn't ordinarily purchase artists of an international caliber."[57]

Jack stayed at Centennial until 1974, when he began to instruct in the teacher training program at Simon Fraser University.[58] In the spring of 1976, he got a job that suited his experience and talent—Director of the Burnaby Art Gallery. Jack had been involved with the arts community in Burnaby for years. In 1958, he'd helped to organize an invitational exhibit of B.C. artists at Burnaby City Hall. The exhibition was so enthusiastically received that a number of artists decided to form the Burnaby Art Society. Jack, who was the first president of the society, thought that the organization should mount Canada's first open-juried print show. It took place at the Centennial Pavilion on Burnaby Mountain in July 1961 and became a biennial event. In 1965, the City of Burnaby purchased the Ceperley Estate at Deer Lake in order to give several arts groups, including the Burnaby Art Society, a permanent home. The Ceperley Mansion became an art gallery operated by the Society.[59]

In the fall of 1976, Jack married Berenice Gilmore.[60] She found him to be "charming, but also mercurial." Berenice shared Jack's passion for art, literature and music. In a phone interview, she recalled, "We both loved opera, and we used often to drive up the Valley looking for antiques, listening to *Saturday Afternoon at the Opera* and trying to guess who the singers were."[61] Berenice had been the wife of Jack Gilmore, a high-school history teacher in north Burnaby. Marya, who met the Gilmores when she was married to Jack, was astonished at the development. "We were all socialists. We had a great deal in common. I didn't realize there was anything wrong with their marriage."[62]

Jack in art room at Centennial High School, 1970s, Burnaby, BC

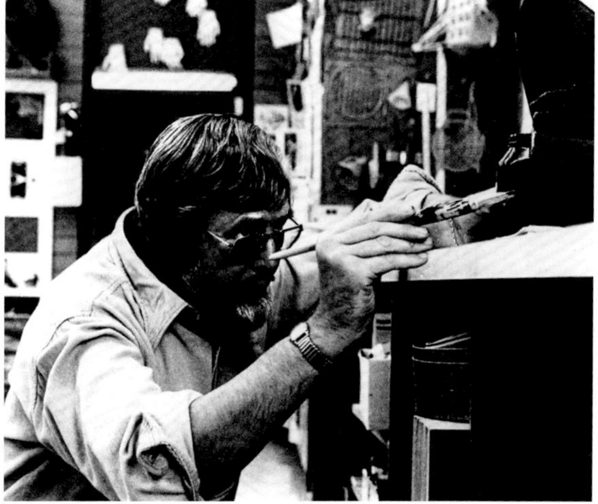

Jack threw himself into his work at the Gallery. Berenice said, "He was very keen to have Canadian artists, particularly B.C. artists, because he really felt that there were a lot of people who hadn't had the exposure they deserved."[63] Jean François Guimond said, "His exhibitions were wonderful, very eclectic. He brought in printmakers, sculptors, painters. He brought in people from all the disciplines, people who were experimental, people who were doing fabric or film cartoons."[64] Jack supported many different kinds of artists, including some of his former students. Both Joe Therrien and Leonard Brett were given a chance to show their work.[65]

In 1977, Jack put on a major show marking the 10th anniversary of the Burnaby Art Gallery. In its catalogue, he wrote, "To mark this milestone in our history, we have attempted to recreate, as closely as possible, the first exhibition held in 1958."[66] He displayed the late-fifties works of artists who in the intervening years had become well-known: Bruno and Molly Bobak, Lawren Harris, Don Jarvis, John Koerner, Joe Plaskett, Jack Shadbolt, Gordon Smith and Tak Tanabe. However, not all of his choices were so safe. He also showed a couple of paintings by Frances Faminow, Jock Hearn, and George Fertig, to whom the past 20 years had not been so kind.

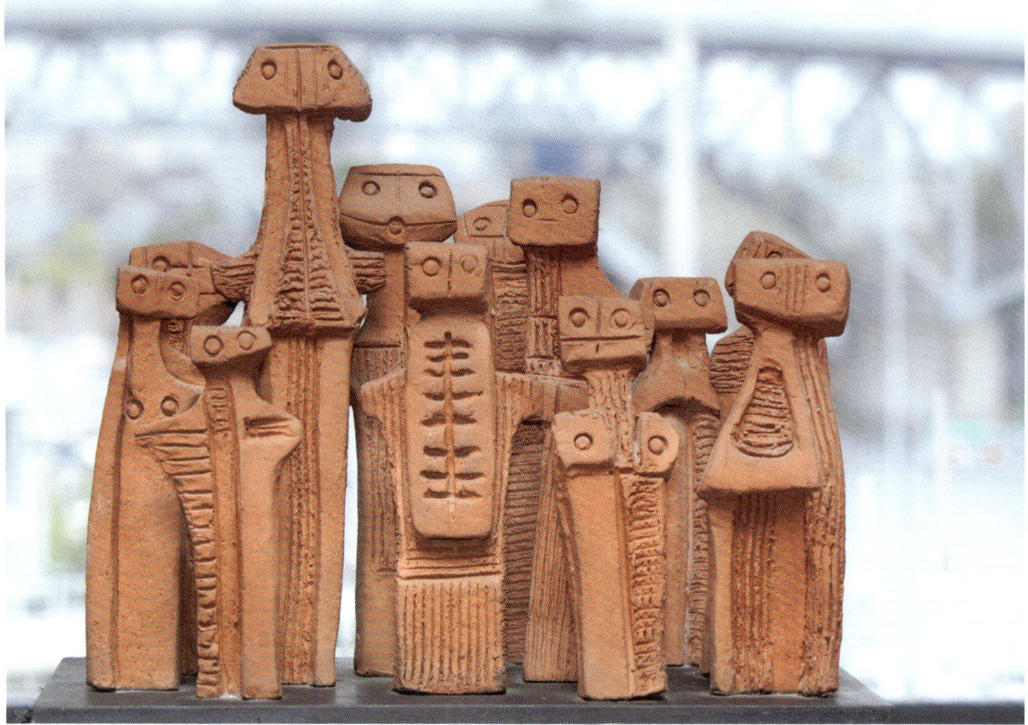

Whatcha Doin' Mister?, 1964, ceramic, 16" x 20" x 12"
PRIVATE COLLECTION OF FRANCES LONG
PHOTO BY INGEBORG HARDMAN

Evelyn Roth, a multi-media artist famous for large innovative textile structures and outdoor festivals, remembers vividly how she benefitted from Jack's willingness to take risks. In an email from Australia where she now lives, Roth wrote:

> Jack Hardman, whom I got to know by being a part of his international festival in 1979, was a generous, outgoing and humorous director of the B.A.G. I don't know if he knew my reputation for far-out works. I had published the *Evelyn Roth Recycling Book* in 1976, drove my car covered with a crocheted recycled video tape car cozy across Canada in 1971 and had just completed 700 street banners, each made by a child in 1979 in Vancouver.
>
> I walked into his office and noticed he had pics of Douglas Cardinal's curvy architecture on the walls of his office. I had just met Douglas and shared a sweat lodge with him and stayed at his curvy house built into the hillside in St. Albert outside of Edmonton. Thus, we shared in the adoration of one of Canada's great men. Douglas went on to design the Museum of Civilization in Hull.
>
> So Jack said, "How about calling it [the festival] the Evelyn Roth International Festival, you can plan eight Sunday events, and here's $8,000 for the works, installation inside, crocheted webs in the outdoor balcony, an all-night drum circle, roving sculpture performance on the lawn, floating ogopogo on

the lake and floating sculptures in the sky. It all came to pass—loved by the general public.[67]

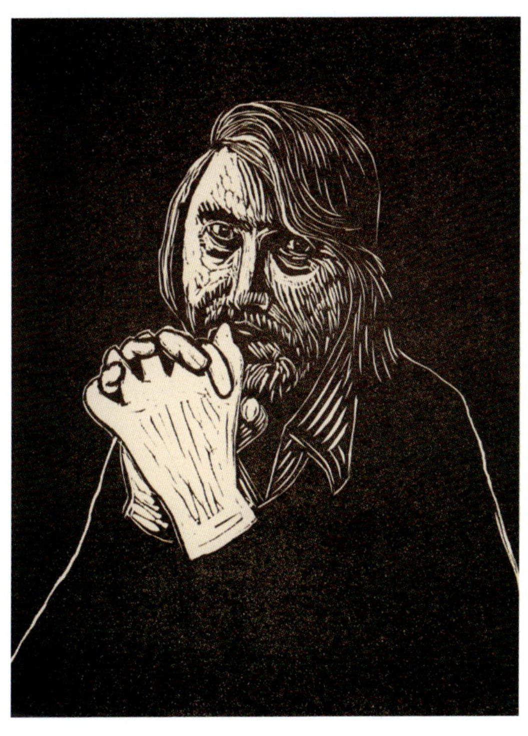

Jack Hardman, 1979, linocut, 12" x 9", COURTESY OF AND BY JOE THERRIEN

Jack also expanded the print collection at the Gallery. When he took over, it owned just 65 artworks. According to *A Quarter Century of Collecting: Burnaby Art Gallery 1967–1992*, "From 1976 to 1981 under Mr. Jack Hardman's directorship, the Burnaby Art Gallery grew in stature, and the collection grew in numbers as 476 new works were given accession numbers."

His list of acquisitions from May 1979 to May 1980 includes artists such as David Milne, Harold Towne, Lawren P. Harris, LeRoy Jensen, Jack Wise, Eric Bergman, John Esler, Laurence Hyde, Jaques Hnizdousky, Jack Shadbolt, Caroline Armington, Pablo Picasso, A.J. Casson, Ina Uhtoff and Irene Whittome (listed in order of the acquisition of their works).[68] Today, the Gallery's collection has expanded to 4,500 works, most of which are still prints.[69]

Jack loved being at the Gallery; he loved what he could do there, he loved being able to give young and unknown artists a chance. But as was so often the case with Jack, his health became an impediment. In the winter of 1978, he suffered a serious stroke.[70] It didn't affect his cognitive abilities, but it did restrict his mobility on his left side. He carried on nonetheless. Berenice helped him by curating two shows about the history of art in British Columbia.[71] Guimond recalled that while he was working at the Bau-Xi, Jack was still keeping abreast of new developments:

> Every Saturday, Jack came into Vancouver and did the gallery tour in his function as director. There were a handful of galleries; Jack visited them all. It was almost a religious thing. You knew that at 10:30 on Saturday morning, Jack would show up. He was always interested in what was new... I was impressed with the extent of his knowledge. He knew all about the different printmakers, why they were important, what kinds of technical breakthroughs different ones had made.[72]

However, by the spring of 1981, a combination of factors led the Board at the Gallery to ask for Jack's resignation. All the reasons for this were never fully made public, but at an acrimonious meeting in May, financial difficulties and a slide in the number of visitors were cited. There were protests. Jack's friend, the sculptor David Marshall, asked members of the Board for a full discussion of the reasons for his dismissal. But in the end, nothing could be done.[73]

Losing the position was both a financial and emotional blow for Jack. Berenice said:

> He really lost everything at once. He enjoyed making his own art, sculpting particularly, and walking. He was unable to do both after the stroke. And then being asked to resign was very hard on him as well. He did enjoy the gallery work. He felt he did have an opportunity to make a difference, especially with local artists.[74]

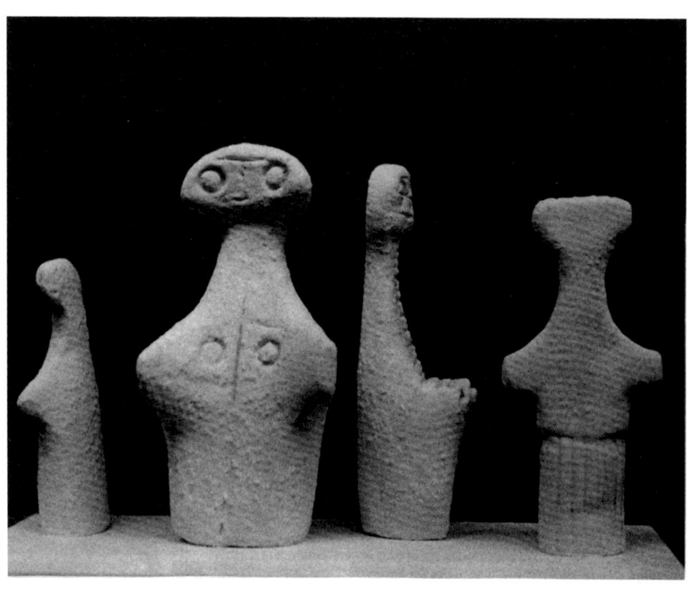

Dmitri's Moon People, mid '50s, ceramic, 12" x 6"
COLLECTION OF VANCOUVER ART GALLERY
PHOTO BY JACK V. LONG

Luckily, his old friend Joe Plaskett stepped in and helped him out financially and invited him to live at a house he had inherited in New Westminster, a small bungalow in a pleasant tree-lined neighbourhood near Queen's Park. A congenial home, it was also loaded with Plaskett pastels.[75] Jack's health continued to deteriorate.

In 1991, Jack moved into a care home[76]; even there, Jack kept up his correspondence with friends around the world. Robin Mathews, a writer who had known him since 1957, said that he hadn't lost his spark—or his diabolical sense of humour. He recalled a time when he rang Jack up and said that he and his wife, Esther, wanted to come and take him out for lunch one day.

"That would be lovely," Jack said.

However, the day before the lunch, Jack phoned, "I can't do it. I'm not well enough. We're going to have to do it on another day."

"That's okay," said Mathews, "I don't mind, because Esther can't come."

"Esther can't come!" Jack exploded. "I'm glad it's cancelled. I don't want to have lunch with you. I don't even like you!"

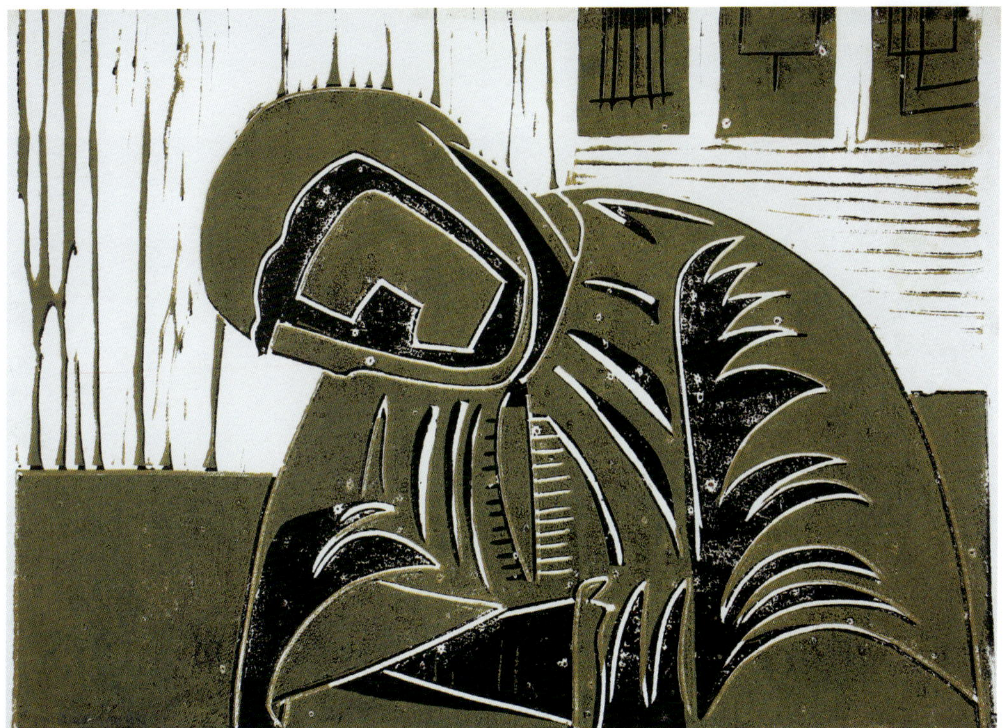

Lazarus, n.d., linocut, 17" x 12", PRIVATE COLLECTION, PHOTO BY INGEBORG HARDMAN

It was vintage Jack, thought Mathews.

In 1996, Jack passed away in Burnaby. A memorial service was held for him in the Burnaby Art Gallery. "It was a charming memorial—a lot of long-time close friends were there," said Mathews. When he was asked to say a few words at the event, one of the stories he told was this last one about the lunch. He remembered that "two or three people came up to me afterwards and said, 'You nailed him. You're the only person who had the courage to say what he was really like.'"[77]

In 2004, Jack's *Family Group* was included in A Modern Life: Art and Design in British Columbia 1945-1960, a Vancouver Art Gallery exhibit.[78] Twelve years after Jack died, the Burnaby Art Gallery organized a retrospective of his prints and exhibited it from November 18, 2008 to January 12, 2009.[79] In a tribute to Jack written for the exhibition, Joe Therrien wrote:

> Jack's passion for art has left several lasting legacies. He was an art maker. He encouraged others to make and appreciate art and he contributed to the establishment of an institution that collects and exhibits the work of others. As a person who has made and exhibited prints, who loves working with clay and who teaches art, I can state unequivocally that Jack Hardman had a major impact on my life.

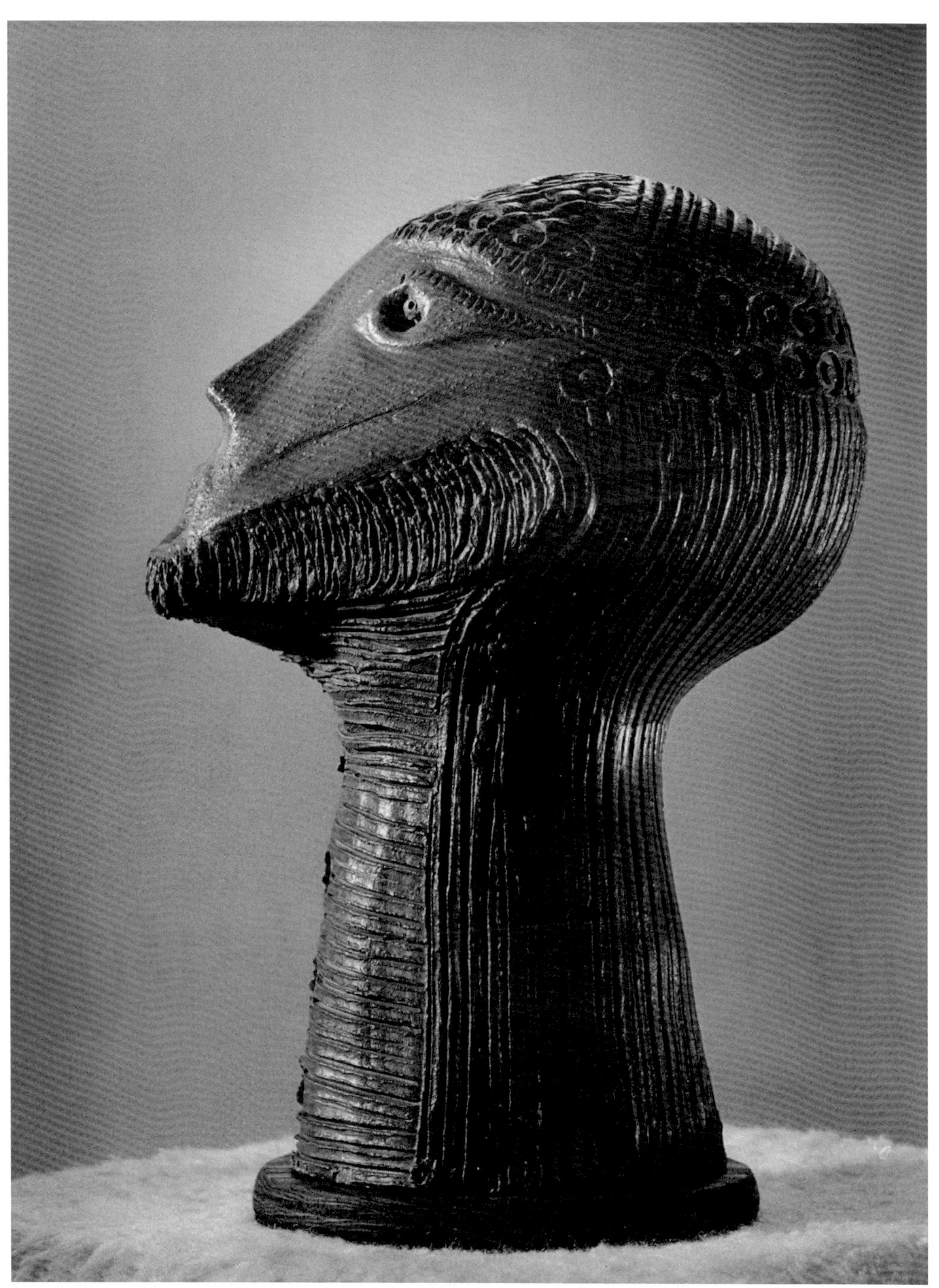

JACK HARDMAN EXHIBITIONS

1947 B.C. Artists, 16th Annual Exhibition, Vancouver Art Gallery

1948 B.C. Artists, 17th Annual Exhibition, Vancouver Art Gallery

1949 B.C. Artists, 18th Annual Exhibition, Vancouver Art Gallery, October 8–30

1950 B.C. Artists, 19th Annual Exhibition, Vancouver Art Gallery, November 28–December 17

1952 B.C. Artists, 21st Annual Exhibition, Vancouver Art Gallery
Photography Exhibition, University of British Columbia, fifty photographs from the Museum of Modern Art in New York, as well as a selection from B.C. photographers, including Jack Hardman and Joe Plaskett

1953 22nd Annual Exhibition, Vancouver Art Gallery

1956 Northwest Institute of Sculpture, conference and exhibition at the Vancouver Art Gallery, March 27–April 19
Northwest Institute of Sculpture, outdoor exhibition, University of British Columbia, opened July 6
Print Prize in Winnipeg Show
25th Annual Exhibition, Vancouver Art Gallery

1958 100 Years of BC Art, Vancouver Art Gallery. Eighty-nine contemporary works, painting and sculptures, were shown.
Sculpture Prize Winner, Northwest Craftsman Exhibition, University of Seattle, Washington
Invitational exhibition of B.C. Painters organized by the Burnaby Centennial Committee
B.C. Society of Artists, Annual Exhibition, Vancouver Art Gallery, June 2–21
27th Annual Exhibition, Vancouver Art Gallery, October 22–November 16

‹ *Dark Prince,* n.d. glazed ceramic, 14"
PRIVATE COLLECTION
PHOTOGRAPHER UNKNOWN

1959 5th Annual Exhibition Northwest Institute of Sculpture, April 7–26
B.C. Society of Artists, Annual Exhibition, Vancouver Art Gallery, June 2–21
President, Burnaby Art Society
President Burnaby Art Teachers Association

1960 46th Annual of Northwest Artists, Seattle Art Museum Exhibition, November 9–December 4

1961 B.C. Society of Artists Annual Exhibition
New Design Gallery, show with Doris Shadbolt, December

1962 B.C. Society of Artists Annual Exhibition
Exhibition, Seattle World's Fair
Exhibition of paintings, prints, ceramics and weaving, Burnaby Public Library, nineteen artists included, December

1963 B.C. Society of Artists Annual Exhibition

1964 B.C. Society of Artists Annual Exhibition
2nd Canadian Sculpture Exhibition, one of seventeen works shown in the National Gallery of Canada, Ottawa, June 5 to September 15
Totemic Number 2, a ceramic sold to Lethbridge Junior College, Alberta
A Trio of Canadian Sculptors, a travelling show organized by the National Gallery of Canada
The New Ceramic Presence, University of British Columbia, three-man show, January 28–February 29
Canadian Water Colours, Drawings and Prints, National Gallery, Ottawa
Six Burnaby Printers, presented by the Burnaby Art Society

1965 The Little Gallery, New Westminster, one-man show, April 4–24
10th Anniversary Exhibition, New Design Gallery, Vancouver, group show, January 11–29
Print Exhibition, Bellingham Public Library, group show, January and February
Canadian Drawings and Prints, Cardiff Commonwealth Arts Festival, group show, sixty-four artists, September 18–October 10

Some B.C. Sculptors, Fine Arts Gallery, University of Alberta, nine sculptors, November 1–20
Exhibition, Children's Gallery, Vancouver Art Gallery, group show, January 15–February 28

1966 B.C. Society of Fine Arts
British Columbia Watercolours, Prints and Drawings, Fine Arts Gallery, University of British Columbia, thirty-seven artists, July 4–August 19
The Studio Art Gallery International, Vancouver, group show, May 10–31

1967 Contemporary Canadian Sculpture, Expo 67. In April, the House of Seagram LTD. bought twenty works from this show, including one by Jack Hardman.
Cybernetic Sculptures, Douglas Gallery, Vancouver, one-man show, May 26 to June 15

1968 52nd Annual Exhibition, Society of Canadian Painter-Etchers and Engravers, The Library of the City Hall, Toronto, March 8–29

1971 Gallery Pascal, Toronto, two-man show with Maxwell Bates, March 4–23

2004 A Modern Life: Art and Design in British Columbia 1945–1960, group show, May 15–October 11

2008 - 09 Jack Hardman, Retrospective Print Show organized by the Burnaby Art Gallery, on display from November 18, 2008 to January 12, 2009

PUBLIC COLLECTIONS

Vancouver Art Gallery, National Gallery of Canada, Burnaby Art Gallery, University of Victoria

PRIVATE COLLECTIONS

Canada, Hawaii, United States, England, France

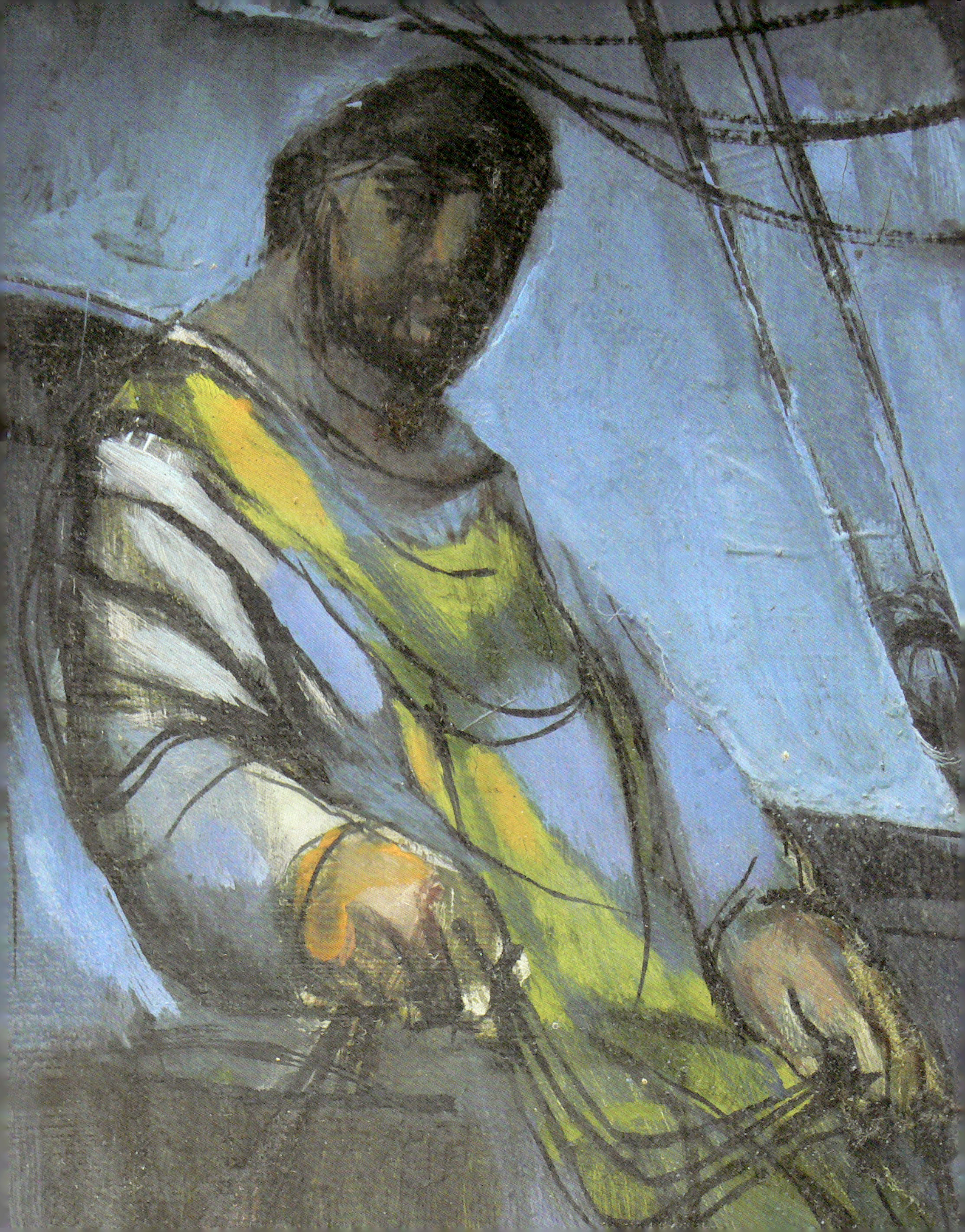

LEROY JENSEN

—WENDY NEWBOLD PATTERSON

preface by ROY PATTERSON

Preface

"Always live to the highest point of your present understanding." —LEROY JENSEN

‹‹ *The Sailor* [detail], 1960s, oil on gesso panel, 8½" x 11"
PRIVATE COLLECTION

MOST DAYS ROLL into each other like gathering fog. Some days stand out like clear beacons. Such was the day I met LeRoy Jensen, a man whose strength of character, compassion, humor and generosity of spirit changed my life. Like many of my generation, I was disillusioned and had dropped out. In September 1970, my friend Don Wunderlee and I hitchhiked across Canada from Cambridge, Massachusetts. We didn't have a plan; Vancouver was the arbitrary destination of our adventure. In Cambridge I had been involved with a group of so-called artists, but it was mostly talk in the cafés and bars. I was searching for depth and substance in my life, but had no idea where to find it.

Shortly after our arrival in Vancouver, Don and I hitchhiked to a small, unassuming house at 7731 French Street. A few days earlier, we had signed up for LeRoy's drawing and painting class at the Vancouver Free University. Reluctant to attend that first class, I remember telling Don that I didn't think I needed any instruction. I made the case for being self-taught and "original." After we knocked on the door and entered that house, my silly concepts dissipated like smoke hitting a brisk wind.

LeRoy's wife Lynda, warmly welcomed us. Inside, paintings covered every inch of wall space, transforming that little house into a faceted jewel exploding with deep, rich color. In the living room, a small charismatic man was holding court. He was absolutely riveting. Within seconds, his huge commanding presence completely overshadowed his stature.

LeRoy's robust approach to life and art was a seminal experience for his students. He gave us a solid foundation to build on and return to throughout our lives. He taught a way to begin, a way to endure and a way of life. He challenged us to live to the highest point of our present understanding, which leaves no room for self-satisfaction.

LeRoy had a deep respect for the masters of art throughout history. He showed us how they too were our teachers and friends. Being a gifted storyteller, he made the history of art live and breathe. With great humor, he admonished us to put the light of our own "genius" temporarily aside in order to absorb the lessons of these giants. He liberated us from the notion that our work was precious and discouraged us from looking for quick results.

He showed us that drawing was the quintessence of all visual art disciplines. Under his guidance, Wendy and I studied drawing exclusively for three years. Then we both began to paint and sculpt simultaneously. The principles we learned from drawing could be applied to either discipline. Later on when the demands of a young family constricted our time, Wendy focused on painting and I chose the path of sculpture.

Above all else LeRoy Jensen was a Master Painter. His depth of knowledge about art and the limitless energy he applied to his craft were surpassed only by his love for humanity. LeRoy poured that love into his canvases. We only have to look at his paintings to see what this rare and remarkable individual was saying to us. I have yet to encounter a bigger man. His gifts were immeasurable.

Roy Patterson is a sculptor and former student of LeRoy Jensen. They were friends for over 30 years.

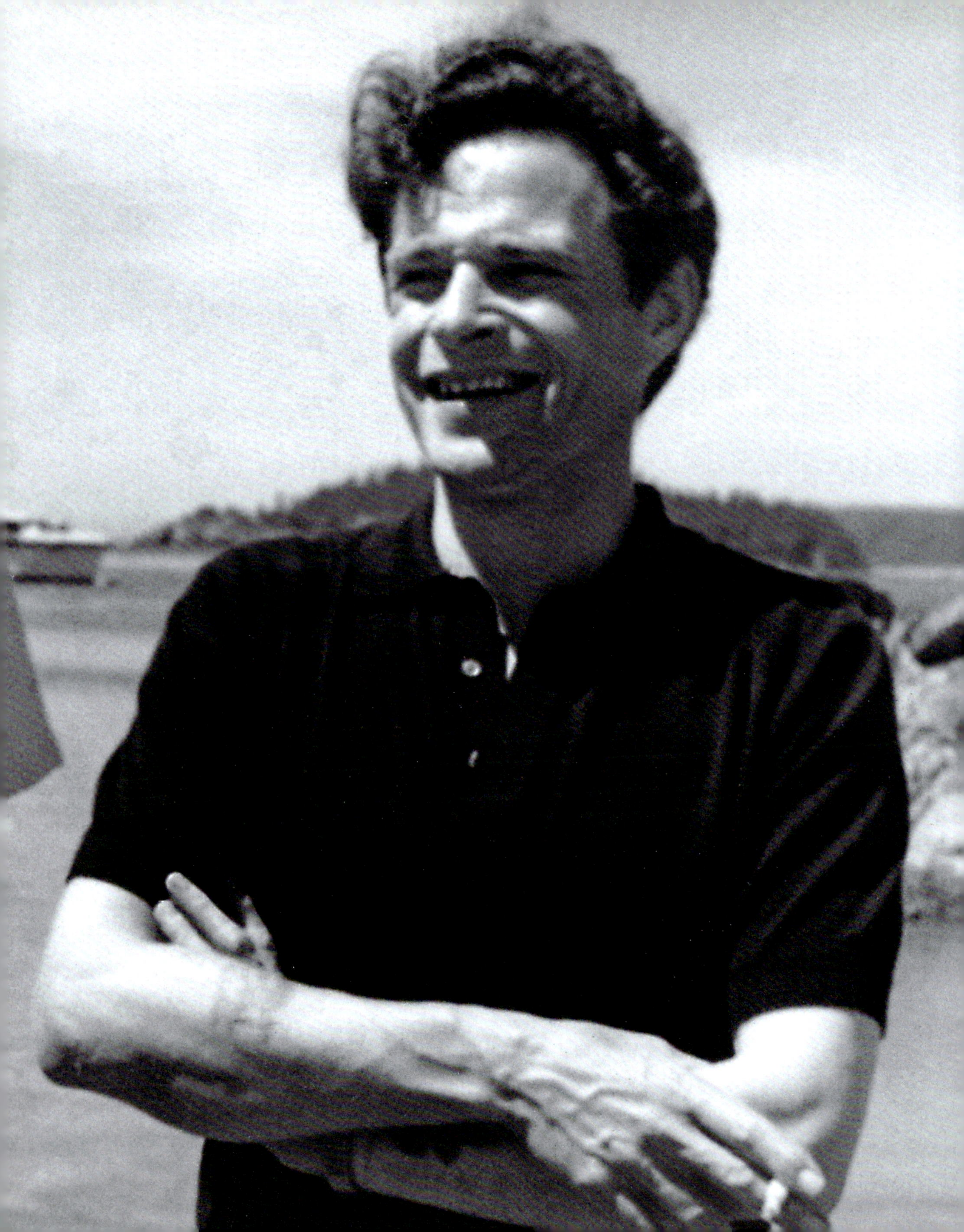

Beginnings in Asia

I paint because my way of life is to paint. Painting for me is the best road to knowledge, the best means of participating profoundly in the life of the world, the best means of communicating with it. —EDOUARD PIGNON

‹ LeRoy Jensen, 1969, Worlcombe Island, BC

When LeRoy Jensen was very young and living in Japan, he became seriously ill with an infection from an eye injury. A doctor from a U.S. navy ship recommended the immediate removal of the eye to save his life. Instead, a family servant brought in a local Oriental healer who examined his eye with a tube and a candle and determined that the eye wasn't the problem. His mother, a registered nurse, realized that he actually had typhoid and tenaciously nursed him back to health, saving both his sight and his life.[1]

LeRoy told me how different his life would have been, if he had lost that eye.[2] The many lives he touched would have also been impoverished, my own, as a painter, included. Vision, insight, his ability to communicate and his principled challenges to authority were always intrinsically connected throughout his work and life.

LeRoy Hackett Jensen was born in Vancouver, British Columbia, August 31, 1927 to Elsie and George Jensen. Elsie Hackett was born in Vancouver in 1893

LeRoy with parents and younger brother Colin on Bowen Island, BC, 1930s
PHOTO COURTESY OF COLIN JENSEN

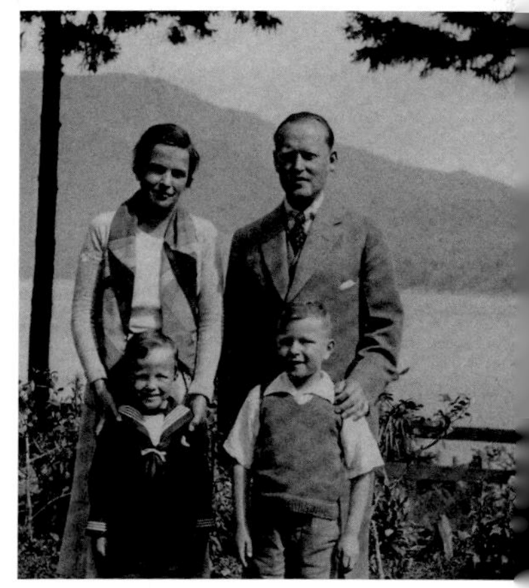

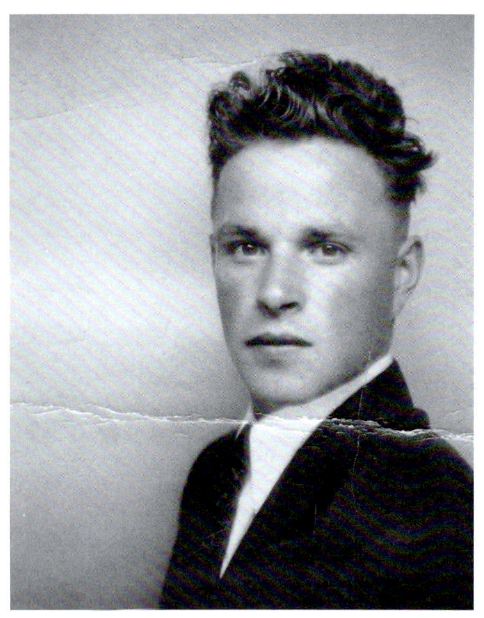

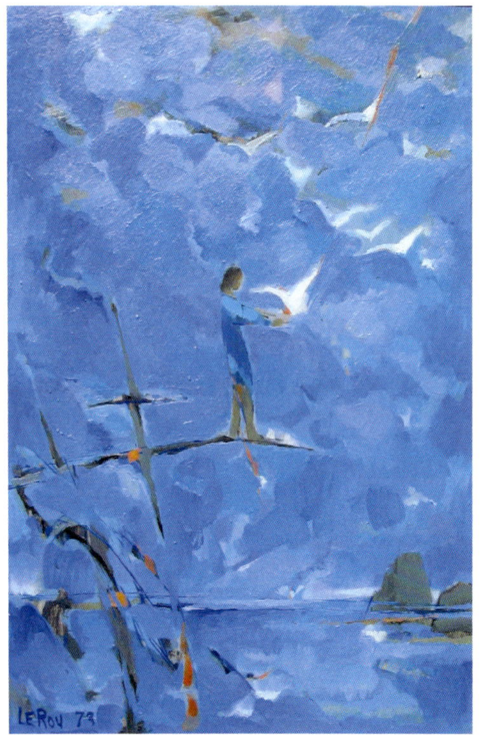

where her father owned and ran the first sawmill. As a young woman, Elsie went to Boston School of Nursing and took a job at the Rockefeller Hospital in Shanghai. George was born in Copenhagen, Denmark, in 1895. He was a telegraph cable engineer working for the Danish company, the Great Northern Telegraph Company, connecting Denmark with the Orient. They met in Shanghai, returning to Vancouver to marry and give birth to their first son, LeRoy. After George signed another contract with the company, the family returned to China. During the politically volatile period from 1928 to 1933, they lived in Shanghai where Colin, LeRoy's brother, was born in 1929.[3]

In 1933, to escape this turmoil, the family moved to Nagasaki, Japan, where they stayed until 1939. On George's comfortable income, the family lived a good lifestyle, and the boys were educated by private tutors. A Japanese gentleman taught LeRoy drawing from age six to ten, his first art lessons. He didn't attend public school until he was ten years old. Drawing became an important healing connection for him during his troubled adolescence and later; the key to his artistic achievements.

This early period of relative calm came to an end when war threatened. In 1939, Elsie took LeRoy and Colin to a boarding school in Vancouver and returned to her husband, then stationed in Hong Kong. Japan's forces attacked Hong Kong eight hours after the Pearl Harbor attacks, occupying Hong Kong on December 25, 1941, "Black Christmas." The Japanese incarcerated Allied nationals, especially British and Canadian, at concentration camps.[4] George and Elsie had Danish passports, and as Denmark had capitulated to German aggression, they were free, but with few resources. Only two letters got out to their sons during the entire six years of war.[5]

The boarding school was "a horrible place"[6] from which LeRoy could hardly wait to escape. In 1941, in the midst of WWII, LeRoy, now 14, lied about his age and managed to join the merchant navy for four years as a "fireman," which was not the adventurous life he imagined.[7] With teams of stokers shoveling coal night and day into the hellish ovens of ships, they sailed the Aleutians and landed at various Pacific Rim ports, avoiding Japanese submarines and Allied reconnaissance.

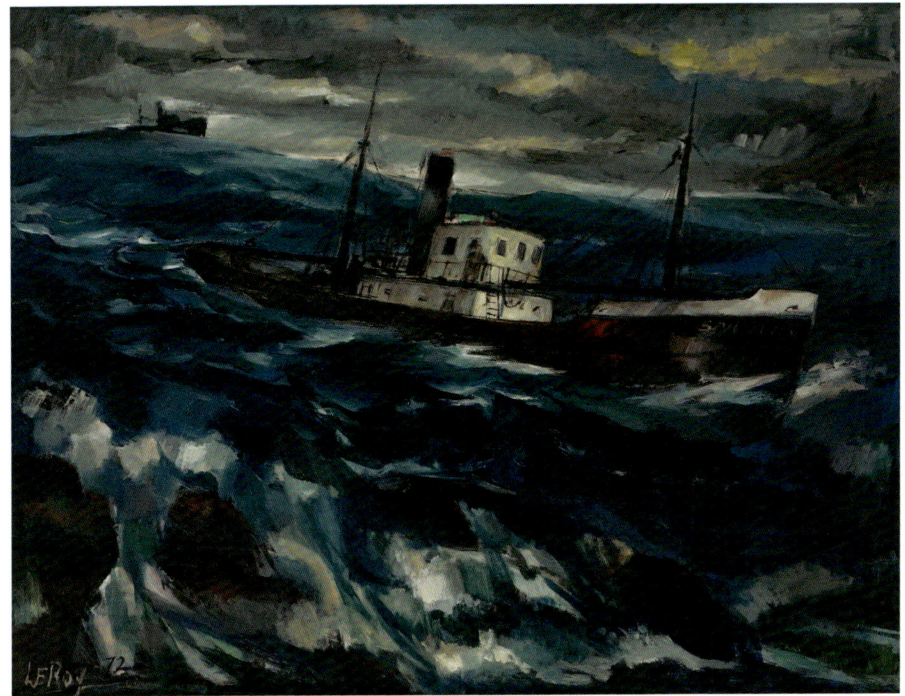

Ship on the High Seas, 1972, oil on canvas, 35" x 46"
PRIVATE COLLECTION
PHOTO BY JANET DWYER

To cope with his situation and the constant conflicts on board, he became a feisty scrapper, using his relatively small size to advantage by grabbing the nostril of his adversary and manipulating him into a position to do serious damage.[8] Reflecting on the harsh reality of life aboard a merchant ship, LeRoy said, "I was made aware of the fact that unless I did something different there was no guarantee my life would be very long."[9]

‹← LeRoy at 18 years

‹ *Boy on Mast,* 1973, oil on board, 35.5" x 23.5"
COLLECTION OF HANK & JAMIE VAN MONTFOORT
PHOTO COURTESY OF HANK VAN MONTFOORT

As the war raged on, LeRoy was unsure if his parents were alive. On layovers, he sometimes visited his maternal grandmother in Vancouver. She had outlived several caregivers, and a new woman always opened the door. One day, there was a woman who recognized him before he recognized her: his mother, Elsie. After years of separation, Elsie convinced her restless son to stay over Christmas and miss his next assignment. To focus his attention, she reminded him that he used to like to draw. Responding to her encouragement, "at age 18, I started to draw again." Initially, he took advantage of this skill to earn some money by selling erotic drawings to sailors.[10] But soon, he rediscovered the sheer pleasure of drawing and acknowledged the healing powers of art in later interviews: "My art restored my sanity after those devastating years."[11]

›› *Copenhagen self portrait,* 1948, egg tempera on prepared paper, 17.75" x 23.5"
PRIVATE COLLECTION
PHOTO BY JANET DWYER

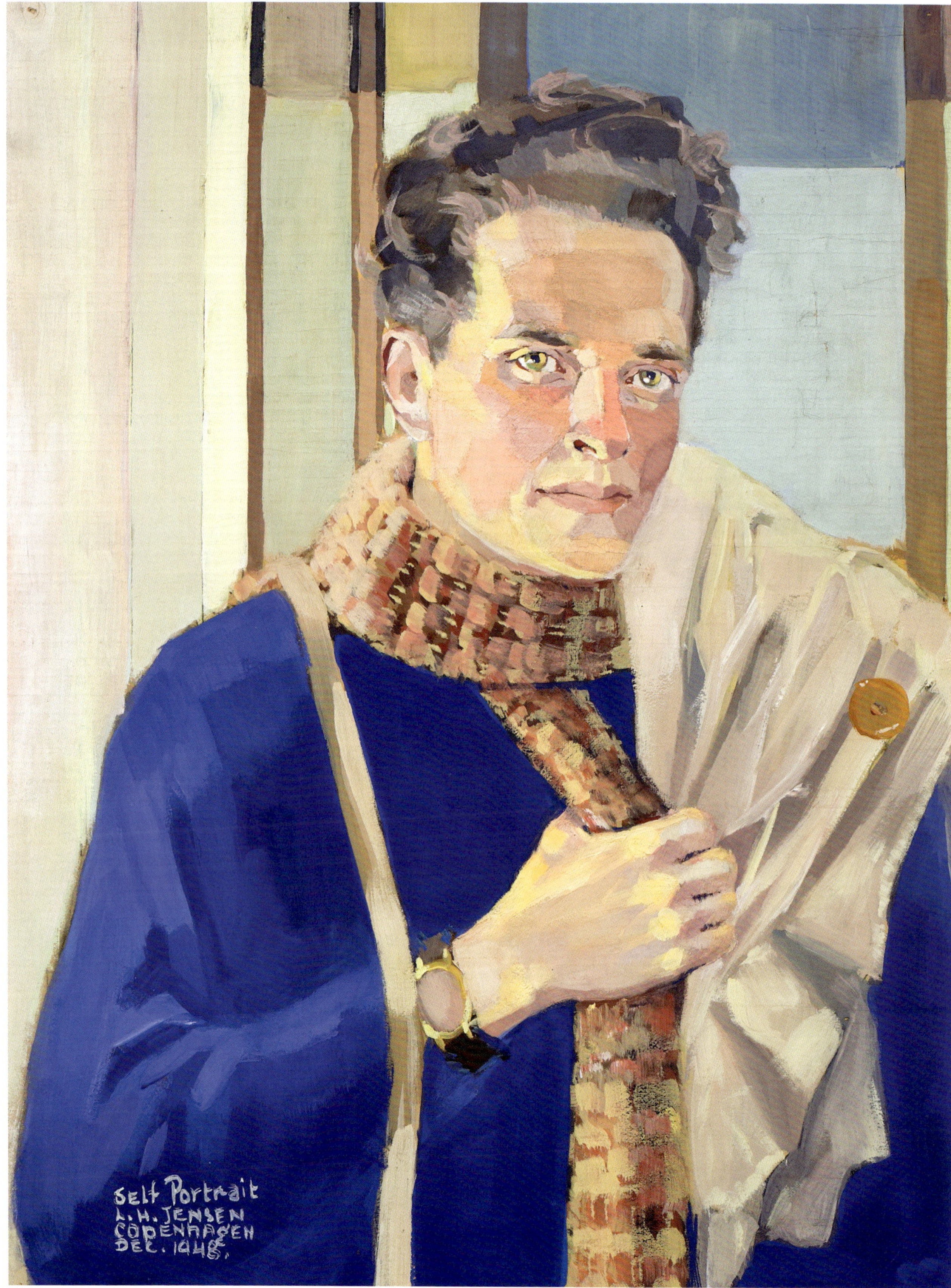
Self Portrait
L. H. JENSEN
COPENHAGEN
DEC. 1948.

Art Student in Denmark and France

I am not a self-made man, and I would like to acknowledge my great debt—to Elsie Jensen, Axel Joergennsen, André Lhote, Edouard Pignon, Herbert Siebner and quite a few others. —LEROY JENSEN.[12]

Encouraged by his mother's support, LeRoy continued to pursue his art, preferring it to his life as a "young seaman on the rocky road to hell."[13] In 1947, he created his first painting, a portrait of his father, and participated in the 16th Annual B.C. Artists' Exhibition at the Vancouver Art Gallery[14] with his painting *Salt Spring, Early Morning.* Other exhibitors included Joe Plaskett, George Fertig, Fred Amess, Charles Scott, Mildred Valley Thornton and Peter Aspell.

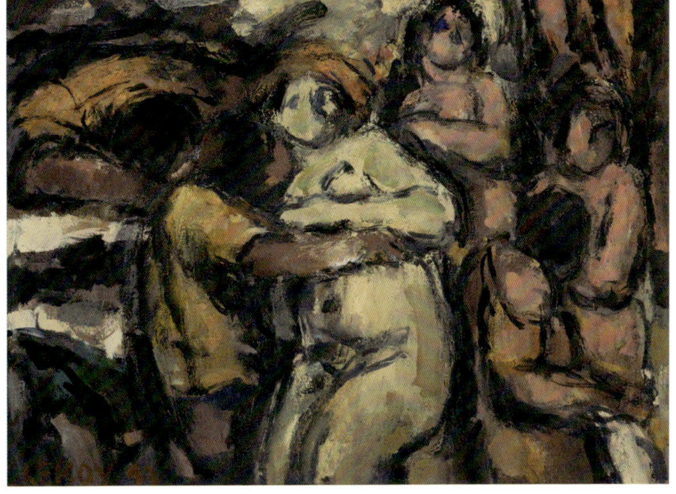

Prodigal Son, 1993, oil on canvas, 18.25" x 24"
PRIVATE COLLECTION
PHOTO BY JANET DWYER

LeRoy attended the Vancouver School of Art (VSA) from 1948 to 1949 but felt that their teachers gave him little direction or foundation in art beyond telling him his work was "good." Restless and hungry to learn, he began searching for a more stimulating environment.

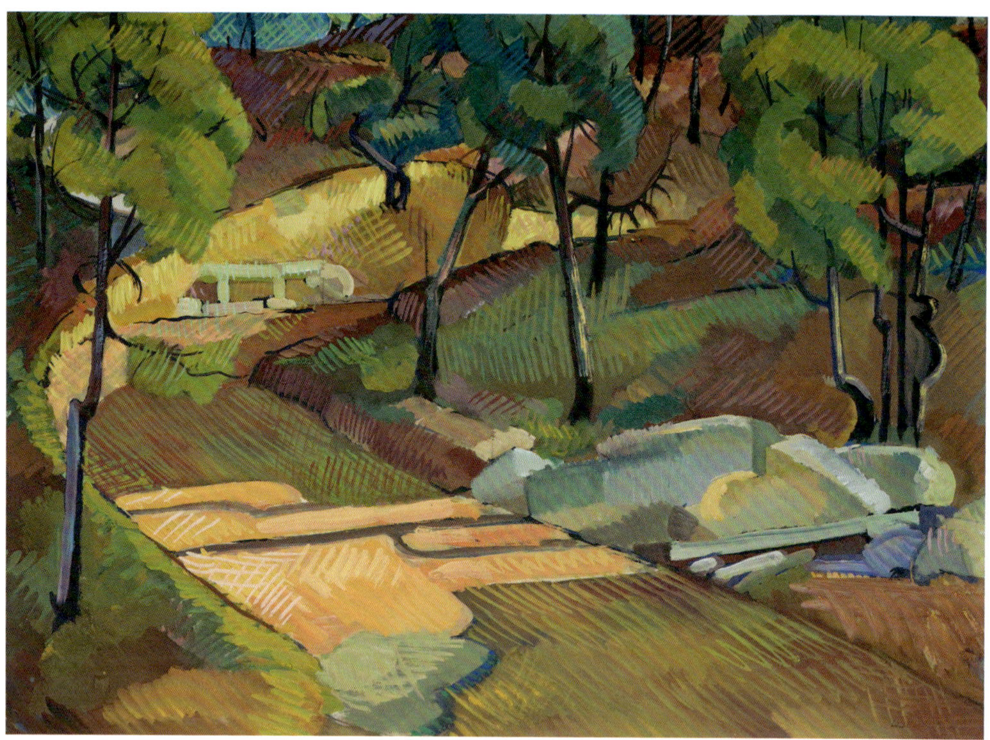

So, France, '50s, gum arabic, 24" x 17.5"
PRIVATE COLLECTION
PHOTO BY JANET DWYER

He was to find it in Denmark. In 1949, LeRoy travelled to his father's homeland with little money and enrolled in the well-respected Royal Danish Academy of Fine Arts in Copenhagen. At first he lived with his Aunt Emmy, his dad's sister, and Uncle Dres at the back of a small shop. Uncle Dres worked as an usher in a theatre, giving LeRoy the opportunity to see many wonderful Danish plays. [15]

Professor Axel Joergennsen, although appalled at the superficiality of LeRoy's Canadian schooling, saw promise in his work and accepted him as a student. LeRoy received a vigorous art education: hours of lectures on art, art history, and drawing—the model, still life, street life, as well as painting and studio work. This was the primer of art education that he used his entire life. Joergennsen taught him to "question everything, to challenge accepted theories, and to scorn trends." [16]

When Joergennsen noticed how thin LeRoy was becoming, he began providing him with school food vouchers, unbeknownst to LeRoy, at his own expense. [17] LeRoy learned a lot from him, especially that there were still kind and caring people in the world. [18]

LeRoy continued to study art in Denmark for two years where he met and married multi-lingual Nonna Bossleman, a drama student who had been born in Shanghai. [19] At 25, he decided it was time to continue his studies in Paris, the hub of artistic

› ~ *France,* '50s, drawing, 15" x 12"
PRIVATE COLLECTION
PHOTO BY JANET DWYER

› LeRoy on a beach at Scheveningan, Holland, 1950, PHOTO COURTESY OF COLIN JENSEN

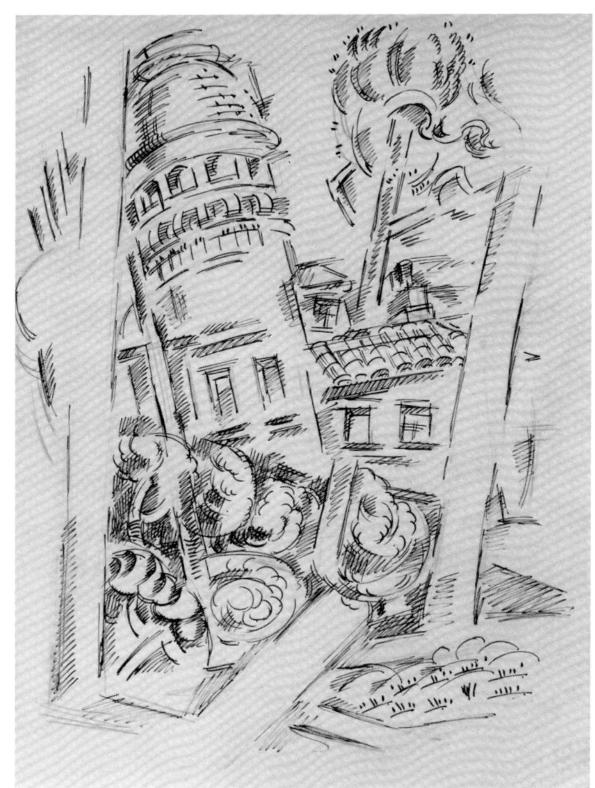

activity in Europe. For two years, the young couple lived in unheated rooms while he studied with André Lhote (1885–1962), the great Cubist painter, as well as Ferdinand Léger. He also worked in the studios of Ossip Zadkine and Jean Metsinger. In spite of their poverty, the energetic recovery in Europe after the destruction of WWII gave vitality to all creative endeavors. LeRoy and his friends would debate art and life in cafes day and night. Everyone endured poverty and hunger, but the intoxicating intellectual stimulation and creative ferment made this experience the focal highlight of his artistic life.

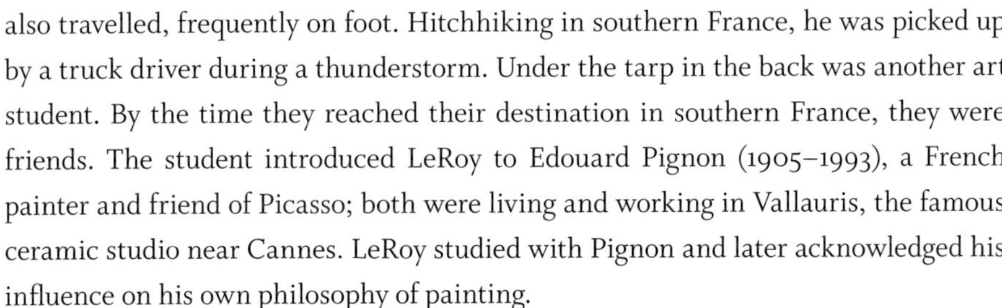

Aside from enjoying the vibrant life in the studios and Paris cafes, LeRoy also travelled, frequently on foot. Hitchhiking in southern France, he was picked up by a truck driver during a thunderstorm. Under the tarp in the back was another art student. By the time they reached their destination in southern France, they were friends. The student introduced LeRoy to Edouard Pignon (1905–1993), a French painter and friend of Picasso; both were living and working in Vallauris, the famous ceramic studio near Cannes. LeRoy studied with Pignon and later acknowledged his influence on his own philosophy of painting.

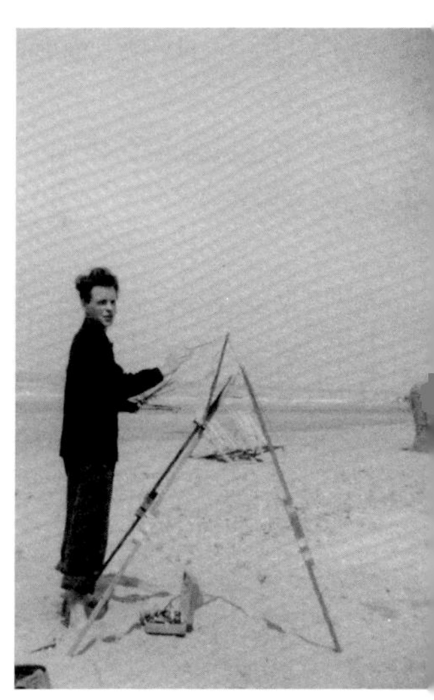

When his parents and his brother Colin came to visit, they toured Europe together. LeRoy and Nonna also visited the French Riviera and the Catalonia Costa Brava region in northeast Spain, where LeRoy found himself deeply moved by the character of the Catalonian people. Years later he did a series of paintings honouring their struggle for freedom.

However, LeRoy still thought of Vancouver as home, so he and Nonna decided it was time to return. Once they had arrived and settled in Vancouver, LeRoy said, "After living in France, it was like coming back to a desert. I almost went back to France. It was so terrible here. I thought, better to starve in France."[20]

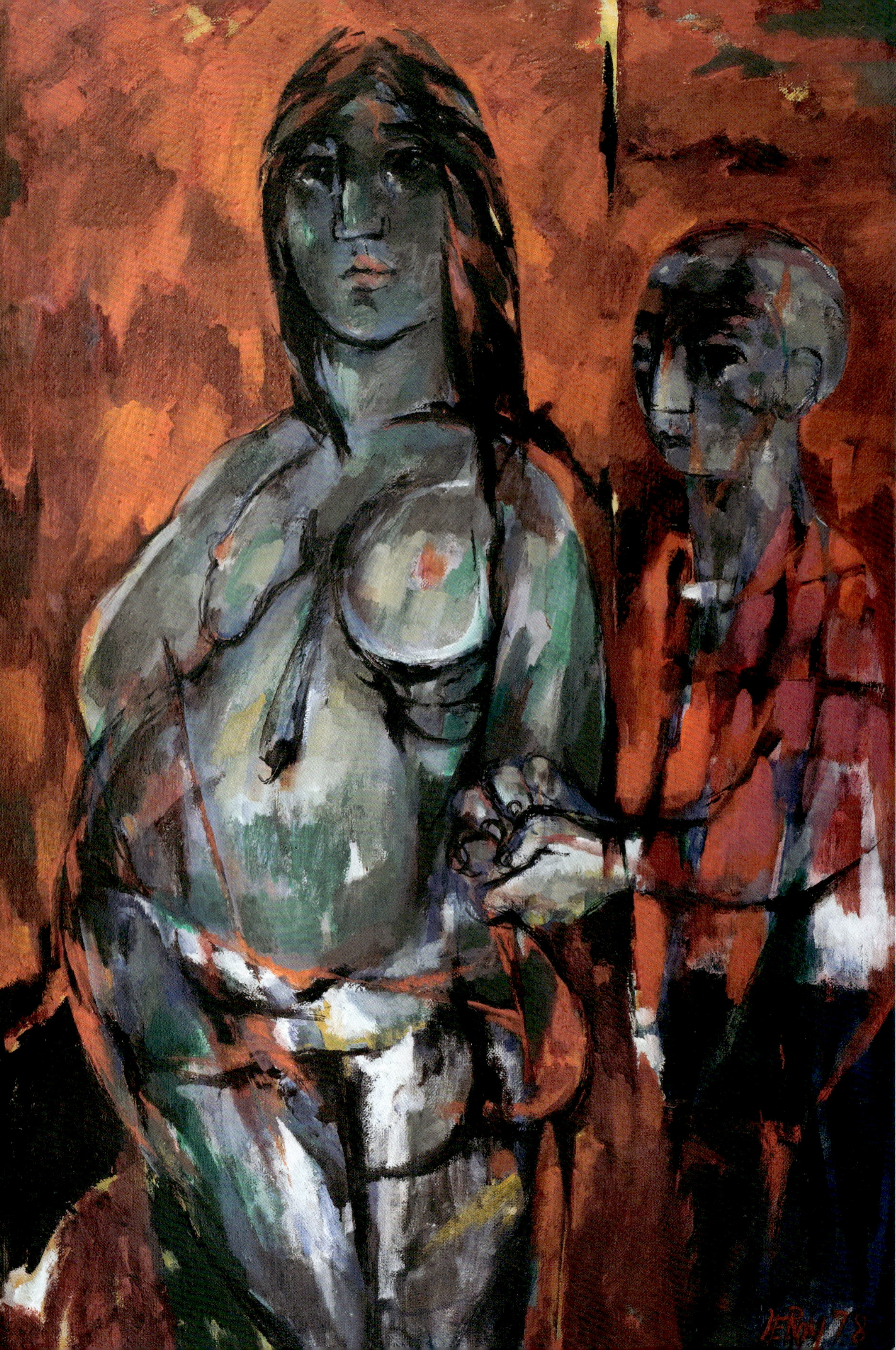

The Price of Success and the Paradigm of Originality

Taste is the stillborn sister of expression. —LEROY JENSEN[21]

Expanding and lush as Vancouver's landscape was, intellectually it appeared desolate to 26-year-old LeRoy when he and his wife returned in 1953, with Nonna becoming a Canadian citizen in 1955. He met the local artists, but "nobody talked about art or anything interesting until I met Jock [Hearn], Dave [Marshall] and George [Fertig]."

<< *The Price,* 1978, oil on canvas on board, 48" x 72"
PRIVATE COLLECTION
PHOTO BY JANET DWYER

> I remember George and I walking and talking all night long in the rain. Suddenly he said, 'An artist needs to deal in honesty like a butcher deals with meat.' These words remained with me all my life. George always expressed that truth in his work.[22]

The small but active local art scene, consisting of over 600 artists in 1949,[23] was dominated by a small clique of male artists and art educators. Over the next few decades they protected and promoted their positions while embracing the latest tastes and trends of New York: Clement Greenberg and abstract expressionism.

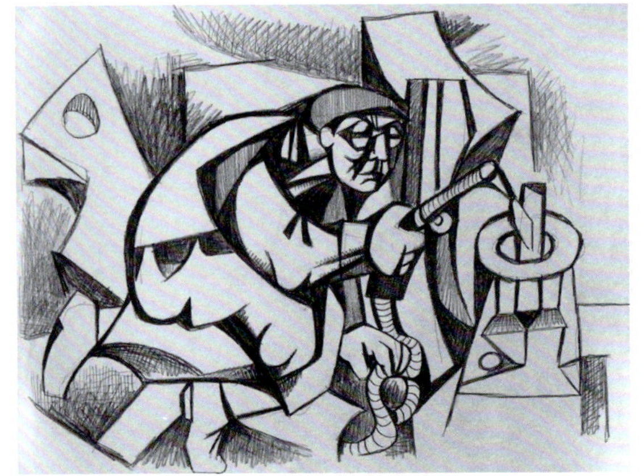

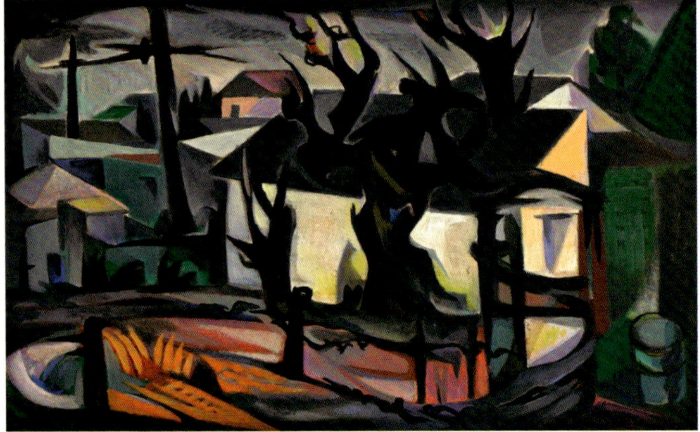

The Sculptor, '50s, pencil on paper, 15" x 12"
PRIVATE COLLECTION
PHOTO BY JANET DWYER

→ *Untitled* 1955, oil on canvas, 36" x 22"
PRIVATE COLLECTION
PHOTO BY JANET DWYER

LeRoy found kinship with the outsider Vancouver artists. Together with Jock Hearn and David Marshall, LeRoy formed the Pendulum Group, spending many hours discussing and gauging the depths of art. In a defiant response to the posturing of others, they used unique pendulum symbols to identify their work: "The Egyptians had the right idea—lots of work, no signatures."[24]

The outsider artists struggled to survive on menial jobs. Hearn worked as a longshoreman and moved furniture for the Vancouver School Board, Marshall did odd jobs, and Fertig worked at a sawmill. LeRoy mowed grass and painted houses. "I survived my first one-man show; the people who came didn't look at the art—they looked at each other and headed for the bar, which I paid for by mowing lawns."[25]

Despite his impressive European resumé, LeRoy met with little success in obtaining an exhibition. His request to participate in a quarterly exhibit at the VAG was rejected in 1955, the same year George Fertig and David Marshall were also declined.

In contrast, the established art bloc were building designer homes, teaching art, entertaining, exhibiting and selling their work to the VAG acquisitions committee.

Scott Watson, contributor in *Vancouver Art & Artists: 1931–1983*, noted the extensive influence of the New York school of abstract expressionism on the prominent Vancouver painters. The New York painters had an urban edginess born from the stresses of big city life. Though Vancouver artists desired to be more cosmopolitan, they retained "the leisure of the suburbs... [the] world of gracious suburban living, job security and contact with nature,"[26] which was reflected in their painterly abstractions. A retrospective view of these artists' work over the years is an interesting microcosm of all the major trends in modern art, but gives little sense of their distinctive vision.

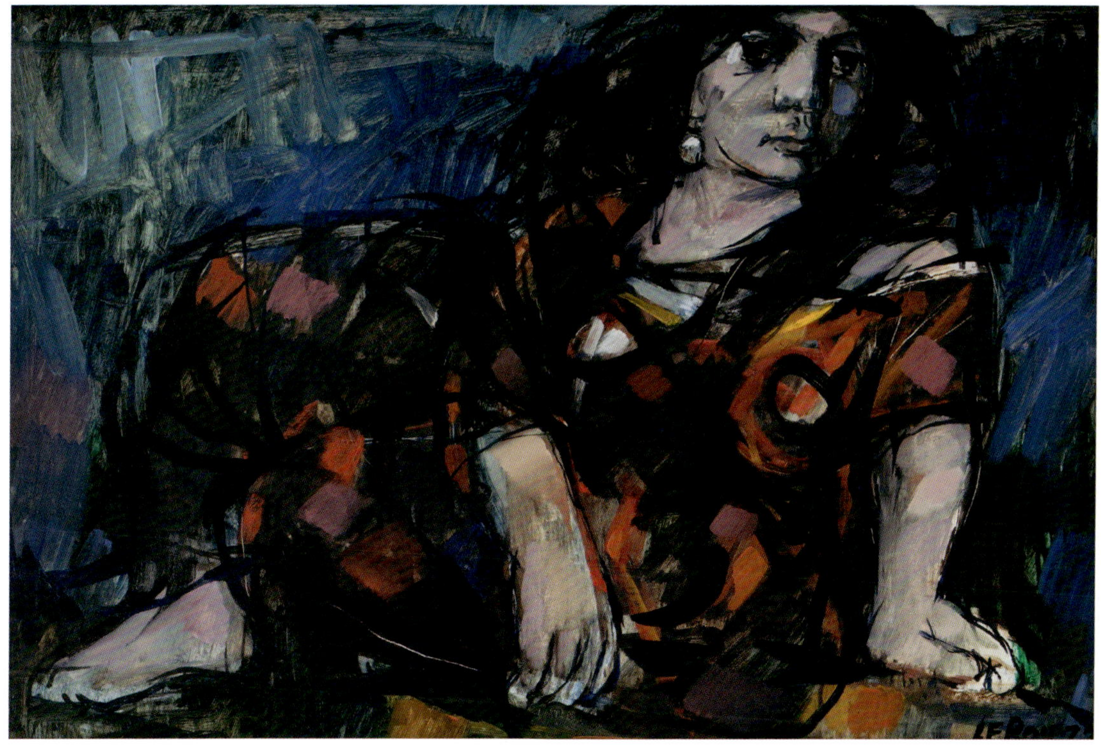

Untitled, 1972, oil on board, 72" x 24"
PRIVATE COLLECTION
PHOTO BY JANET DWYER'

In a rare exhibition opportunity, LeRoy participated in a 1956 exhibition organized by the B.C. Region of the Federation of Canadian Painters at the New Design Gallery, an early private gallery in West Vancouver, started by Alvin Balkind and Abraham Rogatnick that was renowned for its influence on Vancouver art and artists in the '50s and '60s. The show of ten B.C. painters, attempting to call greater attention to the work of those under 30, included Bill Mayrs, Ron Kelly, Herb Gilbert and Heather Spears. Palette, the *Vancouver Sun* art reviewer, stated that "LeRoy Jensen attacks his themes with energy and great freedom."[27]

In time, the Pendulum Group scattered. Jock Hearn gave up art and became a clinical psychologist. David Marshall continued sculpting and began teaching, first art in an elementary school and then sculpture at Capilano College. LeRoy studied ontology, defined by the philosopher, Alexander Baumgarten (1714–1762), as a universal doctrine that analyzes the essence of being and aesthetics.[28] For a short time, LeRoy questioned his involvement in painting and gave lectures about ontology. The French painter Georges Rouault (1871–1958), who greatly influenced LeRoy, also struggled with the ideas of philosophers like Leon Bloy and Baumgarten.

In the early '60s LeRoy lived for a short time in Powell River then for almost four years in Argenta in the central Kootenays, as well as Kelowna. He was very productive and shared several two-man exhibitions with Vancouver sculptor Egon Milinkovich, gave painting demonstrations, lectured on the "Joy of Art" and taught at the Okanagan Landing School of Art.[29]

In 1965, LeRoy separated from his wife, who continued to live with their two sons, Anthony (b. 1962) and Kim (b. 1965), at 100 Mile House, B.C.[30] He moved to Brooklyn, New York, in 1967 to give a six-month lecture series on ontology. There he met Lynda Woolley, whom he married in December 1968.

LeRoy returned to Vancouver with a renewed commitment to painting. He had found that ontology, while fine in principle, seemed to "rattle around in the head." He needed hands and heart to manifest any truth from its substance. Like Rouault, LeRoy could not thrive within a fabricated aesthetic.[31]

In addition to oil painting and etchings, LeRoy started doing frescos, stained glass, floor mosaics and works that were commissioned. He exhibited at the Gallery of B.C. Arts, located across from Stanley Park. The gallery exhibited paintings and sculpture by many of the outsider artists and was also selling pottery, jewellery and native carvings.

invitation: LeRoy Jensen & Frank Poll exhibition, 1969, COURTESY OF THE VANCOUVER ART GALLERY LIBRARY

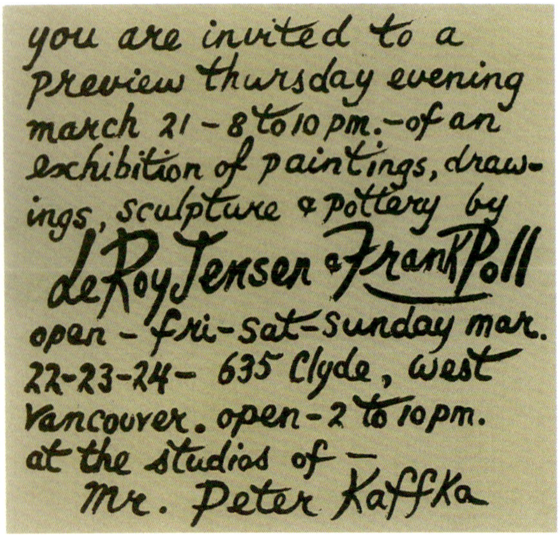

you are invited to a preview thursday evening march 21 - 8 to 10 pm. - of an exhibition of paintings, drawings, sculpture & pottery by LeRoy Jensen & Frank Poll open - fri-sat-sunday mar. 22-23-24 - 635 Clyde, west Vancouver. open - 2 to 10 pm. at the studios of - mr. Peter Kaffka

The Pendulum Group and other independent artists viewed art as an intriguing method of self-discovery and response to the world around them. Honesty was essential about whether a work actually conveyed something legitimately felt or perceived. If it didn't achieve that goal, then it did not function as art, only as decoration. Candor with each other about the work was the currency of exchange. They learned through an open dialogue of ideas and by engaging in serious study of artists who had gone before.

All artists are influenced by their peers and their predecessors. Incorporating an influence into one's work resembles an interior conversation that begins with a resonance. Artists integrate their own insight and perspective into their body of work through a consistent, intuitive and/or logical evolution from previous creations. LeRoy declared, "It takes a long, long time for things to in any way become your property."[32]

A revolutionary reaction to what has gone before begins

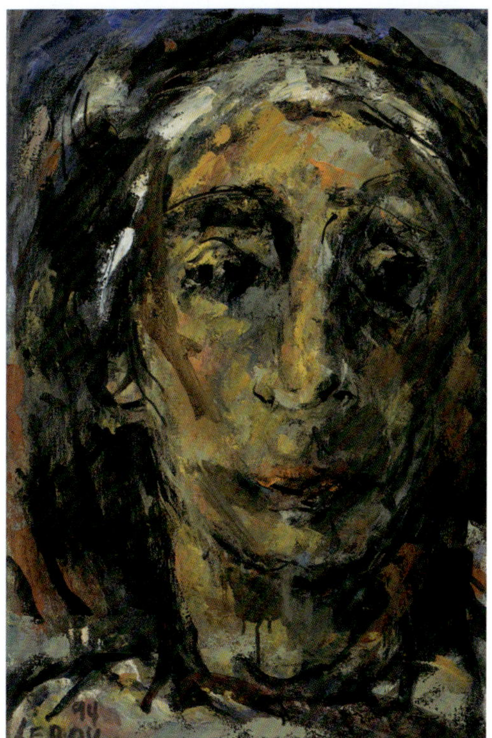

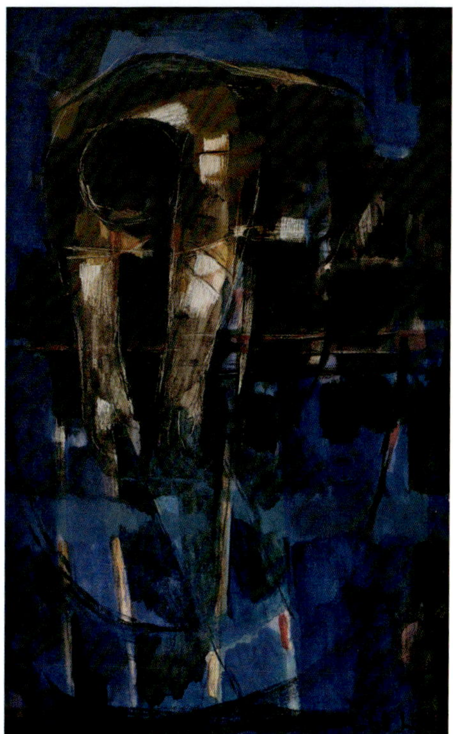

The Deep Net, 1968, oil on canvas, 33.25" x 22"
PRIVATE COLLECTION
PHOTO BY JANET DWYER

⌐(*Wife of Gladiator,* 1994, oil on canvas, 29" x 24"
PRIVATE COLLECTION
PHOTO BY JANET DWYER

with dissonance—a radical departure from the past that opens a new perspective. It emerges from the soil of craft and seeks a new solution with the artist's imprint. Individual pockets of unique artistic searches are often unsupported or marginalized by the established art communities. They flourish only through the dedicated vigor of their authentic quest for artistic expression. The true cultural expression of our time is often a solitary voice, which refuses to be drowned out by the cacophony of the Zeitgeist. For example, the Pendulum Group had agreed it was pretentious to imitate the trends in America and then consider oneself "revolutionary." In contrast, these artists' works reflected their understanding of their craft and inner vision—development that takes a lifetime to complete and requires intense focus.

This was the case with LeRoy: he tended to work alone, evading and deflecting attention. He said, "I have been very fortunate. The closed doors have generally kept me going in a fairly fortuitous direction, a sort of burrow. Perhaps I'm more like a mole, good at burrowing."[33] He transfigured the earthy materials of drawing and painting into a vibrant, living presence. "My only wish is for my work to be seen for what it is, not framed in the clouds of publicity. Only one thing interests me, some humane expression. I believe in the individual, in his or her actual value. I believe in Revolt—primarily in relation to myself. In this I have some childish success"[34]

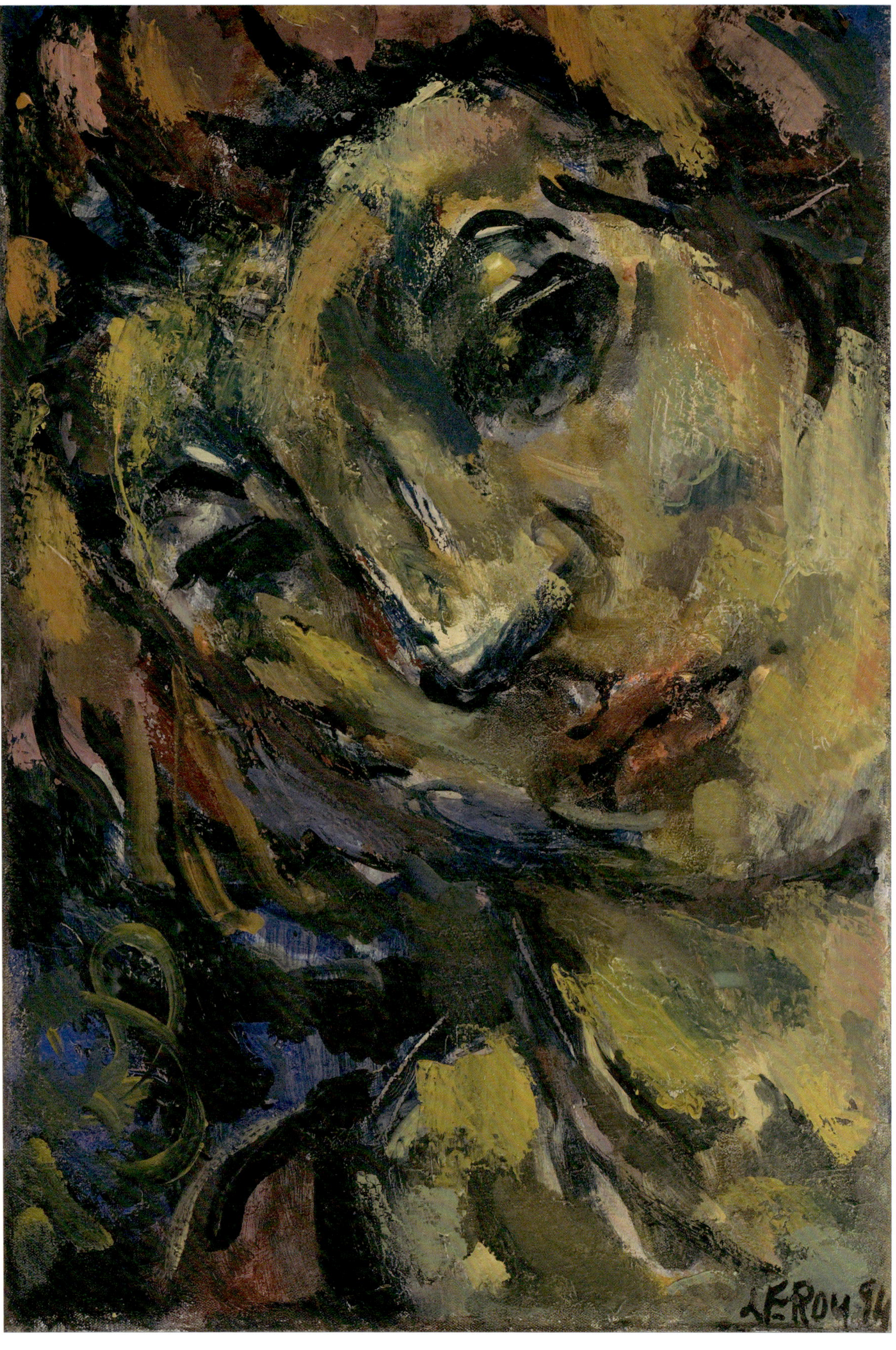

The Teacher and His Students: A Personal Reminiscence

I don't even like the word, "artist." If people ask me what I do, I say, I do "painting work." I think it is presumptuous to assume all the time that one is an artist ... pretending to be something rather exceptional. There is nothing exceptional about it. It is a "simple trade." —LEROY JENSEN[35]

In a filmed interview in 1990, LeRoy denounced the focus of instruction at many art institutions, asserting that art could be taught in two hours per week, thus giving the students and teachers much more studio time. To justify the large tuitions and teacher salaries, contemporary art schools demand many ancillary activities for students and teachers, instead of focusing on crucial solitary work, thus developing dependence on the institution rather than self-reliance.[36] In some art school classes, students are taught that "negotiating interviews, conversations with critics, press releases, catalogues, and wall texts are part of the responsibility of the artist,"[37] all incorporated at the cost of learning the essential language of art.

‹ *Beth,* 1994, oil on canvas, 25" x 17"
PRIVATE COLLECTION
PHOTO BY JANET DWYER

Yet, artist/teachers need to pass on to the next generation the skills and knowledge gained over many years. During the late 1950s LeRoy accepted and then resigned from several teaching posts at UBC and the Banff School of Fine Arts. He found their teaching methods mostly ineffective. "LeRoy's European art education established a philosophy that he never strayed from—that art is an internal journeying, communication and learning from others: that teaching is a sacred trust. When it becomes about ego, its true purpose is lost."[38]

In the fall of 1970, LeRoy offered a class on drawing and painting through the Vancouver Free University at the Vancouver East Cultural Centre, now known as "The Cultch."[39] His wife Lynda said that it was "teaching art the way LeRoy saw fit. He was able to share and pass on not only his skill, but his philosophy as well."[40] LeRoy maintained that, "Art is difficult to teach because it requires an entire change in the person's life."[41] He was an inspiring and sometimes controversial teacher whose students came from all over the world. John Lundgren had evaded the American military draft. Don Wunderlee and Roy Patterson had recently left Cambridge, Massachusetts where anti-war demonstrations in Harvard Square were raging. Xavier had emigrated from Spain. Robert Perrault, Suzanne Savaria and Eddy Raumond arrived from Quebec, having fled the tumult surrounding separatist ambitions and the resulting assassination of Pierre LaPorte.[42] They were all disillusioned and looking for answers; maybe art would hold the key.

› *Genevieve,* n.d. oil on canvas, 24" x 16"
PRIVATE COLLECTION
PHOTO BY DAVID BORROWMAN

›~ *Suzanne,* '70s. oil on canvas, 36" x 48"
PRIVATE COLLECTION
PHOTO BY JANET DWYER

That first evening class at the Free University was a life-transforming experience for Roy, Don and others who had nothing to lose and everything to gain. Some were highly offended by LeRoy's teaching methods and never returned, but a core group attended every week. Roy wrote to me, "We have found the Master Painter you were looking for! Come!" I drove up from Virginia and joined the group. Roy, Don and I lived together in Vancouver. Don first inspired my creativity. He was impressed with LeRoy, but after a few months moved on to start a street theatre in Vancouver. Roy and I continued studying with LeRoy for almost six years, later we married, had children and named our son in honour of him. Our life-long friendship with Lynda and LeRoy parallels our deep and lasting commitment to art.

› *Untitled,* 1988, oil on canvas, 60" x 48"
PRIVATE COLLECTION
PHOTO BY JANET DWYER

LeRoy introduced us to a new visual language and put power and the responsibility to learn into our own hands. He taught that drawing from life provided direct connections between the perceived world, the interior world and one's skills—links that are only accessible through focused work. In order to build upon this new language and develop our originality within it, we hired models; one of the first, Beth Marshall, later joined the group as a student. LeRoy kindled in us a desire to educate ourselves about the art of the past, creating a sense of camaraderie with the ancient fraternity of artists, the "timeless companions."

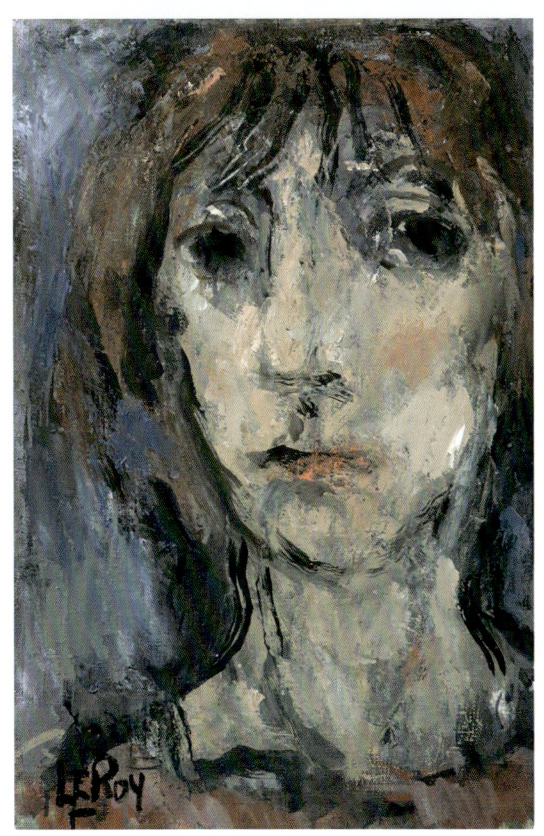
LERoy

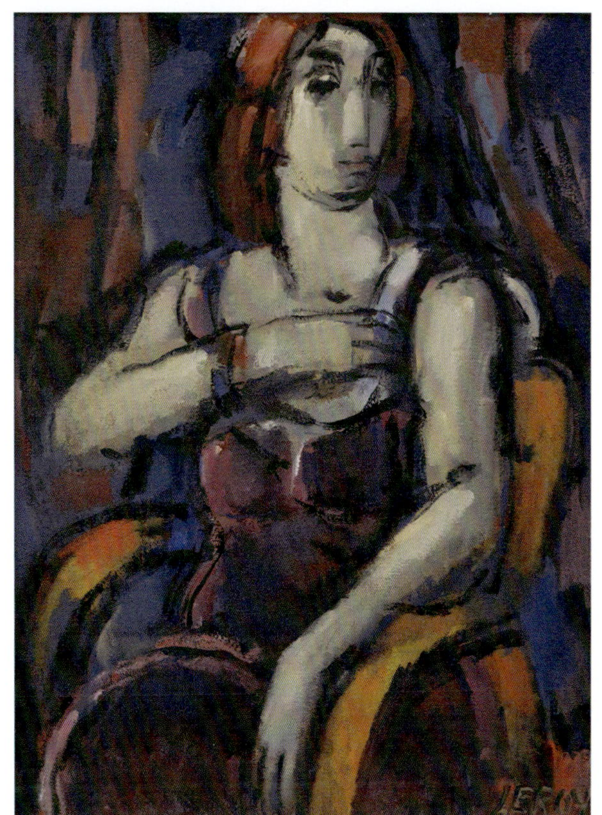
LEROY

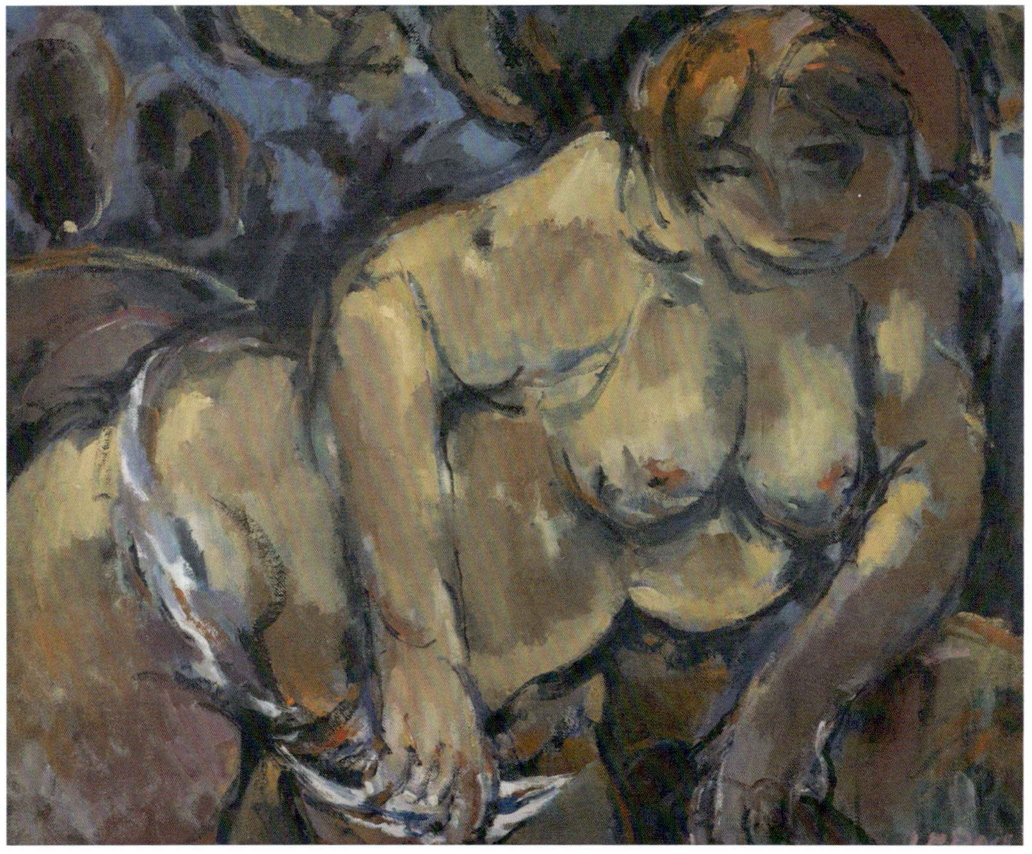

Though our earnest efforts had a certain gravity, LeRoy's classes had a light-hearted quality. "At the core of Jensen's humour lies his most unassailable philosophy—that painting is, and should forever be, a learning experience."[43] He showed us how to be resilient about critique. We laughed often, undefeated by failures, and moved forward, ever stronger. Suzanne Savaria, one of the Quebec students, said, "Slowly, the drawing started to get form, movement, [and strong contrasts]. Even if I didn't understand the language, there was something else passing thru, the essential... LeRoy showed me to see what is the most important."[44] In time, we developed a vocabulary of visual tools, the beginnings of a visual language to express the world around and within us. He had given us a "simple trade."[45]

LeRoy also gave us a "beginner's mind"[46] as an antidote to self-delusion and self-satisfaction. Comparing our work to the masters helped keep our perspective. He also cautioned students against the perils of early success: the expectation to produce work that satisfies patrons instead of the muse.

In the summer of 1971, Suzanne, Robert, Eddy and Xavier tried to camp on Tent Island, near Salt Spring Island, to have access to LeRoy's instructive influence. Sadly, their plans were stymied by several catastrophes, and they returned to Quebec.[47]

Roy and I lived in the machine shed of an old lumber camp on a friend's remote property at Killam Bay on the Sunshine Coast. The rain and isolation helped us focus productively on figure drawing. By the end of the summer, we reconnected with LeRoy before Immigration required us to return to the U.S. For the next few years, we followed the pattern of working and saving money in the U.S. and returning to Vancouver with student visas to study.

Several of LeRoy's students—Beth Marshall, John Lundgren, Ken O'Halloran, Roy Patterson and I—rented cheap studios in the old Empire Building at Hastings and Seymour Street in Vancouver. Though it was a non-residential office building, we built lofts and disguised the fact that we actually lived there.

Down the street in Gastown, Roy and I frequented the Europe Hotel pub where we would draw the old-age pensioners. We inherited our love of drawing street life from LeRoy, who in his youth would sometimes stay up all night drawing at the White Lunch diner on Hastings Street. Later in his life, he wrote that the "greatest artists all remember the special vitality and thrill of their youth, and it continues with them always."[48] It is our "moveable feast."[49]

LeRoy once related a story on the subject of drawing: when he was in Europe, a friend and fellow art student went to Pablo Picasso for help with his work. He took along some paintings to show the master, but Picasso said, "Leave them at the door—anyone can paint. I want to see if you can draw." [50]

In 1973, after three years of disciplined drawing in black and white, we were ready to work with color. That winter, we hired Ruth McLeod to model for several sessions. LeRoy then taught us how to work with powdered pigments and gum arabic on large studies and to grapple with the dynamics of color from real life.

We purchased the powdered pigments, Indian Red, Yellow Ochre, Ultramarine Blue, Titanium White, Raw Umber and Lamp Black, from an old paint store on south Granville Street near LeRoy's house on French Street. The elderly salesman was excited by our interest in a dying trade. Few housepainters knew how to use powdered pigments and mix their own colors anymore. We got a bargain and a blessing from him.

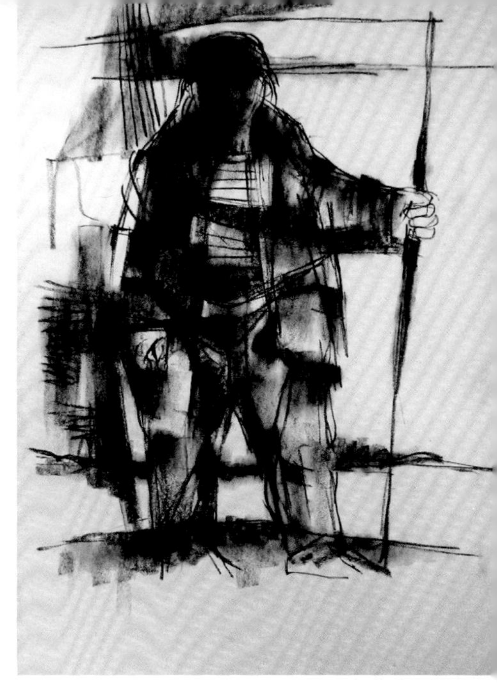

Old Fisherman, 1970s, charcoal on paper, 18" x 24"
PRIVATE COLLECTION

LeRoy showed us how to grind the pigments in linseed oil on glass and store them in small jars or tubes. We learned the particular qualities of different pigments. Ultramarine Blue has the tendency to get very oily; Yellow Ochre tends to be gritty and stiff. Some colors ground quickly, while others took hours to get to the right consistency. A few drops of phenol (a preservative) from the local pharmacy kept the colors from getting moldy or too dry. Years later, I still have some of those pigments. LeRoy continued to grind the non-toxic pigments until the end of his life. Good paint is durable. The basic concept is ancient, simple and close to the source. No technology required.

During that year several of us were hired to work for the New World Jade Company in the carving studio. We worked part-time for $3.25 an hour. Most of the artists they hired were young and learning their craft. When another call went out for artists, we urged LeRoy to submit a piece for consideration. LeRoy offered a model of a simple figure but it was dismissed. We were shocked. How could our experienced artist and teacher be rejected? It was our first encounter with the preference for mediocrity.

All of LeRoy's serious students felt deep respect and gratitude. As Suzanne Savaria said, "After 13 years, I went back to British Columbia… I will always remember that moment I saw him at the ferry; all the years disappeared.… He taught me so much. LeRoy—in French it is pronounced 'Le Roi'—The King." [51]

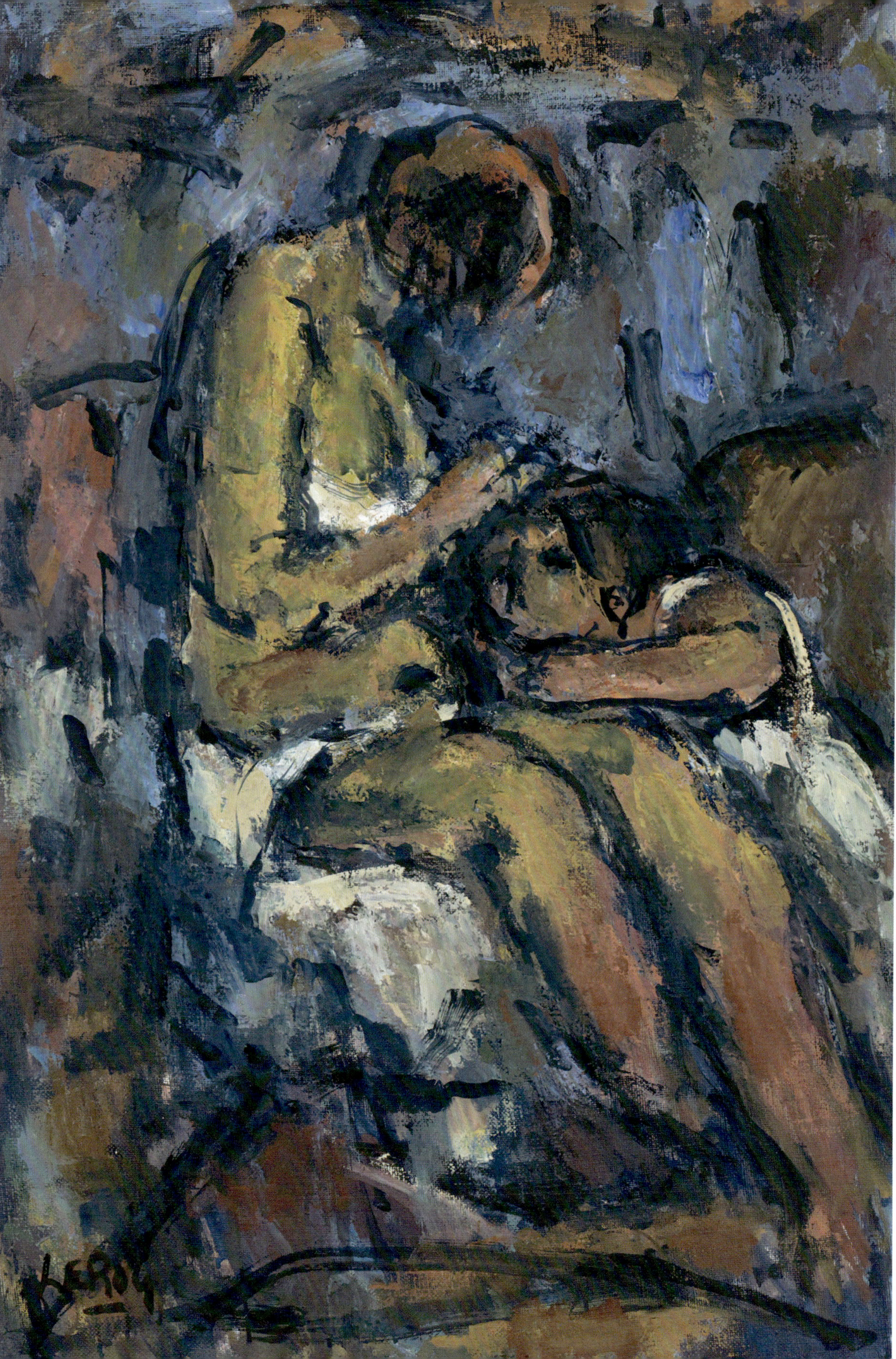

The Work

All that I have to say is in my work, and it is grounded in my constant effort to find suitable language for my expression. For me, painting is movement, luminosity and a discovery of the rhythm that underlies a subject. I must find the proper blend of these forces and set them free; then, the reality appears by itself. —LEROY JENSEN [52]

LeRoy spoke of art as visual language, and like any other language, it can be learned and a vocabulary developed to express oneself. This is the true gift of art. Sandi Johnson, a Salt Spring Island writer, recalls him saying that "everything leading up to the final expression of a [painting] was in the finished work. All the sketches and studies were a necessary part of it." Sandi elaborated, "I think he was saying that the unseen was as important as the seen." [53]

Visual language is a silent communication from the artist to the viewer through the elements of the composition, lines, tones, rhythm and color harmony that an artist develops to suit his sensibility. The viewer may recognize a subject, but senses this silent communication through these visual elements. For instance, LeRoy used the subject of "mother and child" his whole life. But each time, the communication was unique, based on the way he used the elements. One image uses tender visual language, another uses dark and ominous language, all still "mother and child."

‹ *Mother and Child #5*, n.d.
oil on canvas, 26" x 36"
PRIVATE COLLECTION
PHOTO BY JANET DWYER

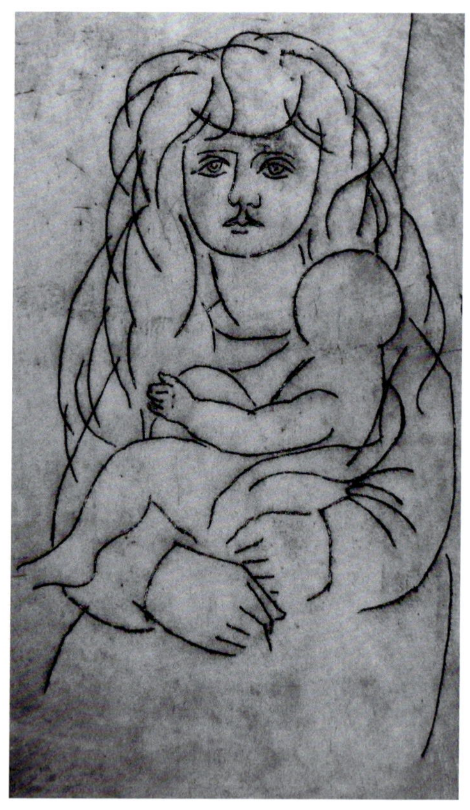

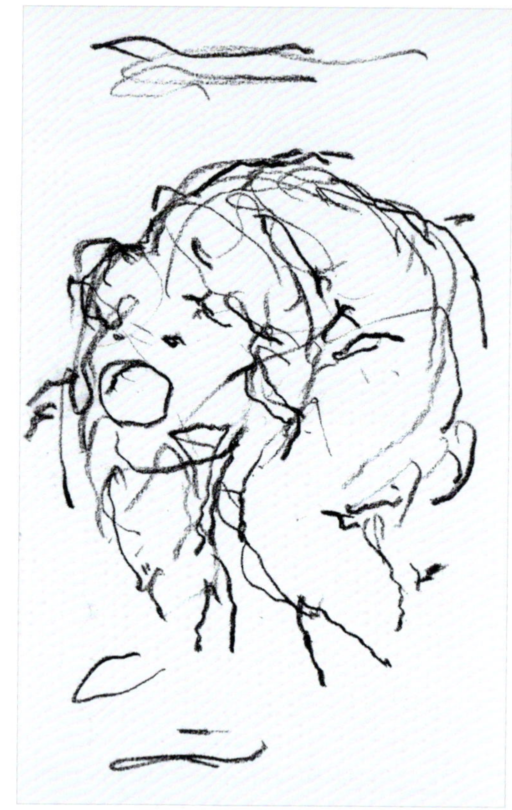

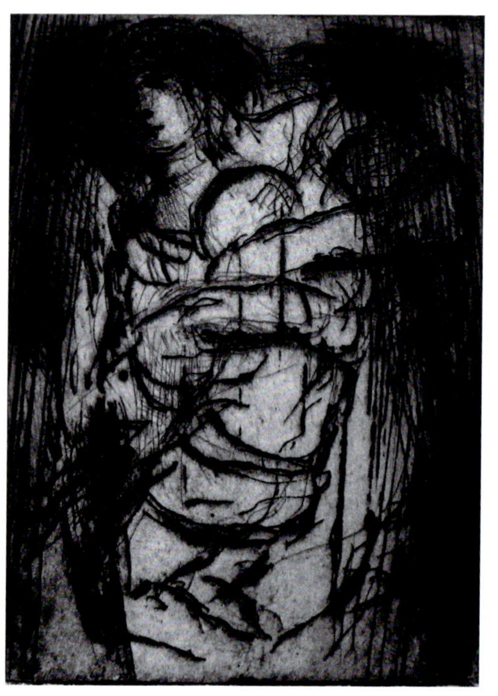

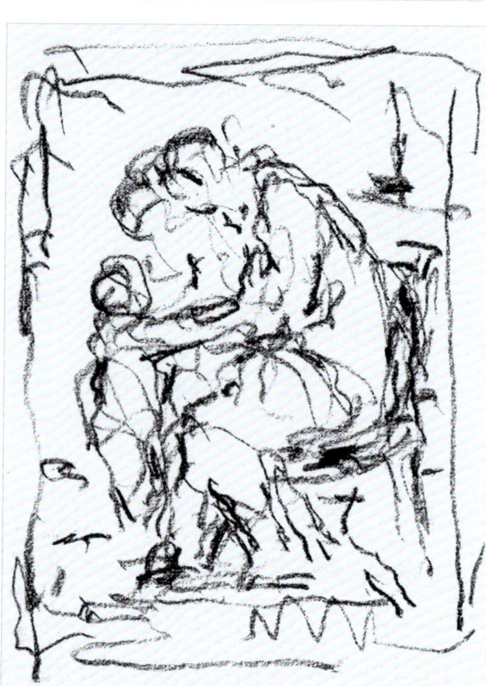

LeRoy said painting (and drawing) was based on Four Forces: *Movement, Luminosity, Rhythm* and *Spirit.*

Movement can be quiet or active. Line is the visual manifestation of movement. These two etchings show different qualities of linear movement.

Mother and Child #1: This etching has a gentle, single line that flows rhythmically around the forms. It is primarily vertical. It is quiet.

Mother and Child #2: This drawing is circular and active, like a whirlwind. There are many lines that vibrate around the forms, expressing a swooping, loving feeling.

Luminosity is an expression of inner light that radiates from the image. Light is created with tones.

Mother and Child #3: This etching has gray tones surrounding the sides and top of the figure of the mother. She is emerging from the tones. The darkest tones are around the head and the shoulders. The lightest are on the child and on the lower part of the mother's face. This arrangement of tones creates a sense of drama.

Rhythm is a pattern; it is repetitive. It is felt and experienced, not copied.

Mother and Child #4: The rhythm of this drawing originates in the curve of the arms from the mother and the child and is repeated in the curve of the chair. The movement is extended and lengthened into the shadow between the mother and the child, creating a rhythm of movement that is like the rocking of a clock's internal mechanism.

LeRoy worked with the above three forces, *movement*, *luminosity* and *rhythm* in painting by what he called "successive attacks." This process required a great insight into craft, each force building on the last, until the fourth force, or *spirit*, was revealed, a source of power that he called the "incandescence of love."[54]

Color is powerful; a little does much work. In this painting, *Mother and Child #5* (overleaf), the coolness of blue focuses the warmth of the mother and child into a rhythmic, moving structure expressing tender attention and love.

LeRoy said, "It is a very absorbing thing to find a means of expressing yourself. You must have enough insight to take what comes from inside and make it understandable to others."[55] He admonished himself and his students to increase the "pressure on our gifts."[56] This requires courage to risk the small gains and push oneself further. Cezanne was our best model of this behavior:

> He pressed his gifts to the limit and goes beyond everyone. We cannot increase

‹‹ *Mother and Child #1,* 1960s, etching
PRIVATE COLLECTIONS
PHOTO BY WENDY NEWBOLD PATTERSON

‹ *Mother and Child #2,* 2005, drawing, 6" x 4", last sketchbook, PHOTO BY WENDY NEWBOLD PATTERSON

‹‹ *Mother and Child #3,* n.d., etching, 6" x 4"
PRIVATE COLLECTIONS
PHOTO BY WENDY NEWBOLD PATTERSON

‹ *Mother and Child #4,* 2005, 6" x 4", last sketchbook
PHOTO BY WENDY NEWBOLD PATTERSON

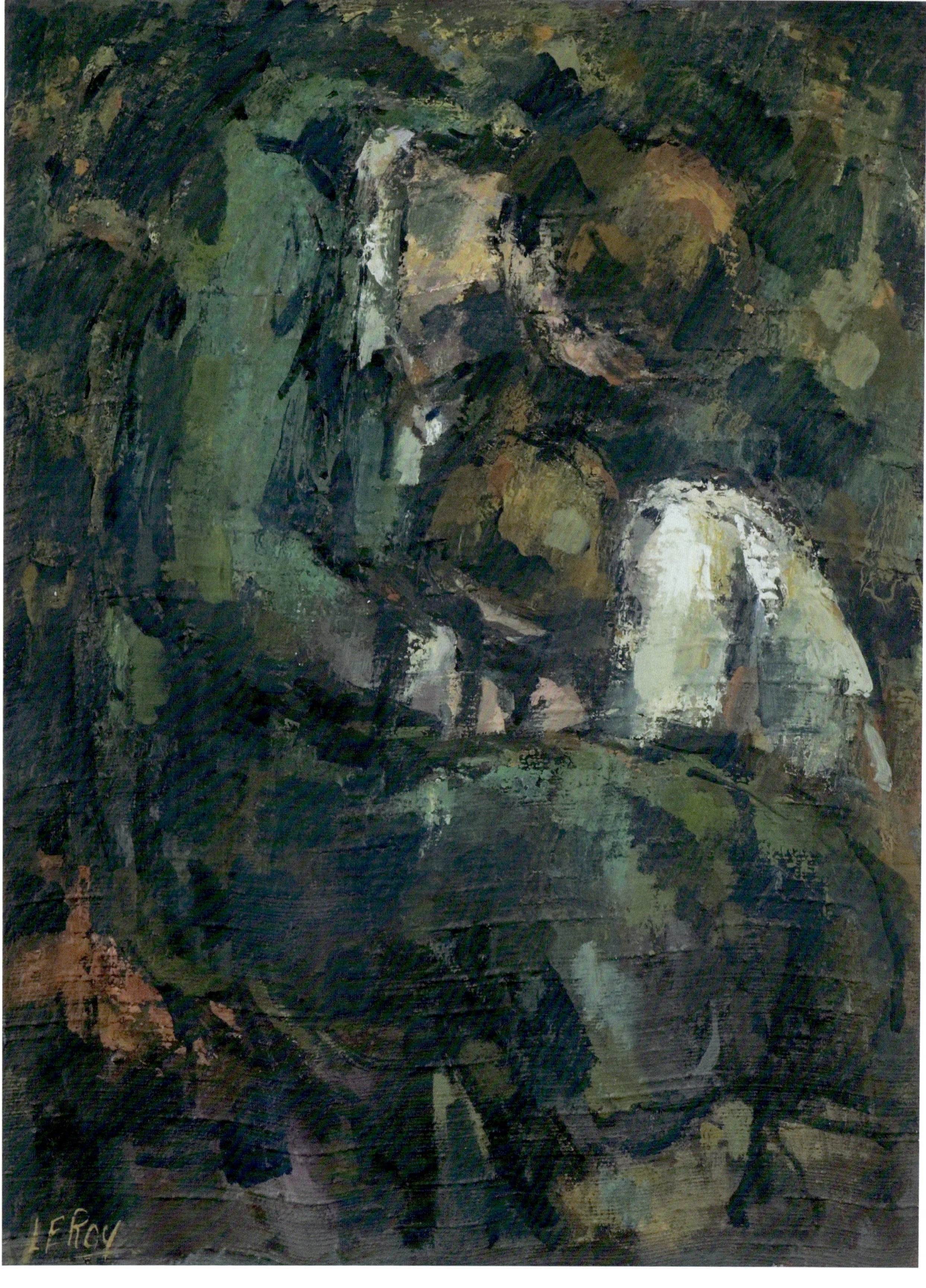
LEROY

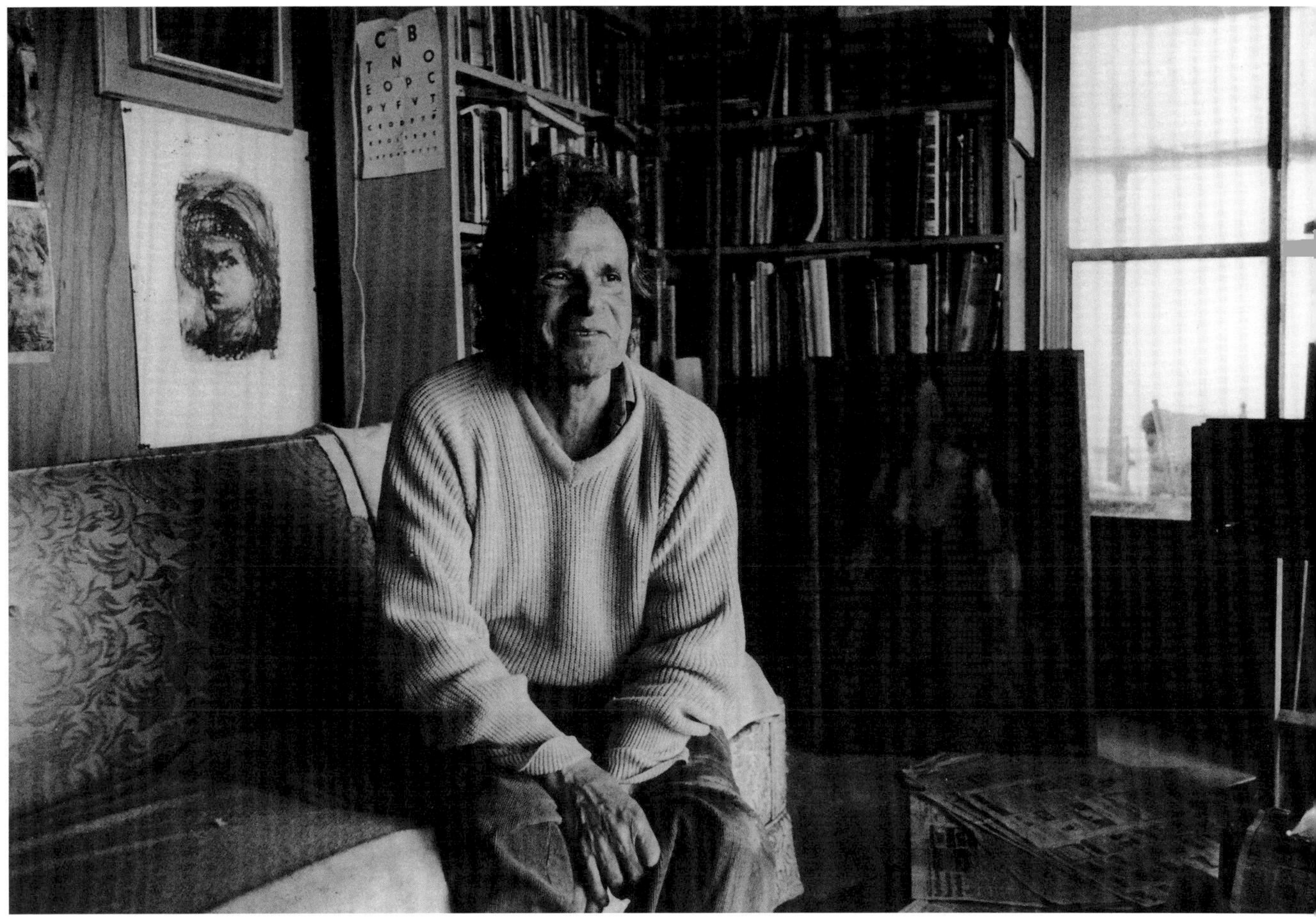

LeRoy in studio, April 16th, 1986, Photo courtesy of *The Driftwood*

> our gifts, but we can increase the pressure on them. Not always pleasant, but in the end, rewarding. In any case, it's all I can do, not being too gifted, but gifted enough. [57]

The long, rich history of art could be likened to an old-growth forest. LeRoy's work is like a strong tree among many trees dwelling in this forest of "timeless companions."

All of LeRoy's visual language was in service to a humane expression. In opposition to those forces of civilization that work toward diminishment of human value, LeRoy dedicated his life's work to strengthen the value of each individual and the beauty of that struggle we bear.

‹‹ *Mother and Child,* 1980s, oil on linen, 29" x 24"
PRIVATE COLLECTION
PHOTO BY JANET DWYER

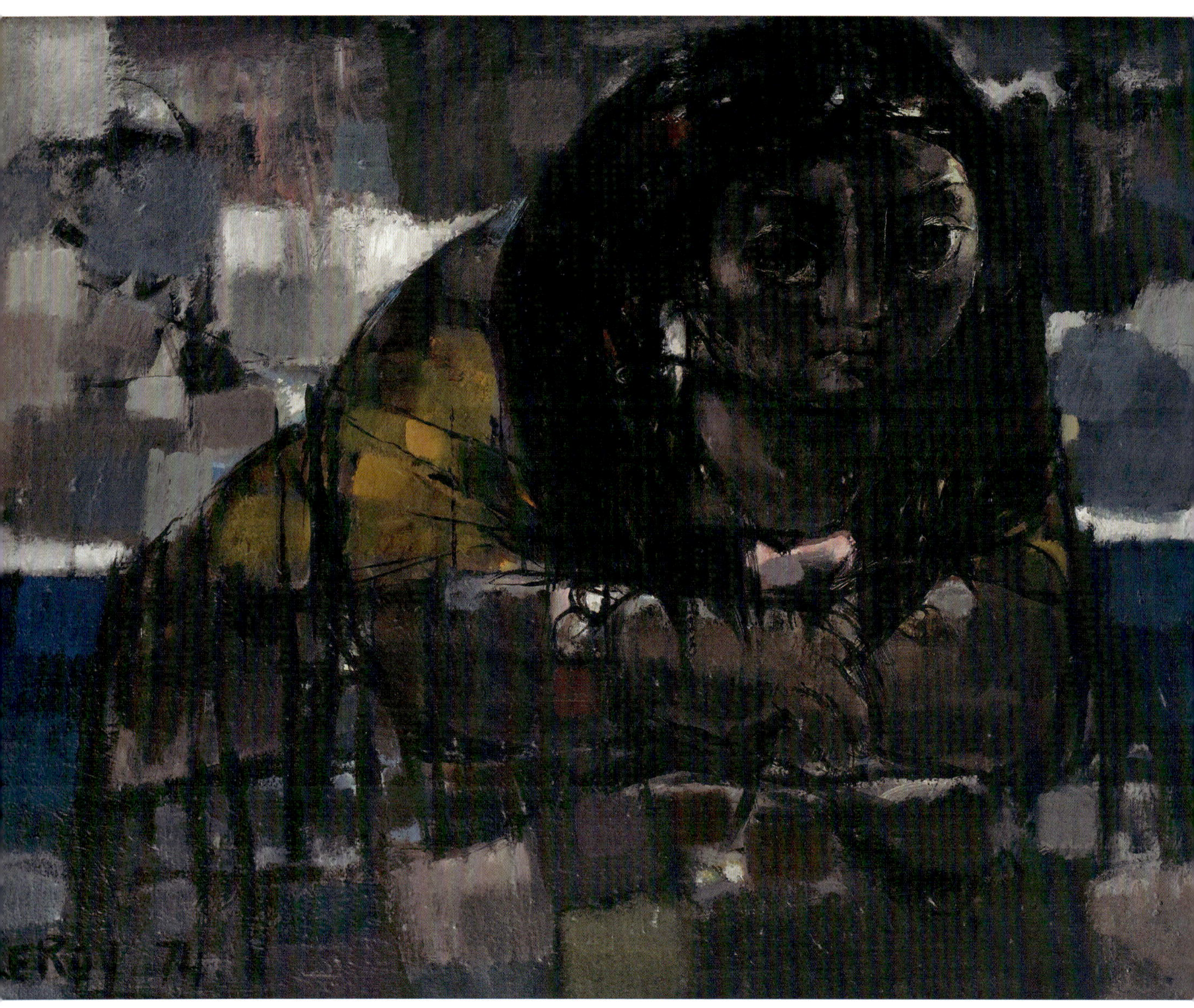

Juggling Art, Family and Activism

Art is the supreme expression of man, no wonder it's not so easy. It's all that's ever left to show what was what in spite of all the wars the murder the horrors the slavery the bestiality the pretend science and the sad sad givingupness of human beings..." —LEROY JENSEN [58]

LeRoy never compartmentalized; family, work and social activism were all interconnected. One looks at his work and sees his family captured with all the love he held for them. He expanded and transformed this love to include all of mankind and never hesitated to get involved in social causes.

LeRoy's young sons, Anthony and Kim, were close companions when Roy and I first met the Jensen family. In December 1970, shortly after we began our studies with him, Lynda gave birth to Gabrielle. Two years later, Amber was born. Now there were four children and two adults living in a small two-bedroom home with a tiny studio on French Street. LeRoy was juggling the roles of father, husband, painter, teacher as well as labourer at the Vancouver Aquarium.

Meanwhile, Lynda, an actress from New York City not yet 30, found herself mothering four young children. They lived on a tight budget so LeRoy could paint as much as possible. Devoted to her family, Lynda did whatever was necessary, even making all their food from scratch—baking bread, granola and cook-

‹ *Woman in the Dunes,* 1974, oil on canvas on board, 35.5" x 47"
PRIVATE COLLECTION,
PHOTO BY JANET DWYER

Lynda & LeRoy, 1990s

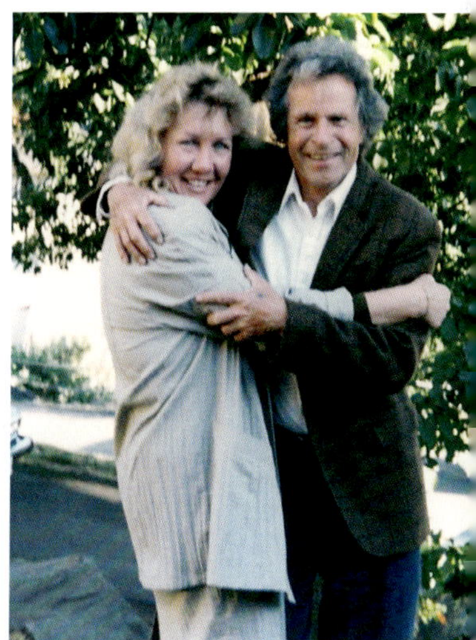

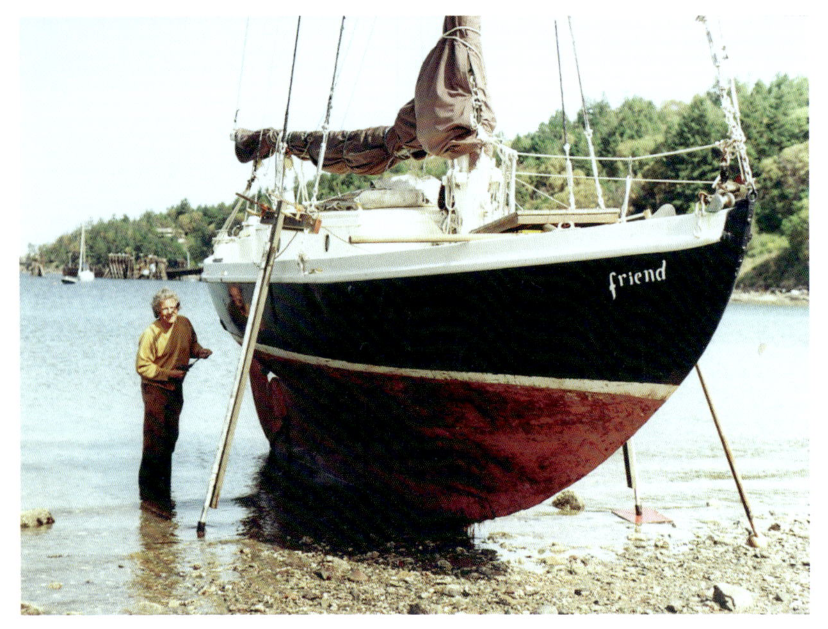

ies and putting up jam. She learned to adapt second-hand clothes and how to make odd cuts of meat delectable. Frequently, LeRoy's hungry art students were guests at the family's table, sharing stories and their meager provisions.

LeRoy had always loved the sea and knew his way around ships, so he decided to build a 26-foot wooden sloop, *Friend*. This ushered in a happy period for the family, as they began to spend their summers sailing around the Strait of Georgia. During two of these summers, LeRoy's art students met them on the Gulf Islands for forays into landscape drawing, with quill pens made from seagull feathers. *Friend* had become an ideal partner in bringing up a family, and on occasion, acted as a floating art school.

Kim, their youngest son, said his favorite memories revolve around summers on *Friend*. It was many years before he could bring himself to buy or eat fish from

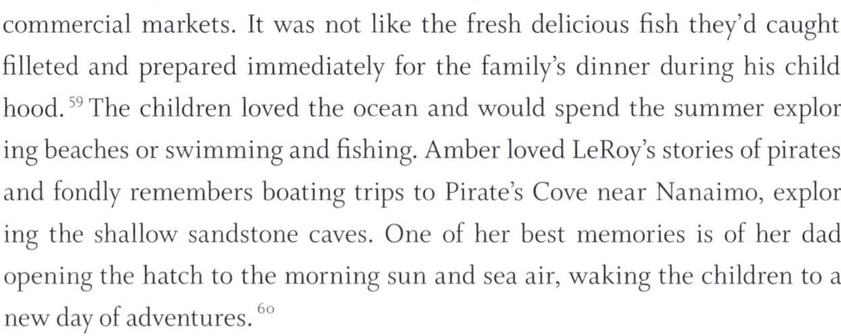

commercial markets. It was not like the fresh delicious fish they'd caught, filleted and prepared immediately for the family's dinner during his childhood.[59] The children loved the ocean and would spend the summer exploring beaches or swimming and fishing. Amber loved LeRoy's stories of pirates and fondly remembers boating trips to Pirate's Cove near Nanaimo, exploring the shallow sandstone caves. One of her best memories is of her dad opening the hatch to the morning sun and sea air, waking the children to a new day of adventures.[60]

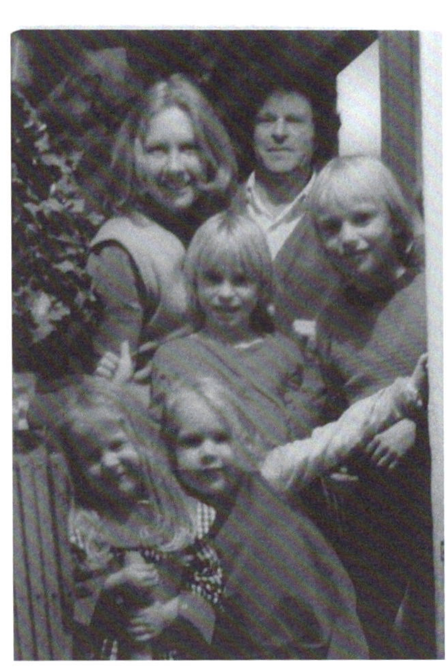

In 1971 LeRoy's powerful sense of social justice found a new outlet with Greenpeace, which was founded in Vancouver for the protection and conservation of the environment. In the fall of that year, he participated in the second Greenpeace expedition, on the *Edgewater Fortune*, to protest and confront U.S. Navy ships doing underwater nuclear testing near Amchitka Island, Alaska. He also participated in another Greenpeace expedition launched to protest and interfere with the whaling ships. His art students were in awe that LeRoy would risk his life, work and his family's security to join these dangerous, often violent confrontations on the high seas. Later he became a supporter of the Green Party.

In 2009 the captain of the *Edgewater Fortune* visited Saturna Island where Amber's young family owns a bed and breakfast. LeRoy's grandson, Izaak toured the boat with the captain, who told him of an experience with LeRoy standing on the ship's bridge and admiring the beauty of sea and sky. LeRoy later painted the image and gave the painting to the captain.[61]

‹ LeRoy and *Friend* in Vesuvius Bay, Salt Spring Island, n.d.
PHOTO BY LYNDA JENSEN

In the late 1970s, LeRoy and his two sons participated in a candlelight vigil in Vancouver's Gastown in support of a native man who had been beaten and kicked by the RCMP. Though very young then, Anthony remembered "feeling compassion and sympathy for someone who was completely unknown to me that was treated unfairly and killed unnecessarily."[62] It was also his first realization that the keepers of order might have 'bloody hands.'[63]

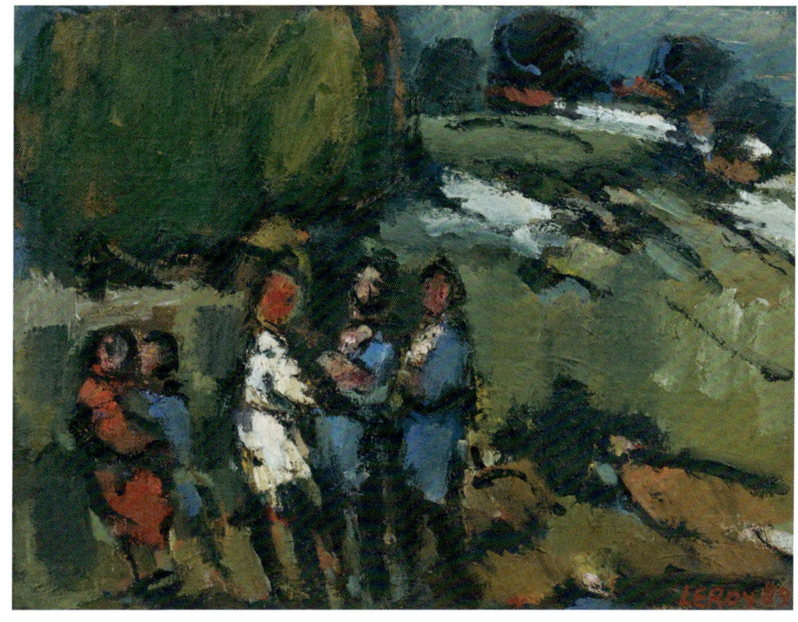

Little Family, 1989,
oil on canvas, 23" x 29"
PRIVATE COLLECTION
PHOTO BY JANET DWYER

As the kids grew older, Lynda augmented the family income by working part-time at a shoe store while they were at school. In the summers, the young Jensen family moored *Friend* in Vesuvius Bay, off Salt Spring Island and visited LeRoy's parents, Elsie and George, on their nearby waterfront property; purchased in the 1930s because it reminded them of Japan.[64] After George died in 1978, Elsie lived alone on the property. In 1982, when his mother's health declined, LeRoy moved his family to her home. It was an old, small, three-bedroom home with a small orchard and garden overlooking Vesuvius Bay. LeRoy's studio was unheated, but it was an austerity he embraced. His mother died at the end of that year.

‹ Whole family—back row: Lynda & LeRoy, middle row: Kim& Anthony, front row: Amber & Gabrielle, 1975, Salt Spring Island

After LeRoy moved to Salt Spring Island, his friend and fellow artist Herbert Siebner invited him to join the Limners, a group of professional artists (sculptors, printmakers, potters, painters, poets and a fabric artist) mostly from Victoria. Helga Grove,

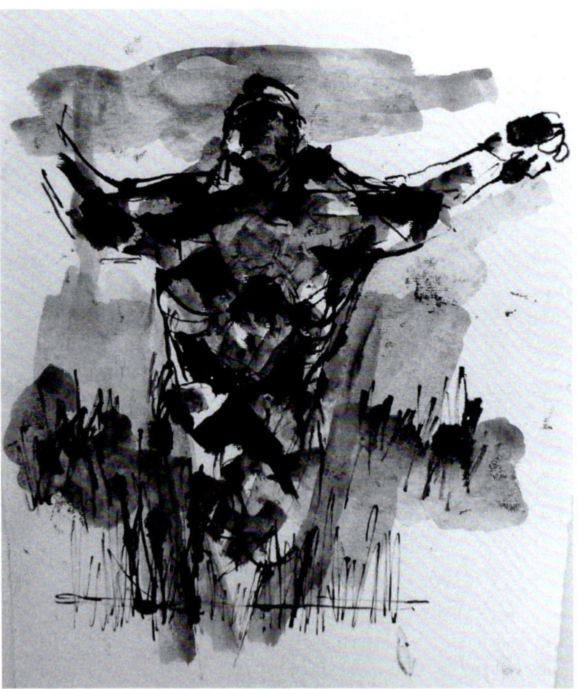

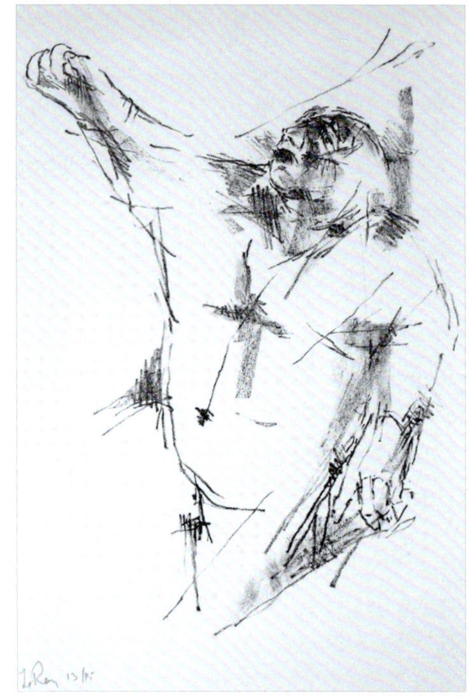

The Juggler, n.d., pen and ink, 8.75" x 11.5"
PRIVATE COLLECTION
PHOTO BY WENDY NEWBOLD PATTERSON

The Activist, 1979, lithograph, 15.3" x 10.6"
FROM THE CITY OF BURNABY PERMANENT ART COLLECTION, JACK HARDMAN SELECTION
PHOTO BY JANET DWYER

one of the group, related that Herbert and LeRoy were great friends and shared lots of "crazy ideas about revolt."[65] In his mid-fifties by this time, LeRoy was as irrepressible as ever and had a wonderful sense of humour. Everyone respected his work and enjoyed his participation in their exhibitions. The Limners had a good history of exhibitions and a loyal following of patrons. However, when a smartly dressed young curator insisted on a curriculum vitae from LeRoy for the Art Gallery of Greater Victoria Limner exhibition, he refused, insisting that all one needed to do was to look at his work, and removed his painting from the show.[66] When he needed more time for work, LeRoy resigned his membership from the Limners.

During his lifetime, LeRoy's work was exhibited in numerous galleries, including the Winchester Gallery in Victoria and the J. Mitchell Gallery on Salt Spring Island. Jack Hardman bought some of his lithographs for the Burnaby Art Gallery. LeRoy recalled, "He was the only one that ever did anything for the artists. He built up a very good collection of prints for the gallery. He would do things like that on his own and not through a committee."[67]

Robin Skelton, in his review of LeRoy's Winchester exhibit said:

> The [women's] bodies are made for labouring, loving, bearing children and surviving the blows of fortune. They are sometimes at rest in a pause between the demanding hours; they are sometimes thinking, perhaps meditating. They sug-

> gest not particular women, but Woman, and they are made more universal by such simple titles as *Dawn* and *Winter*, as if they were not merely caught up in earth's movements but embodiments of it.[68]

As an artist, LeRoy's primary medium was oil, but he also produced etchings on his small etching press in his studio, gouaches, watercolours, lithographs, conté sketches, pastels and volumes of drawings.

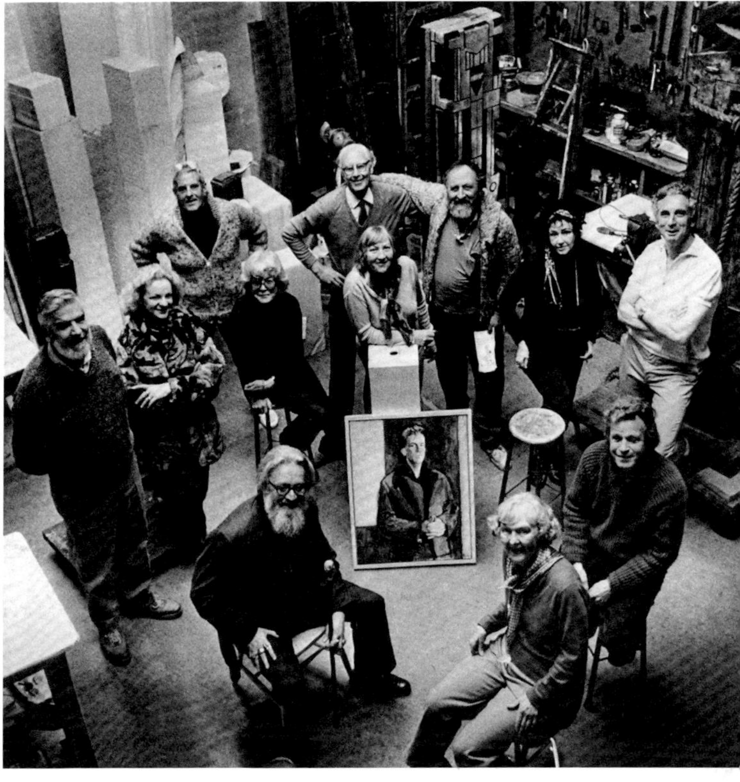

Limners, 1985, left to right, clockwise: Walter Dexter, Carole Sabiston, Karl Spreitz, Myfanwy Pavelić, Colin Graham, Helga Grove, Herbert Siebner, Pat Martin Bates, Jan Grove, LeRoy Jensen, Elza Mayhew, Robin Skelton, Roberto de Castro. PHOTO BY AND COURTESY OF ALEX BARTA

Bernie Raffo, former owner of the Winchester Gallery, wrote:

> I first met LeRoy at a Limner show [1986] and was immediately struck by the deep compassion LeRoy had for art. To me he was a traditionalist and a modernist painter all at the same time. I once expressed to him that I thought his figures had a landscape quality to them, which, to my surprise, he heartily agreed.

He told Bernie, "a painting reaches a point when it takes over and paints itself'"[69]

When LeRoy wasn't involved with painting or family, he wrote lively letters to the local papers. When clear-cutting threatened old-growth forests in B.C.'s Clayoquot Sound and Carmanah Valley, he got involved. He participated in a project for which one hundred artists were taken into the Valley, including fellow Salt Spring artists Simon Camping, Carol Evans, Robert Bateman, Diana Dean and Diana Thompson. The artists' paintings were published in a fundraising book entitled *Carmanah: Artistic Visions of an Ancient Rainforest.*[70]

Texada Lands Corporation, which owned 10 percent of Salt Spring, was clear-cutting on the Island between 1999 and 2001. However, half of the land was saved after intense community protest and with enormous local and nationwide effort. LeRoy's participation in this last protest during inclement weather precipitated a decline in his health.

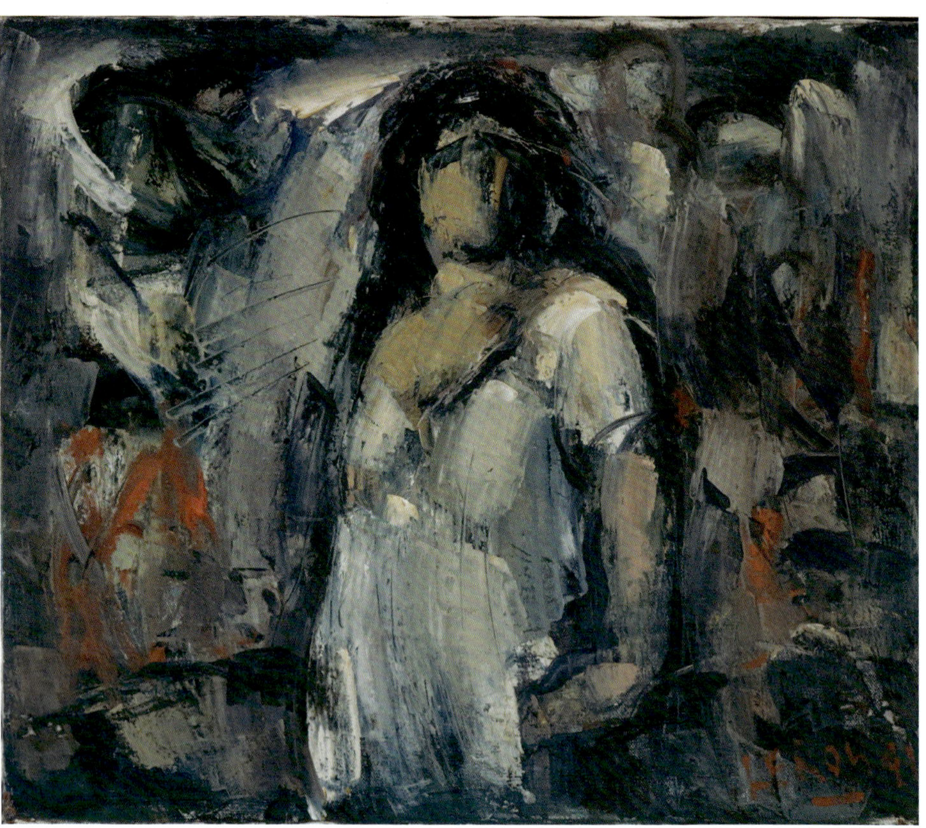

Boudica, 1991, oil on canvas, 18" x 15"
COLLECTION OF EAUVIVRE WINERY BC
PHOTO BY JANET DWYER COURTESY OF THE J. MITCHELL GALLERY

LeRoy became involved with activists because he responded to their courage and generous spirit. The specific details of his activism changed from cause to cause, but his rallying cry remained the same—to support those who stood up against fearful odds; against the aggressors, the oppressors, the experts.

As LeRoy's sons grew up and moved away, his daughters made Salt Spring Island their home. LeRoy, a prolific artist, continued to paint and draw for hours, resisting any interruption. Lynda revived her love of the stage by becoming more involved with local theatre, and when not working in his studio, LeRoy could often be seen cycling to Ganges and back, always keen to have lively conversations with friends. He carried a sketchbook in his backpack to draw whenever he travelled and for several years kept a journal. To replenish his source of imagery and visual vocabulary, he attended model drawing sessions held at Diana Dean's studio.

> LeRoy talked about the construction of a painting, the golden section and how, in the painting *Danaë* by Rembrandt, one can almost smell the room. All this led me to study the old masters, Rembrandt, Titian, Caravaggio, etc. and to see how extraordinary they really were.[71]

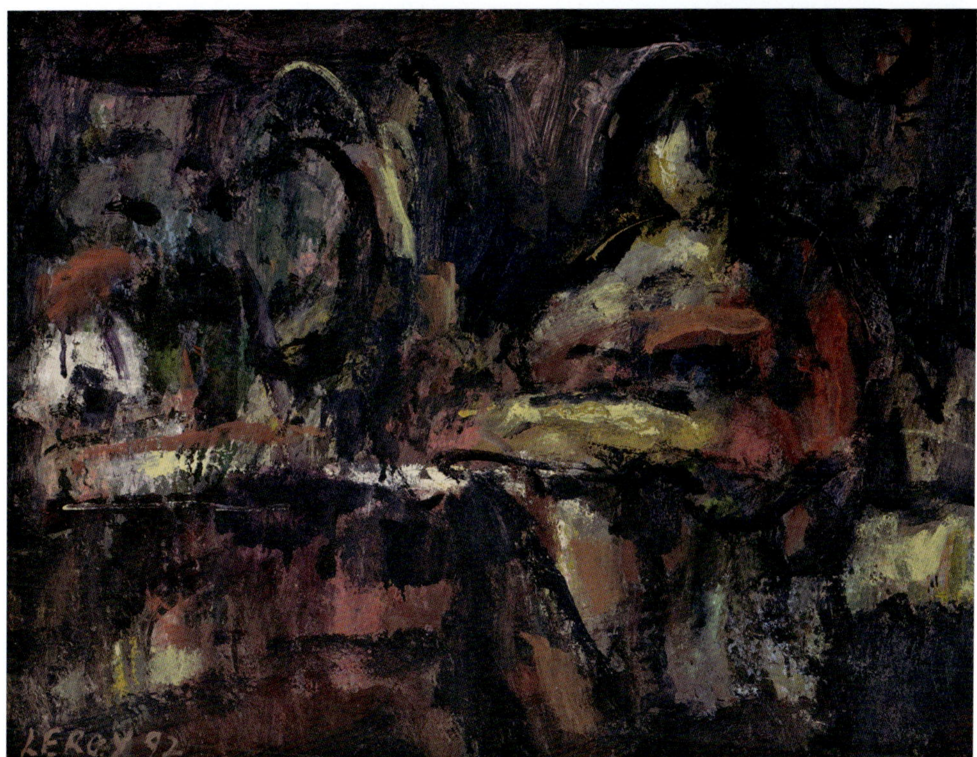

Bread, 1992, oil on canvas, 17.5" x 23"
PRIVATE COLLECTION
PHOTO BY JANET DWYER

He continued to inspire and influence fellow artists. Normand DesRosiers, a Salt Spring ceramist, recalled the time when he was struggling to create in a cold, bird-filled attic. LeRoy told him that "an artist cannot live without a studio,"[72] and a few days later, Windsor Plywood delivered a prefab studio—LeRoy's gift.

As children, Kim, Anthony, Gabrielle and Amber were always welcome in their dad's studio, but it was Gabrielle who became increasingly interested in art, especially drawing. About her drawing she wrote, "Dad, I'm working on the apple again, I guess I better go back to the beginning. I wish I'd never stopped… I realized what life would be like if I stopped."[73] Today on Salt Spring, she frames all of her dad's work at her own framing business. She has begun to exhibit her work and knows that drawing is an important part of her life. When LeRoy passed away, she took on the care of his artistic legacy; a gift as well as an enormous responsibility.

Toward the end of his father's life, Anthony expressed his gratitude for LeRoy's persistence and patience with him, his troublesome first son. To his surprise, LeRoy replied, "And thank you for saving my life!" When Anthony questioned his meaning, LeRoy humbly said, "You saved my life. I was once on the wrong track, and when you came along, you helped me get back on track." That was the last conversation Anthony was to have with his father.[74]

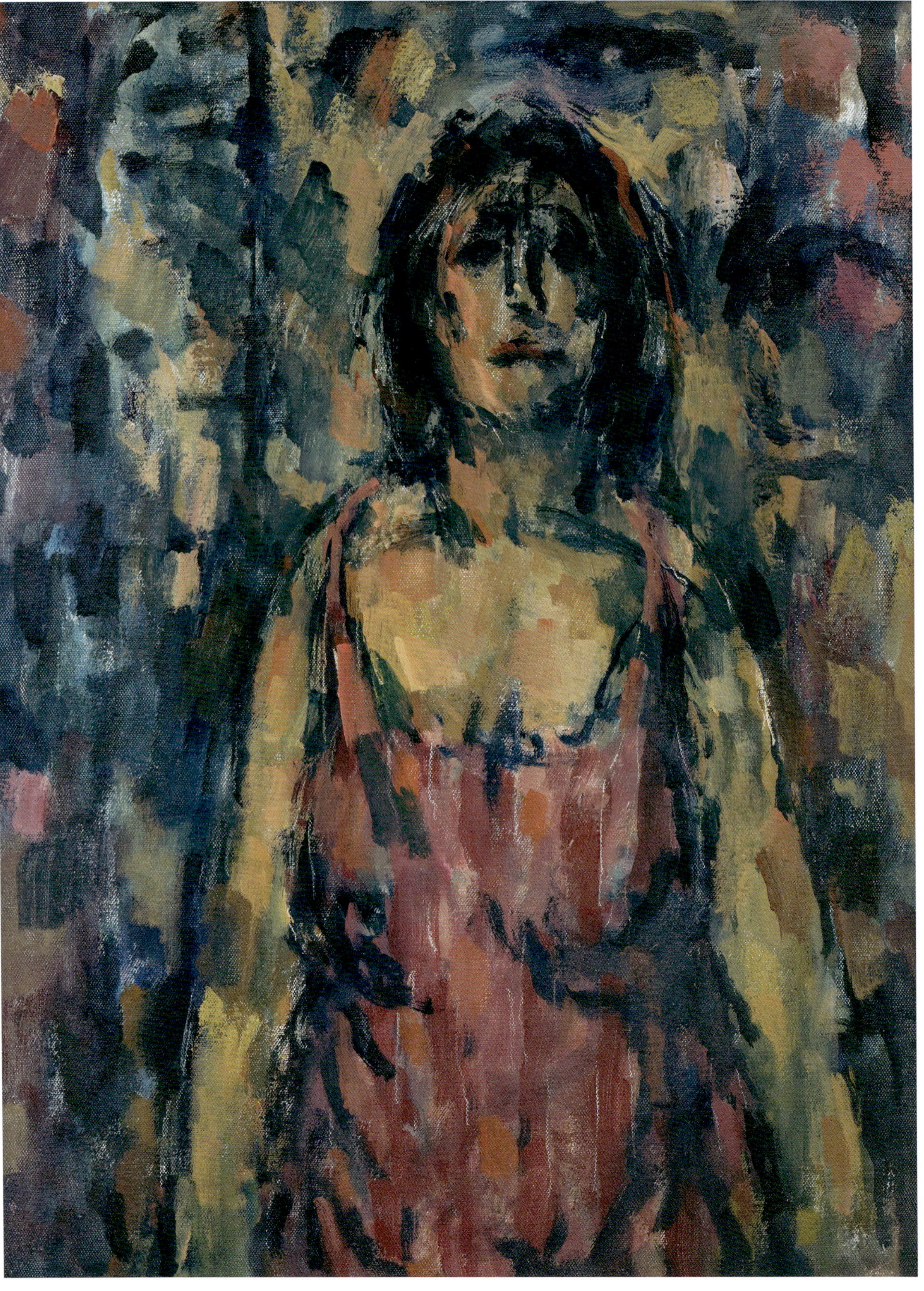

The Last Painting

I believe in invisible things and put my trust there. —LEROY JENSEN [75]

In the spring of 2004, Suzanne [Savaria] and Robert [Perrault], invited LeRoy, Lynda, Roy and I to Lac Lovering, Quebec where they had rented a small camp to reside and work in for a week. We were thrilled by the idea of meeting and working together again after so many years.

‹ *The Last Painting,* 2004–5, oil on canvas, 29" x 24"
PRIVATE COLLECTION
PHOTO BY JANET DWYER

In March, we received an unexpected letter from LeRoy saying that, throughout his life he had been aware of a bad heart valve that had given him little difficulty, but with aging, it was now a problem. As a result, he would not be able to make the journey to Quebec.

Nevertheless, in June, we held our Lac Lovering Art Week. We hired a model, worked all day, shared food and "talked story" long into the night. Suzanne made a video of our event and sent it to LeRoy and Lynda, along with letters and mementoes. It was unfathomable that LeRoy couldn't come because he was too sick. We assumed that it was because he needed to work.

› *The Crucifixion,* 2005, conte on paper, 7" x 5", last sketchbook
PHOTO BY WENDY NEWBOLD PATTERSON

›› *Boy into Light,* 2005, ink on paper, 7" x 5", last sketchbook
PHOTO BY WENDY NEWBOLD PATTERSON

⌣ *The River Styx,* 2005, conte on paper, 7" x 5", last sketchbook
PHOTO BY WENDY NEWBOLD PATTERSON

⌣› *Two Figures,* 2005, conte on paper, 7" x 5", last sketchbook
PHOTO BY WENDY NEWBOLD PATTERSON

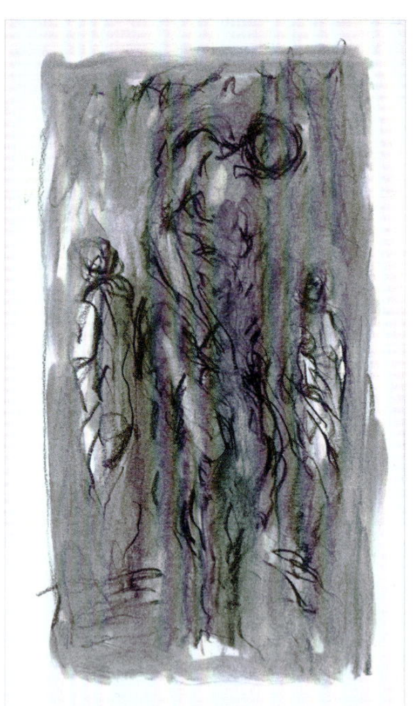

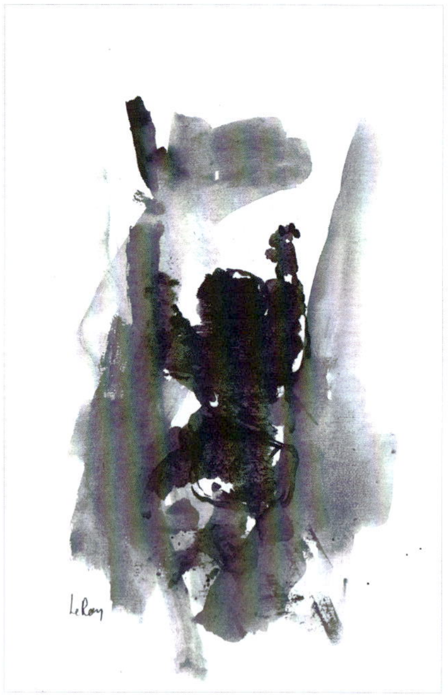

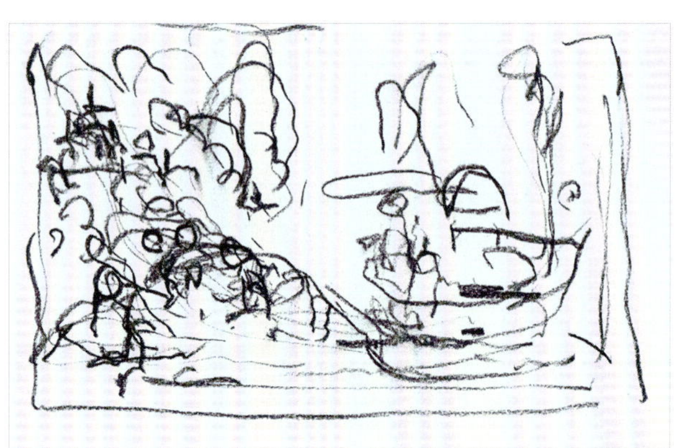

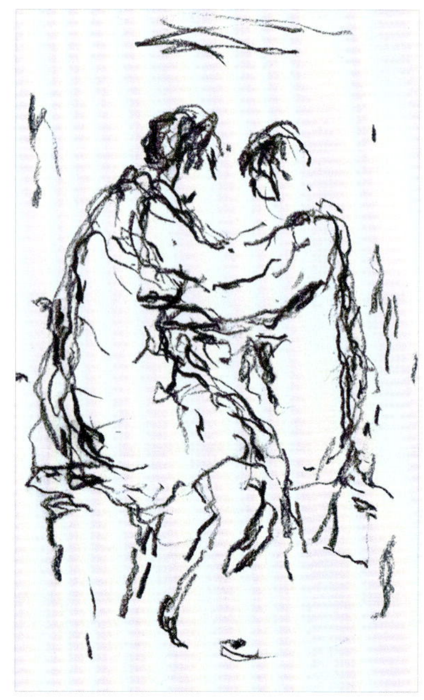

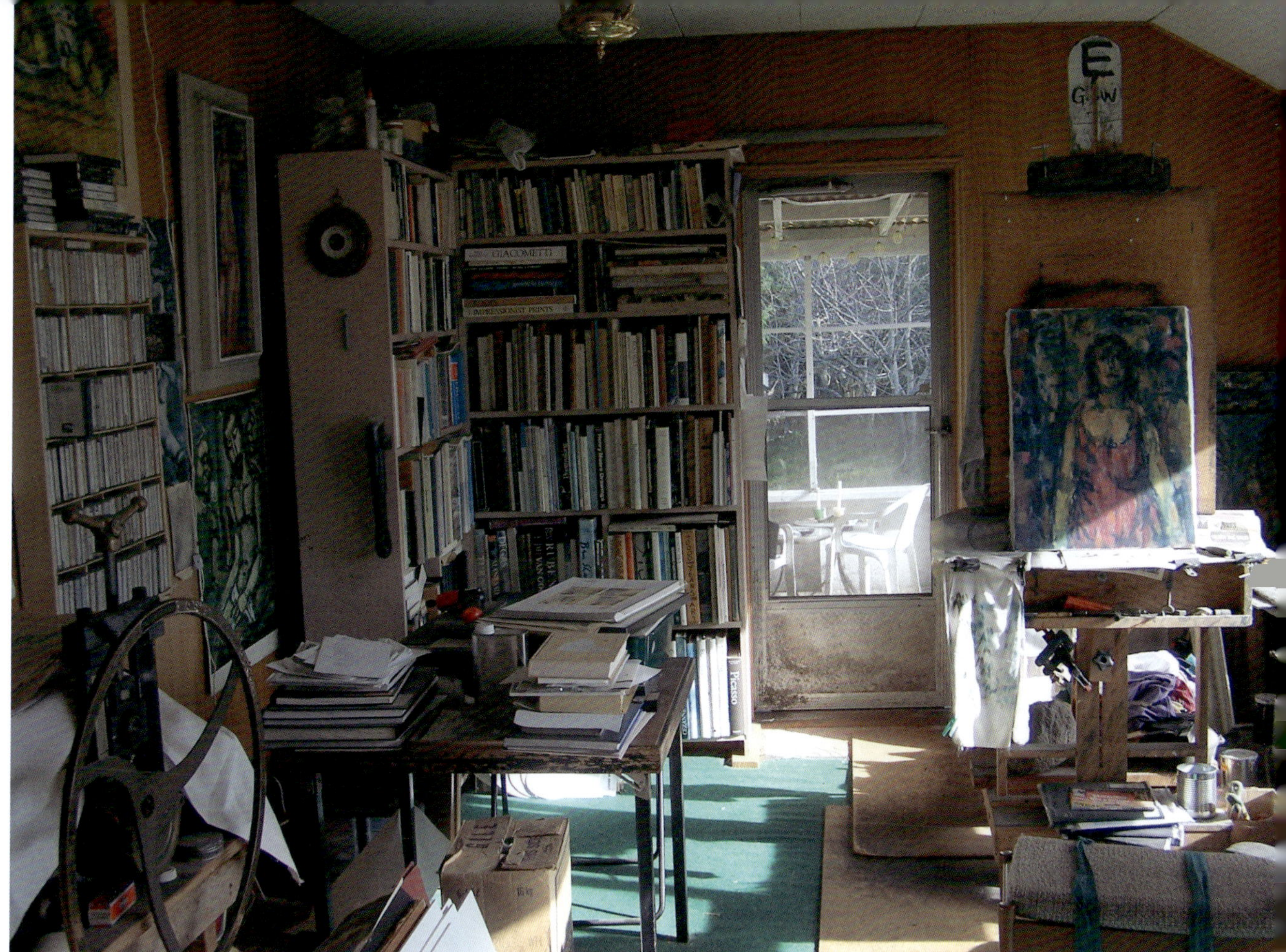

Studio without LeRoy, 2005

PHOTO COURTESY OF DIANA DEAN

But he was, indeed, very ill. After hospitalization and tests, the cardiologist recommended open-heart surgery to replace the valve, but LeRoy declined. In spite of his deteriorating health, he continued to paint and draw. He revisited all of his themes and motifs in his last sketchbook. And he still drew some new things, (The Crucifixion, The River Styx) touched with a fragile and tender love, yet graced with his characteristic energy.

These small drawings speak volumes of the struggles, the comforts and the sorrows that he and his family endured during those last months at home. His art served him to the very end. Like the final masterpieces of Beethoven or Mahler, these drawings say farewell to beloved life and greet the unknown beyond with genuine humanity.

LeRoy's last painting was sitting on the easel when he died in the spring of 2005. It is a complete image of sorrow, compassion, love and hope—a gift of his vision.

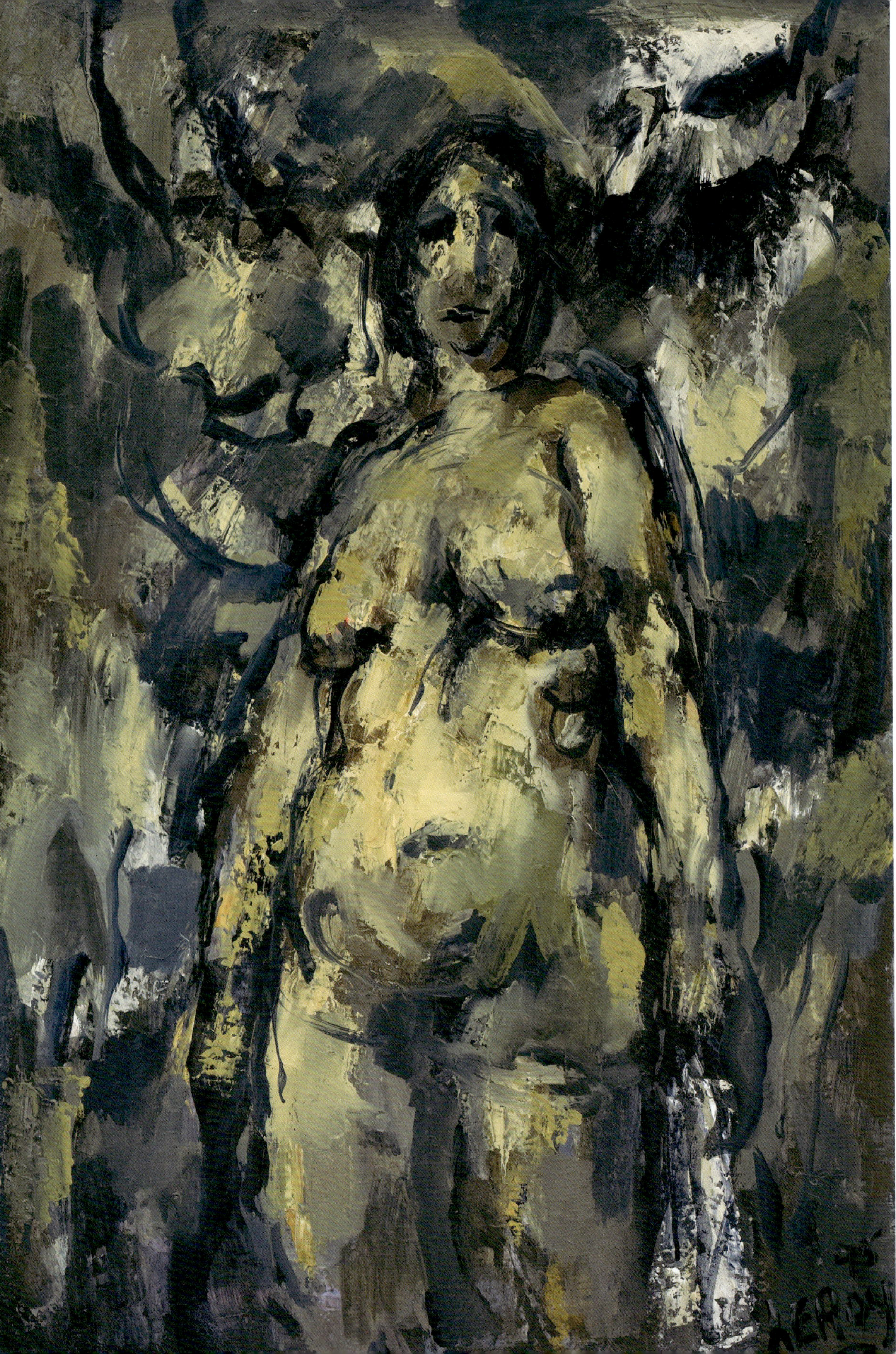

Epilogue: The Dogwood Tree

In the spring of 2009, Roy and I returned to British Columbia, 33 years after we left. Back on Salt Spring Island, I wake before dawn on the fourth anniversary of LeRoy's death. The gathering light in the studio reveals his paintings all around me. With the early dew still on the grass, Roy and I walk to Duck Creek Park near the Jensen home. It is a small rainforest, with a gentle creek and meadows along the banks. Towards the end of the trail, the paths become less travelled, and we are uncertain which one to follow. We ask, "Is this the end?" No, it continues beyond. Then again the path disappears. And again we find a way to carry on. Finally, we emerge onto a meadow just as the sun moves across the treetops. The path has vanished, and we tread through the rough brush.

We turn to look; there to amaze us is a golden shimmering light on an ancient dogwood tree. Long assumed to be dead, it wears a fresh crown of luminous flowers.

‹ *Alone,* 1995, oil on canvas, 25" x 17"
PRIVATE COLLECTION
PHOTO BY JANET DWYER

LEROY JENSEN
EXHIBITIONS

1947 B.C. Artists, 16th Annual Exhibition, Vancouver Art Gallery

1956 Federation of Canadian Artists in B.C., New Design Gallery, 1456 Marine Drive, West Vancouver

1960 Powell River Exhibition

1961 Kelowna, B.C., joint exhibit with Egon Milinkovich, Centennial Hall, November 1-2

1963 Penticton B.C., two-man display with Egon Milinkovich, Jubilee Pavilion, May 2-3

1964 Vernon Exhibition

1965 Danish Art Gallery, Vancouver

1967 Exhibition of 4 Artists: Warren Arthur, LeRoy Jensen, Weldon Munden, Zeljko Kujundzic, Yakima, Washington, Warehouse Gallery

1968 Gallery of B.C. Arts, Vancouver

1969 Studio of Peter Kaffka, W. Vancouver, Man and The Sea, paintings, drawings, sculpture and pottery by LeRoy Jensen and Frank Poll, March 22-24

1972 New Westminster Public Library Gallery

1980 Backroom Gallery, Victoria

1985 J. Arends Gallery, Edmonton, Alberta

1986 Retrospective, Off Centre Stage, Salt Spring Island
Art Gallery at Harbour Park Mall, Victoria
Atelier Gallery, Vancouver, The Limners, May

1987 Art 10 Gallery, Harbour Park Mall, Nanaimo, B.C.
Backroom Gallery, Victoria

1993 Winchester Galleries, Victoria
Peinture Humaine, one-man exhibition, Manse Gallery,
Salt Spring, Island

1994 Winchester Galleries, Victoria, August-September, The Limners
Winchester Galleries, Victoria, September-October, one-man show

2007 J. Mitchell Gallery, Salt Spring Island

2009 J. Mitchell Gallery, Salt Spring Island

PUBLIC COLLECTIONS

Burnaby Art Gallery, Burnaby

Maltwood Art Museum and Gallery, University of Victoria

Art Gallery of Greater Victoria

PRIVATE COLLECTIONS

Canada, United States, England

ACKNOWLEDGEMENTS

Special thanks to Frank and Sylvia Molnar who let me into their home, fed me and patiently answered my questions. To Charles van Sandwyk and Karen Gruninger Shu who shared their memories and showed me their collections. To Frank's former students Cori Creed, Will Rafuse and Andrew McDermott. To Georg Schmerholz, Jean Wolf, Paul Wolf, Peggy Imredy, Joy Aspell, David Maclagan, Kiff Howard and Judith Copithorne, who told me stories about Frank and Vancouver in the '60s and '70s. To Tony Westbridge for answering my questions on art and for Donald Rance at the Art Gallery of Ontario for unearthing a catalogue from 40 years ago. To my family, friends and neighbours for their ongoing support, to Judith Brand for whipping the manuscript into shape, and finally to Mona Fertig for her incredible courage in pursuing this project, her moral support and for all the valuable contacts and long forgotten research materials.

—EVE LAZARUS

Many people helped me, especially Jack's family. Matthew Dmitri Hardman and Ingeborg Hardman were very generous with their time as well as with their photographs, documents and family letters. Marya Fiamengo's lively recollections were inspiring. Elizabeth Swartz and Berenice Gilmore rounded out my understanding of a complex man. Colleagues, fellow artists, and friends, Abraham Rogatnik, Joy Zemel Long, Joe Plaskett, Jean François Guimond, Evelyn Roth and Robin Mathews cheerfully ransacked their memories for me. Former students, Leonard Brett, Ian Lidster, Joe Therrien shed light on Jack's mentoring life. Bob MacIntyre at the Burnaby Art Gallery and Barry Dykes at the New Westminster Museum & Archives were invaluable. I'd also like to acknowledge Judith Brand for her sharp editor's eye and Mona Fertig for her unflagging support, deep knowledge of the artistic scene, and enthusiasm for this project.

—CLAUDIA CORNWALL

My deepest gratitude to LeRoy Jensen, and my dear friend, Lynda Jensen, who trusted me with this responsibility, and for her hospitality and stories upon our return to B.C. To my husband, Roy Patterson, my Best Beloved Collaborator in life and art. Great appreciation to Anthony Jensen for asking appropriate questions, and to Gabrielle, Amber, Allison, Izaak and Kim Jensen along with Tracy Cutler, for their generous spirit, and to Colin Jensen for historical clarity. Warmest gratitude to Beth Marshall for loyal friendship, generosity and hospitality. To Suzanne Savaria, Robert Perrault for old photos and memories shared, to Rachel Ouellette for translations, to John Lundgren who helped me articulate the challenge. Much appreciation to Judy Mitchell and Bernie Raffo, Gail Johnson, Diana Dean, Sandi Johnson and Jamie and Hank van Montfoort for sharing photos and insights, and to Helga Grove for the Limner stories. I am deeply grateful for Mona Fertig's tenacious vision for this project, for her patience to accept, develop and encourage my contribution. To Judith Brand and Monika Ullmann for their heroic editing and re-writing efforts, and to Ann Kimmage for her excellent professional advice.

—WENDY NEWBOLD PATTERSON

A special thank-you to photographers Janet Dwyer, Ingeborg Hardman & Dan Fairchild for their fine photographs of the artists' work. Thanks to Wendy Godley of the Vancouver Public Library, Cheryl Segiel at the Vancouver Art Gallery Library, Peter Bernauer of the Kelowna Library and Colleen at the Penticton Library for important information. To photographers; Alex Barta, Basil King, Marj Trim, Diana Dean, Nicholas Westbridge for permission to use their work. To Robert Keziere for the Limner photo, to Frances Long for permission to use her dad's photographs. To Max Wyman, Charles van Sandwyk, Jean François Guimond, Roy Patterson for the introduction and prefaces. To Judith Brand, Monika Ullmann, Tina Dickey, Sandi Johnson, Bob MacIntyre, Gary Sim, Jan Westendorp for editing and reading ms and moral support. To Shelagh Simpson for indexing. To Ernst Vegt of Coast Imaging Arts for his generosity in photographing the cover painting. To Jan Westendorp for her great book design and eagle eye. To Mark Hand for the cover. To my wonderful husband, Peter Haase, and my family and friends and the supporters, writers and artists of this series who sustain and inspire me to keep climbing that mountain.

—MONA FERTIG

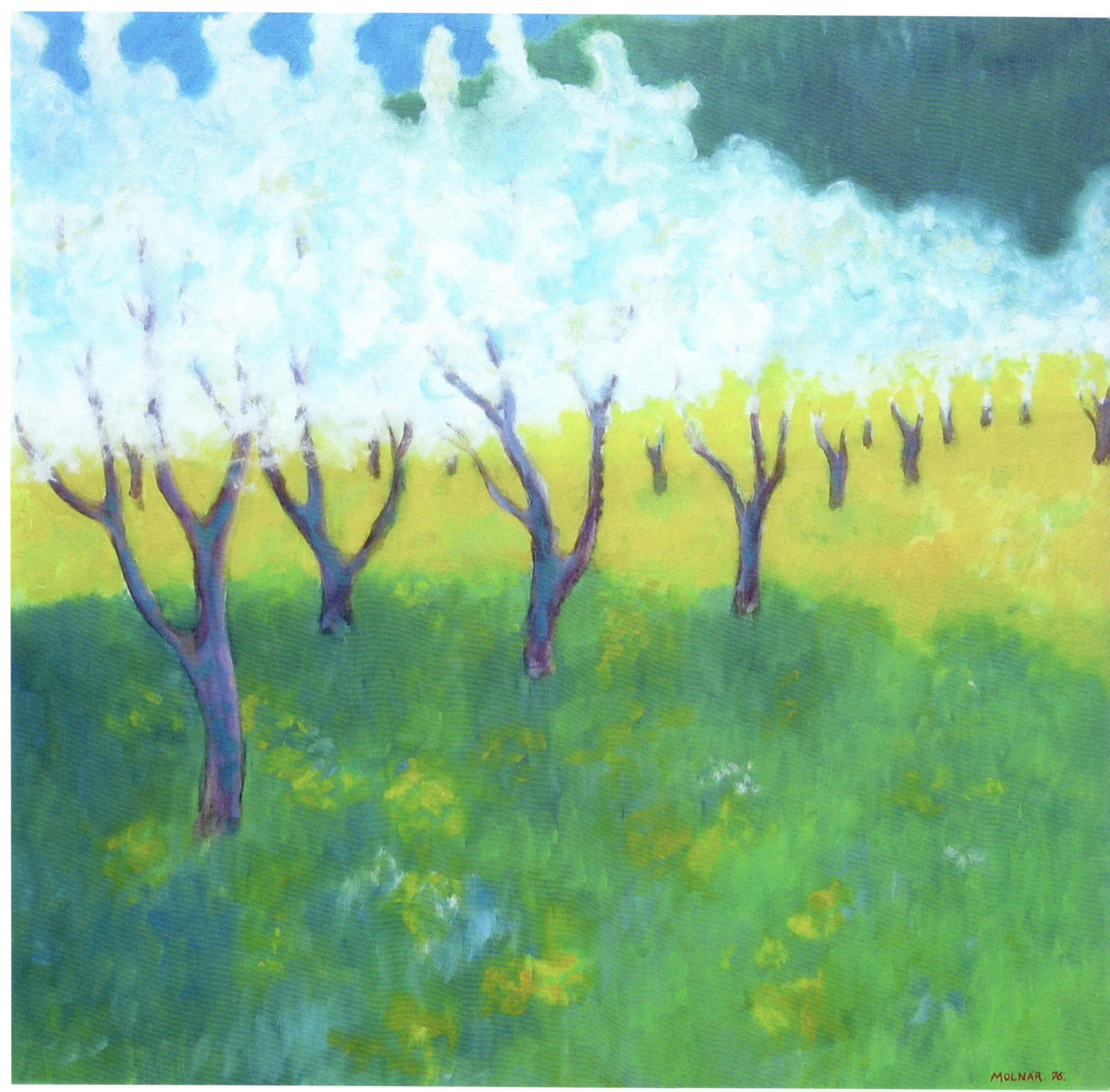
MOLNÁR 76.

ENDNOTES

FRANK MOLNAR

FLIGHT FROM HUNGARY

1 Author interview with Frank Molnar at his home, February 27, 2009
2 Ibid.
3 Author interview with Frank Molnar at his home, May 8, 2009
4 Telephone interview with Paul Wolf, March 9, 2009

AN ARTISTS' COLONY

5 From *Trek Magazine*, UBC Alumni Affairs, Spring 2007
4 Telephone interview with Peggy Imredy, March 30, 2009.
5 Telephone interview with Judith Copithorne, April 4, 2009
6 Author interview with Frank Molnar at his home, February 27, 2009
7 Telephone interview with Frank Molnar, June 24, 2009
8 Ibid.

SYLVIA

11 Author interview with Sylvia Molnar, March 20, 2009
12 Ibid.
13 Ibid.
14 Ullmann, Monika. *The Life and Art of David Marshall.* Mother Tongue Publishing, p. 47

EXHIBITIONS

15 Telephone interview with Jean Wolf, March 9, 2009.
16 Telephone interview with Paul Wolf, March 9, 2009
17 *Survey 70: Realism(e)s: The Montreal Museum of Fine Arts and the Art Gallery of Ontario,* 1970
18 Author interview with Frank Molnar at his home, May 8, 2009

CAPILANO COLLEGE

19 Author interview with Frank Molnar at his home, February 27, 2009
20 Ibid.
21 Author interview with Charles van Sandwyk at his home, April 10, 2009
22 Telephone interview with Andrew McDermott, March 17, 2009
23 Telephone interview with Cori Creed, March 12, 2009
24 Ibid.

CANADIANS AND THE NUDE

25 Telephone interview with David Maclagan, April 1, 2009
26 New Press, Toronto, 1972
27 Author interview with Frank Molnar at his home, March 20, 2009
28 Ibid.
29 Author interview with Sylvia Molnar, March 20, 2009
30 Telephone interview with Karen Gruninger Shu, March 18, 2009
31 Author interview with Charles van Sandwyk at his home, April 10, 2009
32 Ibid.

POINT GREY

33 Telephone interview with Frank Molnar, June 24, 2009
34 Author interview with Frank Molnar at his home, February 27, 2009
35 Ibid.
36 Author interview with Sylvia Molnar, March 20, 2009

FRANK'S LEGACY

37 Telephone interview with Georg Schmerholz, March 5, 2009
38 Author interview with Charles van Sandwyk at his home, April 10, 2009

‹ *Untitled,* 1976, oil on canvas, 40" x 42", Frank Molnar, COURTESY OF THE WESTBRIDGE FINE ART GALLERY
PHOTO BY NICHOLAS WESTBRIDGE

ARTIST, MENTOR, ENFANT TERRIBLE

1 Author interview with Marya Fiamengo, in Gibson's, February 28, 2009
2 *Columbian Supplement,* December, 1903
3 Author phone interview with Elizabeth Swartz in North Vancouver, March 3, 2009
4 Canadian Census, 1911
5 Soldiers of the First World War, Library and Archives Canada, website viewed March 10, 2009
6 Interview with Swartz, March 3, 2009
7 Ibid.
8 Author interview with Abraham Rogatnik in Vancouver, February 26, 2009. Rogatnik died August 30, 2009.
9 Interview with Swartz, March 3, 2009
10 Ibid.
11 Author interview with Fiamengo, February 28, 2009
12 Author phone interview with Joy Zemel Long, in West Vancouver, April 9, 2009
13 Email to author from Joe Plaskett, February 26, 2009
14 Email to Mona Fertig from Joe Plaskett, February 15, 2009
15 Robert Hume, *100 Years of B.C. Art,* catalogue for an exhibition held at the Vancouver Art Gallery to commemorate the British Columbia Centennial, 1958
16 Luke Rombout, *Vancouver: Art and Artists 1931–1983,* catalogue for the inaugural exhibition celebrating the new Vancouver Art Gallery at Robson Square, October 15 to December 31, 1983
17 Author interview with Mathew Dmitri Hardman in Gibson's, February 28, 2009
18 An article in the Columbian, June 1953, reporting on Jack and Marya's wedding, noted that he had been teaching for four years at Edmonds Junior High in Burnaby.
19 Interview with Swartz, March 3, 2009
20 Interview with Fiamengo, February 28, 2009
21 Ibid.
22 Ibid. Information about Plaskett's grant came from the Gallery 78 website, http://www.gallery78.com/jplask.htm, accessed March 22, 2009

BURNABY: AN ARTISTS' ENCLAVE

23 Interview with Fiamengo, February 28, 2009
24 Email from Ingeborg Hardman, March 7, 2009
25 Interview with Fiamengo, February 28, 2009
26 Phone interview with Fiamengo, March 9, 2009
27 Gordon Smith, painter and printmaker, taught in the Faculty of Education at UBC. Geoff Massey was Arthur Erikson's partner. Don Jarvis, painter, taught at the Emily Carr Institute of Art and Design.
28 Interview with Fiamengo, March 9, 2009
29 Author phone interview with Leonard Brett, February 22, 2009
30 Author phone interview with Ian Lidster, February 23, 2009

THE PROFESSIONAL SCULPTOR

31 Registrar's Office, the University of Western Washington
32 Interview with Fiamengo, February 28, 2009
33 Author phone interview with Jean François Guimond, in Vancouver, March 10, 2009
34 Artist file, Vancouver Art Gallery
35 Mathew Dmitri Hardman, private files
36 *Ceramics Monthly,* October 1958, p. 12
37 December 7, 1961, *Vancouver Sun,* p. 4
38 Interview with Rogatnik, February 26, 2009
39 Interview with Fiamengo, February 28, 2009
40 Ibid.
41 Author interview with Guimond, March 10, 2009
42 *Vancouver Sun,* Leisure, February 21, 1964, p. 5
43 *A Dictionary of Canadian Artists,* VOL.2, by Colin S. MacDonald (June 1989). For the months the show ran, see the National Gallery website, http://www.gallery.ca/english/494.htm, viewed May 25, 2009
44 *Columbian,* June 6, 1961, pp. 5–6
45 *Toronto Telegram,* August 22, 1964, article by Dorothy Howarth
46 *Vancouver Sun,* April 6, 1965, p. 44
47 Author interview with Fiamengo, February 28, 2009
48 Ibid.
49 Email from Mathew Dmitri Hardman, March 8, 2009
50 *Columbian,* March 1, 1996
51 Author interview with Fiamengo, February 28, 2009
52 Email from Mathew Dmitri Hardman, March 18, 2009

53 *Vancouver Sun*, April 29, 1967, p. 16

54 Douglas Christmas was a flamboyant art promoter whose gallery showcased contemporary American art as well as local talent. He also opened the Ace Gallery in Los Angeles. Today it is the city's oldest and largest. See *L.A. Weekly*, October 16, 2003, on-line edition. Christmas also opened a gallery in New York and in 1997 collaborated with the Guggenheim on a Rauschenberg retrospective. See *New York Times*, October 3, 1997, p. E32

A MENTOR'S LIFE

55 Email from Mathew Dmitri Hardman, March 18, 2009

56 Author phone interview with Marya Fiamengo, March 9, 2009. Though Jack's work was often well received, there were also indifferent reviews that wouldn't have helped his frame of mind. See the *Sun*, June 2, 1967, p. 32 for a review of Cybernetic Sculptures. Ian Wallace wrote, "They offer a rather pleasing and tasteful example of Hardman's sensibility for textural surfaces, but they are neither didactic, informative, nor esthetically challenging."

57 Excerpt from 'Jack Hardman: an appreciation' by Joseph Therrien, 2008, written for Burnaby Art Gallery exhibit and website, http://www.burnabyartgallery.ca/Home/Exhibitions/PastExhibitions.aspx

58 Author interview with Joe Therrien in Coquitlam, February 22, 2009

59 Author interview with Mathew Dmitri Hardman, February 28, 2009

60 The Burnaby Art Society disbanded in 1968 and was replaced by the Burnaby Art Gallery Association. See 10th Anniversary Show, the catalogue for an exhibition that took place in the Burnaby Art Gallery from September 14 to October 9, 1977. In 1998, the City of Burnaby took over the management of the Gallery. See History of Burnaby Art Gallery, website, http://www.burnabyartgallery.ca/Home/AboutUs/HistoryofBurnabyArtGallery.aspx, viewed March 23, 2009

61 Author interview with Mathew Dmitri Hardman, February 28, 2009

62 Email from Berenice Gilmore, May 25, 2009

63 Author interview with Fiamengo, in Gibson's, February 28, 2009

64 Author phone interview with Berenice Gilmore (she has reverted to her first married name) in Victoria, April 24, 2009

65 Author interview with Guimond, March 10, 2009

66 Joe Therrien was part of a group show in 1979, and Leonard Brett got a print exhibit in 1980.

67 10th Anniversary Show, Burnaby Art Gallery, September 14–October 8, 1977

68 Email from Evelyn Roth, April 6, 2009

69 *The Paper Bag*, Summer 1980, Burnaby Art Gallery newsletter

70 Email from Bob MacIntyre, Preparator/Exhibition Coordinator, Burnaby Art Gallery, March 13, 2009

71 Author interview with Mathew Dmitri Hardman, February 28, 2009

72 Berenice Gilmore wrote two catalogues for Burnaby Art Gallery exhibitions that reflect her historical bent. They were *Artists from the Sea, 1778–1793* [July 26–September 3, 1978] and *Artists Overland: A Visual Record of British Columbia, 1793–1886* [Sept 10–Oct. 18, 1980]

73 Author interview with Guimond, March 10, 2009

74 Minutes, AGM, May 26, 1981, Burnaby Art Gallery archive

75 Author phone interview with Berenice Gilmore in Victoria, May 20, 2009

76 Author interview with Joe Therrien, February 22, 2009

77 Private papers, Mathew Dmitri Hardman

78 Author phone interview with Robin Mathews in Vancouver, March 4, 2009

79 Alan C. Elder et al., *A Modern Life: Art and Design British Columbia 1945–1960*, Vancouver: Vancouver Art Gallery/Arsenal Pulp Press, 2004, p. 110. *Dmitri's Moon People* is titled *Family Group*.

80 Email from Bob MacIntyre, March 16, 2009

LEROY JENSEN

BEGINNINGS IN ASIA

1 Lynda Jensen, telephone conversation with the author, March 13, 2009
2 Story told by LeRoy to the author
3 Colin Jensen, Timeline
4 www.wikipedia.org/wiki/Battle_of_Hong_Kong
5 Colin Jensen, telephone conversation with the author, July 27, 2009
6 Interview with LeRoy by Gary Cherneff, Gulf Islands Driftwood, April 16, 1986
7 Lynda Jensen in conversation with the author, July 2009
8 LeRoy in conversation with the author
9 *Nanaimo Daily Free Press*, January 14, 1987
10 Story told by LeRoy to the author in 1970s
11 *The Times*, Nanaimo, January 8, 1987, 8A

ART STUDENT IN DENMARK AND FRANCE

12 LeRoy Jensen, hand-printed statement
13 Judy Harper interview with LeRoy, 2004
14 16th Annual B.C. Artists' Exhibition Catalogue, September 20-October 12, 1947, Vancouver Art Gallery archives
15 Lynda Jensen, telephone conversation with the author, spring 2009
16 Andrea Rabinovitch, *Gulf Islands Driftwood*, September 20, 2006, B18
17 Lynda Jensen, telephone conversation with the author, March 13, 2009
18 Student conversation with Roy Patterson in the '70s.
19 Anthony Jensen, email July 6, 2009
20 Interview with LeRoy Jensen and Mona Fertig, June 24, 1997

THE PRICE OF SUCCESS AND THE PARADIGM OF ORIGINALITY

21 LeRoy Jensen in conversation with Wendy and Roy Patterson in the 70s
22 Interview with LeRoy Jensen by Mona Fertig, June 24, 1997
23 October 6, 1949 letter to Frank Taylor from the curator, Vancouver Art Gallery archives.
24 Letter from LeRoy to Wendy and Roy Patterson, undated
25 Excerpt from interview with LeRoy Jensen by Judy Harper, February, 20, 2004 for the *Salt Spring Village Views*
26 Scott Watson, "Art in the Fifties: Design, Leisure and Painting in the Age of Anxiety" from *Vancouver Art and Artists: 1931-1983*
27 Palette, the Vancouver *Sun*, "Young Painters Work in Current City Show," June 18, 1956
28 William L Reese, *Dictionary of Philosophy and Religion*, Humanity Books, Amherst, NY, 1999, p. 535
29 Hank van Montfoort, email to Mona Fertig July 30, 2009, and *Penticton Herald*, 1953
30 Anthony Jensen, email to the author, May 14, 2009
31 Student conversation with Wendy Patterson, 1970s
32 Letter from LeRoy to Wendy and Roy Patterson, July 8, 1983
33 Letter from LeRoy to Wendy and Roy Patterson, May 5, 1996
34 (m)Öthêr Tøñgué Press publication, 1992, Issue 4, p. 13

THE TEACHER AND HIS STUDENTS: A PERSONAL REMINISCENCE

35 Public Broadcasting Station (PBS), filmed interview, excerpt from The Limners, 1990, Augustine Luviano-Cordero, Executive Producer
36 Ibid.
37 Sarah Thornton, *Seven Days in the Art World*, W.W. Norton, 2008, p. 55
38 Judy Harper interview with LeRoy Jensen, Salt Spring Village Views, February 20, 2004
39 www.thecultch.com, formerly the East End Cultural Centre
40 Andrea Rabinovitch, *Gulf Islands Driftwood*, September 20, 2006, B18
41 PBS filmed interview, 1990
42 Robert Perrault, written statement, undated
43 Judy Harper Interview with LeRoy Jensen, *Salt Spring Village Views*, Feb 20th, 2004
44 Suzanne Savaria, written statement, undated.
45 PBS filmed interview, 1990
46 Letter from LeRoy to Wendy and Roy Patterson, October 12, 2004
47 Story told to Wendy Patterson by Suzanne Savaria
48 Letter from LeRoy to Wendy and Roy Patterson, May 5, 1996
49 Ernest Hemingway, *A Moveable Feast*, Scribner, NY, 1964.

50 Judy Harper interview with LeRoy Jensen, *Salt Spring Village Views*, February 29, 2004
51 Suzanne Savaria, written statement, undated

THE WORK

52 LeRoy Jensen, Artist Statement
53 Sandi Johnson, email to the author, July 2, 2009
54 LeRoy's Journal, October 14, 1984, p. 18
55 *Nanaimo Daily Free Press*, January 14, 1987
56 LeRoy's journal, October 22, 1984, p. 21
57 Ibid.

JUGGLING ART, FAMILY AND ACTIVISM

58 Letter from LeRoy Jensen to Roy and Wendy Patterson, n.d.
59 Kim Jensen, conversation with the author, May 4, 2009
60 Amber Jensen, telephone conversation with the author, July 11, 2009
61 Amber Jensen, telephone conversation with the author, July2, 2009
62 Anthony Jensen, email to the author, May 25, 2009
63 Ibid.
64 Lynda Jensen, conversation with the author, April 29, 2009
65 Helga Grove, telephone conversation with the author, May 10, 2009
66 Lynda Jensen, conversation with the author, May 2, 2009
67 Interview with LeRoy Jensen by Mona Fertig, June 24, 1997
68 From a magazine published in Victoria, March 25-31, 1993
69 Letter from Bernie Raffo to Lynda Jensen, 2009
70 *Carmanah: Artistic Visions of an Ancient Rainforest*, Western Canada Wilderness Committee and Ken Budd, 1989
71 Diana Dean, email to Mona Fertig, June 26, 2009
72 Normand DesRosiers in conversation with Mona Fertig June 24, 2009
73 Letter from Gabrielle Jensen to LeRoy, n.d.
74 Anthony Jensen, email, March 20, 2009
75 Letter from LeRoy to Suzanne Savaria and Peter Perrault, n.d.

The first books in the series; *The Unheralded Artists of BC:*

1 *The Life & Art of David Marshall*—Monika Ullmann (2008)
2 *The Life & Art of Frank Molnar, Jack Hardman, LeRoy Jensen*—Eve Lazarus, Claudia Cornwall, Wendy Newbold Patterson (2009)
3 *The Life & Art of George Fertig*—Mona Fertig (forthcoming; 2010)

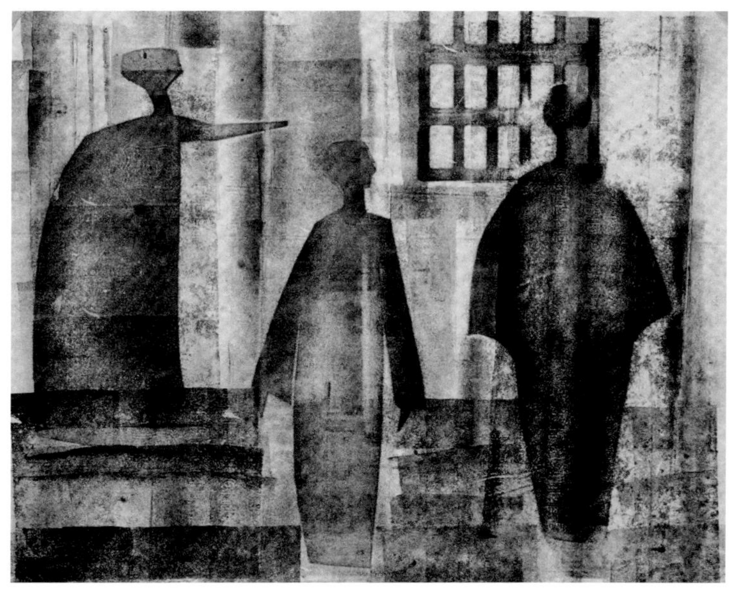

Beneficiaire #4 of 8, 1968, linocut, 17"x14", Jack Hardman

PHOTO BY INGEBORG HARDMAN

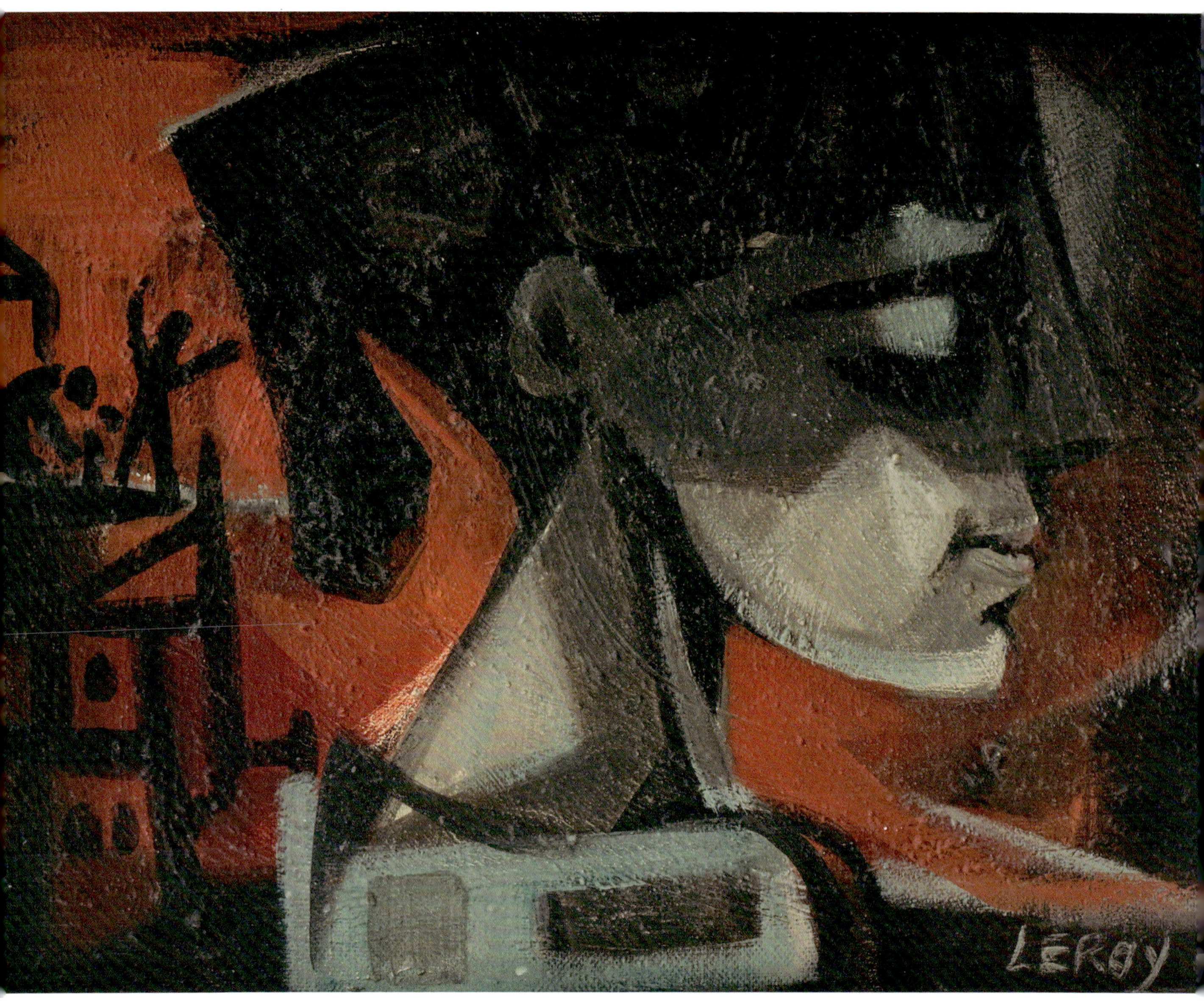

Gladiator, 1962,
oil on gesso panel,
23½" x 17½",
LeRoy Jensen
PRIVATE COLLECTION
PHOTO BY JANET DWYER

ITALICS INDICATE AN IMAGE OR PHOTOGRAPH

INDEX

Abstract (Hardman), 52
Activist, The (Jensen), 122
Akroyd, Jack, 10–11, 15, 17, 19, 21, 31, 42
Alone (Jensen), 129
Amaya, Mario, 19, 21
Amess, Fred, 97
Apt, Eddie, 9
Archipenko, Alexander, 66, 78
Armington, Caroline, 81
art and artists
  the art scene, 52–53, 101
  the establishment, 7, 46, 58, 101
  and fame, x–xi
  influences on, 102–3, 104–5
  nudes, Canadian attitudes, 27–28
  as outsiders, x–xi, 15, 24, 37, 39, 46, 77 (See also Pendulum Group)
  styles, 25, 27, 37, 52, 65–66
Arthur, Warren, 132
Artists West, 19
Aspell, Peter, 21, 97
Assyrian, The (Hardman), 70
At Home (Hardman), 52

Balkind, Alvin, 66–67, 103
Bateman, Robert, 123
Bau-Xi Gallery, 67, 81–82
Baumgarten, Alexander, 103
B.C. Society of Artists Annual Exhibition, 78–79, 85, 86
B.C. Society of Fine Arts, 66
Beneficiaire #4 of 8 (Hardman), 141
Bergman, Eric, 81
Beth (Jensen), 106
Binning, B.C., 7
bissett, bill, 10
Blocking (Hardman), 72
Blossoms (Molnar), 11
Bobak, Bruno, 79
Bobak, Molly Lamb, 57–58, 79
Bonnard, Pierre, 2, 33–34
Boudica (Jensen), 124
Boy into Light (Jensen), 128
Boy on Mast (Jensen), 94
Bread (Jensen), 125
Brett, Leonard, 60, 79
Bunting, Rosamund, 54
Burnaby Art Gallery (B.A.G.), 46–47, 78–81, 83, 87, 122
  invitation, print show, 61
Burnaby Art Society, 78–79, 86

Camping, Simon, 123
Canada Council, 54, 75
Capilano College, 18, 21, 23–25
Cardinal, Douglas, 80
Carmanah: Artistic Visions of an Ancient Rainforest (Wilderness Committee and Ken Budd), 123
Casson, A.J., 81
Ceperley Mansion. See Burnaby Art Gallery
Charcoal on paper (Molnar), 20, 22
Copenhagen self portrait (Jensen), 96
Copithorne, Judith, 10
Creed, Cori, on Molnar, 25
Crucifixion, The (Jensen), 128, 129
Cultch, The, 108
cultural elite (artistic). See art and artists: the establishment (artistic)
Cybernetic Sculptures, 75

Dale, Jack, 10
Damaged Family (Hardman), 50
Danby, Ken, 19
Danish Art Gallery, 17, 28, 42, 132
de Castro, Roberto, 123
Dean, Diana, 123, 124
Deep Net, The (Jensen), 105
Delacroix, Eugene, 21, 33–34
Denby, David, 10, 19
DesRosiers, Normand, 125
Dexter, Walter, 123
Dmitri's Moon People (series, Hardman), 74, 82
Dorothy Cameron Gallery, 28, 71
Douglas Gallery, 75, 87

Eleven Saints (Hardman), 66
Erikson, Arthur, 58
Esler, John, 81
Evans, Carol, 123
exhibitions. See under Hardman, Jackson, Molnar

Familia No. 3 (Hardman), 70
Familia No. 11 (Hardman), 72
Family, The (Hardman), 61
Family Group (Hardman), 83
Faminow, Frances, 79
Father and Son (Hardman), 55
Federation of Canadian Painters, B.C. Region, 103
Fertig, George, 15, 29, 77, 79, 97, 101, 102
Fertig, Mona, 77
4 Penises (Hardman), 74
France (Jensen), 99
Frank & Sylvia, at home, 38

Frank Molnar studio
Friend (sailboat), 120

Gallery of B.C. Arts, 17, 42, 104, 132
Gallery Pascal, 71, 87
Gauguin, Paul, 2, 33–34, 39
Genevieve (Jensen), 109
George Schmerholz Studio Gallery, 43
Gilbert, Herb, 103
Gilmore, Berenice (wife, Hardman), 79, 81, 82
Girl in a Wetsuit (Imredy), 10
Graham, Colin, 123
Greenberg, Clement, 58, 101
Greenpeace, 120
Group, The (Hardman), 66
Grove, Helga, 121–22, 123
Grove, Jan, 123
Gruninger Shu, Karen, 28–29
Guimond, Jean François, 46–47, 65–66, 67, 79, 81

Harbour, Calais (Hardman), 54
Hardman, Alfred and Annie (grandparents), 49–50
Hardman, Gordon and Irene (parents), 50, 72
Hardman, Jack Nelson, 48, 50, 51, 53, 58, 71, 75, 79
his art
acclaim and neglect, xi, 46–47, 67, 77
the artist and, 50–51, 53
education, influences on, 65
exhibitions, 70–72, 75, 83, 85–87, 102, 187
his legacy, 83
sculptor and printmaker, 46, 52, 65–67, 70–72, 75, 78–79, 81, 83
themes, 72
the artists' enclave, 57–58
director, B.A.G., 46–47, 78–82
early life, illness, death, 46, 49–51, 65, 72, 75, 81–83
European tour, 53–54
marriage, family life (See Gilmore, Berenice; Hardman, Marya)
as teacher and mentor, 53, 60, 63, 78–81
See also art and artists: as outsiders
Hardman, Marya (nee Fiamengo, wife), 53–54, 57–58, 60, 67, 70–71, 72, 75, 77, 79
Hardman, Matthew "Dmitri" (son), 57, 75, 77
Harris, Lawren P., 81
Harris, Lawren S., 79
Hearn, Jock, 10, 18–19, 79, 101, 102, 103
Hepworth, Barbara, 65
Heriot, George, 46
Hnizdousky, Jaques, 81
Huba, Paul, 10

Hungarian Revolution, 5–6
Hyde, Laurence, 81

Imredy, Peggy and Elek, 10, 31
invitation: Jack Hardman exhibition, 70
invitation: LeRoy Jensen & Frank Poll exhibition, 104
invitation: Molnar and Akroyd exhibition, 19
invitation, 2nd National Burnaby Print Show, 61
Israel, Charles, 75

J. Mitchell Gallery, 122, 133
Jack Hardman (Therrien), 81
Jackson, A.Y., 78
Jarvis, Don, 58, 79
Jeffery, Mildred, 70–71
Jensen, Amber (daughter), 119, 120, 121, 125
Jensen, Anthony (son), 104, 119, 120, 121, 125
Jensen, Colin (brother), 93, 94, 99
Jensen, Elsie and George (parents), 93–95, 99, 121
Jensen, Gabrielle (daughter), 119, 120, 125
Jensen, Isaak (grandson), 121
Jensen, Kim (son), 104, 119, 120, 125
Jensen, LeRoy Hackett, 92, 93, 94, 96, 99, 117, 120, 123
his art
education, influences on, 95, 97, 98–99, 103, 107–8, 124
exhibitions, 97, 103, 122–23, 132–33
legacy, 125
painting and drawing, 104, 110–11, 123
teachers and mentors, 91, 98
themes, 113, 129
art, a visual language, 108, 110, 113, 117, 129
the artists' group, 121–22
early life, illness, death, 93–95, 127, 129
European tour, 97–99, 110–11
Four Forces (in painting), 115
marriage, family life (See Jensen, Lynda; Jensen, Nonna)
quotes, about art and life, 90, 97, 101, 107, 113, 119, 127
and social activism, 119, 120–21, 123–24
as teacher and mentor, 90–91, 93, 107–8, 110–11, 125
See also art and artists: as outsiders; Pendulum Group
Jensen, Lynda (nee Woolley, wife), 90, 104, 108, 119–120, 121, 124, 127
Jensen, Nonna (nee Bossleman, wife), 98–99, 101
Joergennsen, Axel, 97, 98
Johnson, Sandi, 113
Juggler, The (Jensen), 122

Kahane, Anne, 70
Kalamalka Lake (Molnar), 19
Kelly, Ron, 103
Kincaid, Sheila, 46
King and Child (Hardman), 59
Kiyooka, Roy, 10, 19
Koerner, John, 79

Lamb, Harold Mortimer, 57–58
Last Painting, The (Jensen), 126
Leda and the Swan, series (Molnar), 6, 7, 29, 32–33
Léger, Ferdinand, 99
Leskard, Stephen, 21
Lhote, André, 97, 99
Lidster, Ian, 60, 63
Limners (artists' group), 121–22, 123, 133
Little Family (Jensen), 121
Little Gallery, 71, 86
Long, Joy Zemel, 51
Lundgren, John, 108, 110

Maclagan, David, 27
Marshall, Beth, 108, 110
Marshall, Carel, 58
Marshall, David, 15, 19, 24, 39, 47, 58, 82, 102, 103
Martin, Pat, 123
Mask (Hardman), 67
Mathews, Robin, 82–83
Mayhew, Elza, 123
Mayrs, Bill, 103
McDermott, Andrew, on Molnar, 25
McLeod, Ruth, 111
McNairn, Ian, 52
Metsinger, Jean, 99
Mews, Peter, 75
Milinkovich, Egon, 104, 132
Milne, David, 81
Modigliani, Amedeo, x
Molnar, Ferrence and Maria (parents), 5–6, 21
Molnar, Frank Stephan, 4, 7, 10, 13, 15, 18, 19, 32
his art
education, influences on, 2–3, 6, 7, 13, 24, 34
exhibitions, 17–19, 21, 28–29, 31, 42–43
legacy, 37, 39
the man and, 2–3, 6, 9–11, 13, 21, 31–35
nudes, colour, sensuality, 7, 11, 19, 27–29, 32–35
self-portraits, 2, 21, 24, 32
teachers and mentors, 7, 24
the artists' colony, 9–11
European tour, 21
marriage, family life (See Molnar, Sylvia)
as teacher and mentor, 2, 18, 21, 23–25, 29
young adulthood, 5–7, 9–10
See also art and artists: as outsiders
Molnar, Ilona (sister), 5
Molnar, Sylvia (nee Pidraziuk, wife), 3, 13–15, 17, 18, 21, 28, 32, 34, 39
Moore, Henry, 65
Morris, Jerrold, 27–28
Mother and Child (Jensen), 116
Mother and Child #5 (Jensen), 112, 115
Mother and Child #s 1, 2, 3 and *4* (Jensen), 114, 115
Mulatto Nude with Yellow Flowers (Molnar), 26

National Gallery of Canada, 28, 53, 67, 70–71, 86, 87
Nelson, Emma (grandmother, Hardman), 50
New Design Gallery, 66–67, 86, 103, 132
New World Jade Company, 111
Newlove, John, 10
Northwest Institute of Sculpture, 66
Nude Against the Light (Molnar), 29
Nude in Canadian Painting, The (Morris), 27–28
Nude With Cat 1964 (Molnar), xii

Ochs, Peter Paul, 78
O'Halloran, Ken, 110
Old Fisherman (Jensen), 111
100 Years of B.C. Art (McNairn), 52
Onley, Toni, 7, 19
Open and Closed Form (Hardman), 66

Palettc (art reviewer), 103
Patterson, Roy, 90–91, 108, 110, 127, 131
Pavelió, Myfanwy Spencer, 47, 123
Pedersen, Peder and Anne, 17
Pendulum Group, 102–5
See also art and artists: as outsiders
Perrault, Robert, 108, 127
Persephone series (Molnar), 31, 32–33, 35
Picasso, Pablo, 78, 81, 99, 111
Pignon, Edouard, 93, 97, 99
Plaskett, Joe, 46, 51–52, 53, 54, 71, 79, 82, 85, 97
Portelance, Don, 78
Portrait of Elizabeth Mihalik (Molnar), 24
Price, The (Jensen), 100
Prodigal Son (Jensen), 97

Quarter Century of Collecting, A: Burnaby Art Gallery 1967-1992, 81

Raffo, Bernie, 123
Rammel, George, 47

Raumond, Eddy, 108
Reclining Nude (Molnar), 9
Rembrandt van Rijn, 21, 78, 124–25
Richards, Cecil, 70
River Styx, The (Jensen), 128, 129
Rogatnik, Abraham, 50, 66–67, 103
Roth, Evelyn, 80–81
Rouault, Georges, 103, 104

Sailor, The (Jensen), 88
Salt Spring, Early Morning (Jensen), 97
Satyr (Hardman), 70
Savaria, Suzanne, 108, 110, 111, 127
Schmerholz, Georg, 15, 17, 31, 37, 43
Scott, Charles, 97
Sculptor, The (Jensen), 102
Sebiston, Carole, 123
Seurat, Georges, 33
Shadbolt, Doris, 58, 66, 67, 86
Shadbolt, Jack, 7, 58, 79, 81
Ship on the High Seas (Jensen), 95
Shu, Maurice, 29
Siebner, Herbert, 97, 121–22, 123
Skelton, Robin, 122–23
Slough, The (Molnar), 19
Smith, Gordon, 7, 58, 79
Snow, Michael, 19
So, France (Jensen), 98
Spears, Heather, 103
Spreitz, Karl, 123
Spurrier, Steven, 54
Standing Woman (Jensen), 128
Stilted (Hardman), 63
Studio without LeRoy Jensen, 131
Survey 70: Realism(e)s, 19, 21
Susan (Hardman), 52
Suzanne (Jensen), 109
Swartz, Elizabeth (nee Hardman, sister), 50, 53
Sylvia (Molnar), 12

Tanabe, Takao "Tak," 54, 79
themes, in book, xi
Therrien, Joe, 78, 79, 83
Thompson, Diana, 123
Thornton, Mildred Valley, 97
Three Hundred Years of Canadian Art (exhibition), 28
Totemic #2 (Hardman), 64, 67, 70, 86
Totemic #3 (Hardman), 68
Totemic Baroque (Hardman), 70
Totemic Figure (Hardman), 67
Totemic Insect (Hardman), 60
Two-Fold Astarte (Hardman), 66
Two Women & Ralph (Molnar), 39

Uhtoff, Ina, 81
Untitled (Hardman), 52, 56, 60, 62, 68, 76, 78
Untitled (Jensen), 102, 103, 109
Untitled (Molnar), iv, 8, 16, 20, 24, 25, 28, 29, 30, 35, 36, 38, 40, 41, 137
Untitled Man (Hardman), 61, 74
Untitled Woman (Hardman), 61
Urquhart, Tony, 19

Van Gogh, Vincent, 2
van Sandwyk, Charles, 2–3, 24–25, 29, 39
Vancouver Art and Artists: 1931-1983 (Watson), 53
Vancouver Art Gallery (VAG), 7, 24, 53, 58
exhibitions, 52, 66, 83, 85, 86, 87, 97, 132
Vancouver East Cultural Centre/Vancouver Free University. See Cultch, The
Vancouver School of Art, 7, 23, 58, 97
Varley, Frederich H., 39, 58
View from Mission Abbey (Molnar), 19
Visceral Totem (Hardman), vii

Watercolour (Molnar), 11
Watkins, Franklin Chenault, 6
Watmough, David, 71–72
Watson, Scott, 52–53, 102
Weatherbie, Vera, 58
Whatcha Doin' Mister? (Hardman), 80
Whittome, Irene, 81
Whole Family (Jensen), 120
Wieland, Joyce, 19
Wife of Gladiator (Jensen), 105
Williams, Dorothy, 51
Winchester Galleries, 122–23, 133
Wise, Jack, 81
Wolf, Jean, x–xi, 18–19
Wolf, Paul, 7, 18–19
Woman & Child (Hardman), 51
Woman by Bathtub (Molnar), 14
Woman in the Dunes (Jensen), 118
Woolley, Lynda (see wife, Jensen)
Wunderlee, Don, 90, 108
Wyman, Max, x–xi

Xavier, 108, 110

Zadkine, Ossip, 99